COMPLETE BOOK OF BULB GARDENING

COMPLETE BOOK OF BULB GARDENING

Frederic Doerflinger

Stackpole Books

COMPLETE BOOK OF BULB GARDENING
© 1973 by Frederic Doerflinger;
illustrations © 1973 by Associated
Bulb Growers of Holland

First published (1973) by David & Charles (Holdings) Limited, South Devon House, Newton Abbot Devon, England and printed in Great Britain by The Pitman Press Bath, this edition was printed in the U.S.A. and published by The Stackpole Company, Cameron and Kelker Streets, Harrisburg, Pennsylvania 17105 through special arrangement with David & Charles (Holdings) Limited.

Library of Congress Cataloging in Publication Data

Doerflinger, Frederic.
   Complete book of bulb gardening.

   1. Bulbs. I. Title.
SB425.D64 1973   635.9'44   73-13513
ISBN 0-8117-0416-5

CONTENTS

LIST OF ILLUSTRATIONS

PHOTOGRAPHS

Page

LINE DRAWINGS

Photographs are copyright by the Bulb Information Desk of the Associated Bulb Growers of Holland

INTRODUCTION

THIS BOOK is the inevitable result of the founding of the Bulb Information Desk in London in 1959 as a service to the amateur gardener. Although I developed a particular affinity towards Dutch bulbs at a very early age—my grandparents were nurserymen and florists in southern Wisconsin—it was not the miraculous transformation from bulb to flower that first captured my interest. That came later. My earliest recollection of bulbs was the arrival from Holland of large wooden crates of lily bulbs, which when opened inevitably included one or two red-waxed Edam cheeses with the compliments of the Dutch growers. It was frankly these cheeses that roused my curiosity about their fellow travellers, the bulbs themselves.

My preoccupation with bulbs began with the birth of the Bulb Information Desk. During the wartime occupation of Holland the famous Dutch bulb industry had sadly declined. Despite a rapid restoration of production in the early postwar years the industry was seriously hampered in recovering pre-war export markets because of restrictive trade agreements and limiting import quotas such as Britain imposed. It was not until 1959 that the British Government finally lifted the import quota on Dutch bulbs to give the Dutch free access to the important British market again. After two decades of severe bulb shortages, during which another generation set up homes, there was an obvious need for the Dutch bulb growers to inform the British public of the availability, advantages and applications of Dutch bulbs.

This became my responsibility under Walter Roozen, Director of Information for the Associated Bulb Growers of Holland, with whom I established the Bulb Information Desk in London. Becoming associated with Walter was almost like coming home to the greenhouses of my youth again. Like my own family Walter lives and loves flowers and has been only too willing to share with me his extensive specialist knowledge and lifetime experience of the world of bulbs. Without his valued guidance, the entré he afforded me into all aspects and areas of the fascinating Dutch bulb industry, as well as the real friendship he and his wife, Rose, have given me, my work on the Bulb Information Desk would not be so enjoyable nor would this book have been written.

In writing literally millions of words about bulbs for publication in newspapers and magazines and for broadcast by radio and television, in providing hundreds of thousands of photographs, in preparing and circulating leaflets and pamphlets, in devising and distributing films and slide lectures, in judging bulb competitions, in conducting surveys and organising exhibitions, and in answering countless inquiries about bulbs, I have learned a good deal both about the latest developments in the growing world of bulbs and about the problems and needs of gardeners.

It has been the questions over the years, in particular, which have provided a unique insight into what most gardeners most want to know about bulbs and which have served as a guide to me in writing this book. I have found that gardeners—whether beginners, those who do a bit and get fun and satisfaction from the results, or confirmed addicts—are down-to-earth people with inquiring minds but with no pretensions of being botanists, and consequently want information in plain language rather than in technical jargon. In so far as it is possible and consistent with accuracy I have, therefore, sought to express myself in gardening rather than in botanical terms.

When gardeners refer to bulbs they tend to interpret the word more liberally than botanists, and include not only true bulbs but other related organs which have the common characteristic of an underground food store. This book, too, accepts the gardeners' broad definition of bulbs and includes corms, rhizomes and tubers.

Nothing can be more frustrating than to read about or see a photograph of a beautiful plant and then, when ownership of such a specimen becomes a craving, disappointingly discover it is either unobtainable or such a rarity that it costs a fortune. The world of bulbs, using the term in its widest sense, is incredibly large and not all species and varieties of bulbous and tuberous plants included in classified lists and international registers are in fact commercially cultivated in such quantities as to make them generally or easily available to the home gardener. There is, nevertheless, such a tremendous choice of Dutch bulbs regularly on sale at reasonable prices that any gardener would find a lifetime too short to bring all of them into flower.

Particular care has been taken to ensure that all bulbs mentioned or illustrated are obtainable both in Britain and in North America. While the fully comprehensive range cannot be stocked by every local retailer the catalogues of the larger and specialist retail suppliers will offer wide selections.

The primary purpose of this book is to create a wider awareness of the amazing adaptability of this unique group of flowering plants and, by providing both concomitant and practical information, enable even the most uncertain and impatient of gardeners to achieve and enjoy the miracle of the bulb in and around their own homes.

THE EFFECT OF CLIMATE ON BULB GARDENING

The information in the following pages is basically as valid for North American as for British gardeners for, with few exceptions both hardy bulbs, which can survive freezing weather when left in the ground through the winter, and non-hardy or 'tender' bulbs, which must be lifted in areas subjected to frosts for frost-free winter storage, can be brought successfully into bloom throughout the United States and southern Canada as they can everywhere in Britain.

The sequence of bloom or flowering order of all bulbs is the same in Britain, Canada and the United States, with minor exceptions in the warmer climates of the United States. Much more detailed data than has hitherto been made available to amateur gardeners on the flowering order of bulbs is contained in this book.

Variations in climate, however, affect the date of bloom and the length of the flowering season but, with few exceptions, neither the sequence of flowering nor the choice of bulbs.

Climate is an incredibly variable factor. Even in a small garden, one corner will differ from another because of exposure or soil composition, nearby structures or the amount of moisture in the ground. A species may flower two weeks earlier in one garden than in another only a few miles away because of differences in altitude or in the positions of the gardens. And the seasons themselves will differ from year to year; one spring will be very early, mild and dry, and another year it will be unusually late, cold or wet.

Although it is impossible to forecast the exact date any bulb will bloom, gardeners want to have some mean or standard on which to base initial estimates of flowering time—until experience and observation fosters more accurate local forecasting.

The date when any bulb blooms and the length of its flowering period depends upon the climate in which it is grown and whether the seasons are cool or warm. Flowers tend to bloom earlier in the south than in the north, but this is not always true, because of local variations of soil, moisture or winds. In general, spring or autumn advances about one week for every 100 miles as you go north or south, and about the same variation occurs in every 500ft of altitude in hilly or mountainous regions. But the proximity of large bodies of water can influence this considerably. It can, for example, be freezing in central Ohio or New York State and at the same time be relatively mild in Cleveland or New York City. Bulbs come into bloom sooner in warm weather than in cool weather. A very early warm spring can cause bulbs to bloom out of sequence and may bring different classes of tulips into flower at the same time.

Because Britain is relatively small with a fairly uniform climate I have been able throughout the text to cite normal or average flowering times— and planting times—as a specific guide to British gardeners. Naturally, bulbs will bloom a little earlier in gardens at Land's End, Cornwall than in gardens at John O'Groats, Caithness but with a common sense approach Britain can be treated as a single climatic zone.

This means that the dates given in the year-round bulb calendar in Chapter 2 are relatively precise for Britain but, although the sequence of bloom is identical, the dates are subject to extensive fluctuations in respect of North America. The same bulbs that bloom together in Britain, however, will in general also flower together in North America. Allowance must be made for differences in the length of flowering seasons and for the effects of unusual climatic behaviour in certain areas of North America.

Nevertheless, by relating the regular sequence of bulb bloom to the arrival of the seasons in their area, North American gardeners can estimate the dates to expect bloom from the various bulbs. If, for example, crocuses bloom in Baltimore and St. Louis early in March they will flower approximately 3–4 weeks later in New York City, Kalamazoo and Milwaukee. By then there will be daffodils and hyacinths in bloom in Baltimore and St. Louis.

Because of the sprawling expanse of North America with its king-size physical features ranging from high mountain chains through vast plains, great swamplands and burning deserts to giant bodies of water, it is pointless to attempt to provide dated year-round bulb calendars for particular areas of the United States and southern Canada in the face of such varied climates and such extensive distorting influences. Warnings not to plant dahlia tubers outdoors before June ·1—in New York City—when by that time they are already in bloom—in California —would, I fear, also tend to hopelessly confuse.

But by discussing climatic factors in detail in this introduction, incorporating particular methods for the cultivation and care of bulbs planted in extreme climates and including the results of the latest research into the adaptability of bulbs in North American gardens, I have sought to simplify and make it easy for North American gardeners to relate the dates in the text to the arrival of the seasons in their local area.

With this information North American gardeners, wherever they live, can effectively compile their own local year-round bulb calendars as, over the years, they become better acquainted with the fascinating world of bulbs.

There are two things every gardener, and especially North American gardeners, can do to contribute to most successful bulb gardening. The first is to observe bulbs growing, not only in one's own garden but in other gardens in the area. The second is to purchase bulbs from reliable local suppliers or large reputable specialist suppliers who are familiar with local climatic conditions.

Having grown Dutch bulbs both in North America and Britain I feel there is one particular natural phenomenon I should bring to the attention of readers. Plants—flowers, shrubs and even trees—move faster on the Western side of the Atlantic Ocean. Throughout most of North America spring brings swift climatic changes that speed the growth of plants. In consequence North American gardeners witness a procession of flowers accelerated in their development to a degree that is not really appreciated unless they are aware of the slower growth pattern in climates like that of Britain. This phenomenon is exciting and rewarding —after 30 years I still find spring sluggish in Britain—but it has one drawback. Flowers do not last as long in North America as they do in Britain. The same factors that speed their growth hasten their passing. Flowers that remain in bloom for a month in Britain may fade after only two weeks in North America. The tulip season, for example, stretches over several months in Britain while in North America it lasts only over a matter of weeks.

Thus while North American gardeners benefit from a spectacular emergence of bloom and British gardeners from a longer flowering period, North American gardeners do have a more exacting task than their British counterparts in achieving continuous colour or combinations of colour in their gardens. It means that careful observation and planning are of particular importance but the greater challenge has its compensation in greater satisfaction.

Climatic Zones in North America. The United States and southern Canada can be divided into five climatic zones. Zone One lies north of a line stretching from Portland through Toronto, Green Bay, Minneapolis and Miles City, then down to Cheyenne and Denver and back up again through Rawling, Livingston, Lethbridge and Calgary.

Zone Two is that area lying south of Zone One and north of a line from New York City through Cleveland, Chicago and Sioux City, then down through North Platte and La Junta to Sante Fe and back up again through Salt Lake City, Wallace and on through Prince George.

Zone Three lies to the south of the above line and north of a line running from Atlantic City through Baltimore, Charlotte, Middlesboro, Harrison, Amarillo, Albuquerque, Las Vegas and Tacoma to Cape Flattery in an undulating arc. Within this zone, however, the area round the Grand Canyon National Park and the eastern third of Oregon are both comparable to Zone Two climate.

Zone Four is the area between the above line and north of a line from Cape Hatteras through Columbia, Macon, El Dorado, Dallas, San Angelo, El Paso, Phoenix, Fresno and Sacramento to Cape Blanco.

And Zone Five is the deep south and western United States below the Zone Four line.

The vast majority of hardy and tender bulbs can easily be grown in Zones Two, Three and Four—the north, mid-south and south. It is in Zones One and Five—the far north and deep south—that climate presents special problems for bulb gardeners and to which particular attention will be given.

In the far north winters can be so severe that some of the normally hardy spring-flowering bulbs, like hyacinths, cannot always cope effectively and may not always give consistently good bloom. But others, including tulips, narcissi, muscari and scillas, when properly planted and cared for, bloom superbly year after year. If the right kinds are chosen they will give 2–3 months of brilliant colour in the garden. Tender summer-flowering bulbs like gladioli and dahlias can also be grown successfully although their flowering season is inevitably shortened by late frost in spring and early frost in autumn (fall).

In the deep south gladioli can be grown virtually round the year in some areas and the hippeastrum, an indoors-only plant in Britain, can be grown outdoors. But the hardy spring-flowering bulbs, which have chilling requirements which must be met before they will surge to life and start to develop roots and eventually flower, will bloom most effectively if they are pre-cooled. In the deep south and other warm areas of the United States where there is no winter or autumn weather remaining below 40° F (5° C) for more than 6 weeks, it is advisable and often absolutely necessary to create a cold period through artificial means. I will explain this procedure in detail later.

There are also methods of lengthening the normally short season of summer flower in the far north. Tender bulbs like dahlias and begonias can be started indoors in early spring and kept inside until it is safe to set the plants out in the garden. In this way bloom can be achieved for an extra month or more than is possible from bulbs planted directly outdoors after the last frost.

Autumn is the traditional time to plant spring-flowering bulbs. However, since autumn weather arrives over an extended period across North America, a more precise planting time is when the soil cools down to 50–55° F (10–13° C); which means about the end of September in the far north and about the end of December in the deep south. Bulbs need at least a month in the soil to develop a good root system before really deep frost sets in.

Spring is the proper time for planting summer-flowering bulbs and always after the last killing frost. Most of these are tender bulbs and should not be left in the ground during winter except in such warm areas as Florida, the Gulf Coast and southwestern areas of the United States. There are certain exceptions about planting summer-flowering bulbs in the warmer climates too, which will be dealt with later.

Spring arrives earliest in the south and moves gradually and irregularly north. This is when the mean daily temperature rises above 40° F (5° C) and occurs before 1 February in the deep south, between 1 February and 1 March in the south, between 1 March and 1 April in the mid-south, between 1 and 15 April in the north and between 15 April and 15 May in the far north. Frosts can and often do occur after the arrival of spring. While this will not affect the hardy bulbs which begin to bloom with the arrival of spring in each climatic zone, it will affect tender bulbs just planted for summer flower and it is essential to postpone spring planting until the danger from frosts has passed. In fact 'frost' is the key word for summer-flowering bulbs. Planting time is always after the last killing frost of spring and the flowering season comes to an end with the first killing frost in autumn.

Frost is no handicap to gardening with the hardy spring-flowering bulbs. They may be planted throughout the autumn and—when properly stored—may even be planted during winter thaws for spring bloom. As the soil does not steadily grow colder from the first autumn frost onward—there usually are both warm spells and cold snaps—it is normally quite late in the season before the soil temperature is cold enough to stop roots growing. Generally, however, early autumn planting is advisable both to ensure that the bulbs get that month in the soil to develop proper roots before growth is halted by cold weather and to prevent bulbs—particularly the small ones—from drying up through lengthy exposure out of the ground. Daffodils and the smaller spring-flowering bulbs should always be planted early. Tulips, however, prefer later planting.

Bulbs in Cold Climates. There are a number of general hints for bulb gardening in cold climates. Throughout the text I have given indications where winter protection is welcome. Early spring-flowering bulbs always do best where late winter sun is warmest and where they are sheltered by walls, boulders and other plants. All spring-flowering bulbs will grow beautifully in temperate parts of Canada and on the mild Pacific coast they will bloom even earlier and last longer. The University of Alberta in Edmonton has been most successful in cultivating tulips and even in the cold Peace River country, narcissi or daffodils and many small or miscellaneous spring-flowering bulbs have each year provided wonderful colour and display. In addition to looking at your own and neighbours gardens, do visit the many fine bulb displays in Canadian public parks and botanical gardens and make a note of the bulbs you would like for your own garden.

Generally, bulbs will not send up sprouts until the weather has warmed up and consequently there is very little risk of damage from severely cold temperatures and snow. The freezing spells of spring in southern Canada and northern United States usually last only a short time and therefore will not seriously damage blooms or stems. The worst that can happen is that frost will sometimes darken the tip of a hyacinth or the foliage of spring-flowering bulbs. The small bulbs of spring, in particular muscari, will sometimes send up foliage in the autumn but the freezing temperatures of winter and snows will rarely if ever cause any damage, for their foliage has an insulation against low temperatures.

The earlier flowering spring bulbs are available from late August or early September and should always be planted then in cold climates. These include bulbs like snowdrops, winter aconites, species iris, crocuses, narcissi, glory of the snow, scilla and puschkinia. Tulips are best planted in the Canadian prairies and the far north in mid-to-late September; in eastern Canada in late September to late October and on the west coast in October and November. Hyacinths can be planted in October.

Many summer-flowering bulbs will thrive in southern Canada too but of course must not be planted before the danger of frost is past. Their season of flower will be shorter than in warmer climates because autumn frosts arrive earlier, but quite a number can be potted up early and brought on in greenhouses or indoors to extend their period of display in the garden.

In short, if you look around you, consult your local bulb supplier and do a bit of experimenting in your choice of bulbs, you will be genuinely surprised at the wide range of bulbs that can be grown successfully in cold climates.

Bulbs in Zones Two, Three and Four. Planting times will vary somewhat but in general spring-flowering bulbs will appear in the shops and be available from specialist suppliers in late August or early September as they are in Britain. As in the cold climates the earlier flowering spring bulbs should be planted early. Tulips should be planted in the north from mid-to-late September; in central United States in late September to late October and on the west coast in October and November. Hyacinth planting time is October.

A regional planting guide worked out for gladioli provides a clue to the planting of summer-flowering bulbs. The first gladioli planting of the year in the Northeast, Middle Atlantic States and Midwest generally is about the third week of April. The flowers will begin to bloom shortly after the Fourth of July. Succession planting can continue every two or three weeks until mid-July.

In the Rocky Mountain states gladioli planting can also begin in late April but succession planting should not be continued beyond the end of June. In the Northwest planting can begin about mid-March as it can in southern states like Virginia. But in Florida, along the Gulf Coast and in the Southwest gladioli bulbs are planted in December. In fact, gardeners in southern California can have gladioli in bloom right round the year.

Summer-flowering bulbs like anemones and ranunculi can be planted in early spring in the north, mid-south and south whereas in the deep south they may be planted from September through January for bloom from March to May.

Bulbs in Warm Climates. Many bulbs will produce glorious blooms even in the deep south when proper planting and pre-planting procedures are adopted. I cannot emphasise too strongly that in the deep south and other warm areas of the country where there is not a prolonged 6-week period of weather below 40° F (5° C) spring-flowering bulbs should be pre-cooled. Scientists do not fully understand why all spring-flowering bulbs need a period of cold in their life cycle but it is an indisputable fact that they do.

Bulbs will be found on sale in warm climates at the same time of the year as in colder climates but planting time must be delayed until the soil has cooled. This usually occurs in October in the upper south, in October and November in the mid-south and in November or December in the lower south. Some suppliers offer pre-cooled bulbs later in the year but distribution is not all that extensive as yet. Gardeners in warm climates can quite easily pre-cool bulbs themselves. Pre-cooling is a treatment that provides some of the 'cold period' spring-flowering bulbs require in their life cycle. All it involves is placing bulbs—in their original bags as long as there are air holes for circulation—in the bottom of the refrigerator for 6–9 weeks prior to planting. The vegetable crisper is a good venue but do not place bulbs under any circumstances in the freezing compartment of a refrigerator or in a deep freeze. Be sure all bags of bulbs are clearly marked and it is a good idea to add the date on which the bags are first placed in the refrigerator. Some warm climate gardeners use second-hand refrigerators to pre-cool large quantities of bulbs. The average American refrigerator will take as many as 2,000 bulbs.

Tulips, hyacinths, narcissi—in fact all hardy bulbs—should be pre-cooled at 40–45° F (5–7° C). Tulips require 6–9 weeks while the others can get by with a minimum of 4 weeks, though 6 weeks is better. Although, technically, hyacinths and some varieties of narcissi do not have to be pre-cooled it is wiser to do so, for pre-cooling almost guarantees results.

The cultivation of spring-flowering bulbs in warm climates is little different from that in other parts of North America. Most large bulbs—tulips, hyacinths and narcissi—do best at a depth of 5–6in in heavier soils and 6–7in in sandy soils. The smaller bulbs can be planted 2–3in deep. After covering with soil a light mulch will help to keep the soil cool.

The applications of bulbs in the garden in warm climates is as wide as in other areas. Spring-flowering bulbs also make superb and inexpensive cut flowers and there is no reason why they cannot be planted in a cutting garden in warm climates.

Where the weather gets really hot in the deep south it is advisable to plant bulbs where they get some light shade. Densely shaded positions should be avoided if the bulbs are expected to flower for a number of years, however.

If shady and cool locations are selected and proper watering procedures are pursued bulbs will do well. Thorough watering is necessary after planting. In light, sandy soils it is advisable to water weekly if the soil becomes dry. Do ensure that plants are well watered during the flowering period. And don't forget to water spring-flowering bulbs after they have bloomed, because food for next year's flowers is being manufactured at this time. Try to keep the leaves green as long as possible. In addition to watering, a mulch helps to retain soil moisture after flowering.

In warm climates spring-flowering bulbs can be left in the ground from year to year. But each winter when rooting starts established bulbs should be given a light dressing of general garden fertiliser and another light dressing when the first shoots appear in spring.

Although there are bulbs which can be grown outdoors in warm climates that will not thrive elsewhere—the whole range of freesias and paper-white narcissus for example—very little information has been collated on the adaptability of the various types, species and varieties of bulbs to warmer climates. All available data on choosing bulbs for warm climates has been included in this book under the respective headings. Enterprising gardeners are encouraged to experiment with others and the Bulb Information Desk in London will welcome any data forwarded. Gardeners in warm climates have, in one sense, a distinct advantage over gardeners elsewhere. As far as many bulbs are concerned they are living in an age of discovery and one of the most exciting rewards of any kind of gardening is the fun of finding out.

Chapter One

BULB BASICS

To ME the most wonderful thing about bulbs is that anyone, even the beginner at gardening, can have and enjoy a continuous succession of beautiful, spectacular and fascinating flowers outdoors or indoors virtually round the year with a minimum of effort.

It is quite possible to drop a bulb casually in a hole in the ground, push some soil over it carelessly with a shoe, and be rewarded in a remarkably short time with a lovely flower. Whatever kind of soil you have, if it will grow anything, it will provide a home for some kinds of bulbs. Indeed, I have seen bulbs inadvertently dumped with weeds onto a compost heap in the autumn produce the lushest blooms the following spring.

Of course, it is not quite as simple as that to get the most from bulbs, which is what this book is all about, but these examples do illustrate how remarkably adaptable bulbs are, how easy they are to grow and why they have come to be regarded by so many as miracles of nature.

Bulbs will thrive in almost every conceivable position or situation in the garden, in sun or partial shade, in moist or drier conditions. And it is not even necessary to have a garden for bulbs for they will flourish indoors in pans, pots or bowls and outdoors in windowboxes and in a variety of containers on porches, staircases, terraces, balconies and even rooftops.

Bulbs provide infinite variety in colour, texture and form. When in flower they range from a mere inch or two to upwards of eight feet and the characteristics of their foliage are as diverse as their blooms. The flowers of most bulbs last surprisingly well when cut and are ideal for flower arrangements.

Gardening with bulbs requires a minimum of effort, and the bulk of that at those times of the year when it is pleasant to potter in the garden. They are easy to cultivate. In most cases the flowers are already formed in embryo in the bulbs before we purchase them, so that providing bulbs are of sufficient size and we treat them reasonably we are almost guaranteed to get flowers in the first year after planting. There is no other group of plants with such a built-in success factor and consequently bulbs are invaluable to beginners as to newly formed gardens.

Bulbs are easily obtainable in great variety and inexpensive too. The dividends in beauty and pleasure they provide are out of all proportion to your modest investment of money and care. Many bulbs, once established in a happy home, increase and multiply to produce a bonus of delight year after year.

What actually lies behind this miracle? What is a bulb? Gardening usage has for so long applied the term 'bulb' to all bulb-like organs that it has now generically come to include a vast array of flowering plants that are sold to the public in a dormant condition. The majority of bulbs we cultivate are native to countries where the weather enforces on them a dormant, resting period underground. In our case this is the winter, but in the case of many bulbs originating in Asia Minor or countries bordering the Mediterranean, the hot dry summer, sometimes both. Therefore they need a rapid growing cycle and a means of storing nutriment before they are dormant so that they may have a good start when growth begins again. This is very relevant to their cultivation in the garden and in the home for without their resting period the majority will not succeed.

There is considerable uncertainty in the minds of many gardeners as to the difference between bulbs, corms, rhizomes and tubers because their function is identical—to tide the plant over a period of adverse conditions like winter cold and summer drought. All have common factors—food storage; quick growth under suitable conditions; and the same life-cycle, in that during growth and flowering, the following year's flower is formed in miniature, the foliage soon reaching maturity and dying away, as do the roots in most cases when the plant enters its period of rest.

As the differences between them are less significant than the fundamental similarities they share, there is therefore no reason why we should not conveniently continue to call them all bulbs. It is useful, however, to be able to distinguish one from the other, for this leads to a better understanding of the particular requirements of the various bulb-like plants and consequently to achieving the most favourable results from their cultivation.

The determination of whether or not a particular plant is technically a bulb depends upon the structure of the storage organ.

The True Bulb like that of the hyacinth, narcissus or tulip, is a bud sheathed in layers of food-storing fleshy white leaves called scales attached to a tough flat disc or basal plate. From this base emerge both the roots and the stem of the flower. It is usually ovoid or conical in shape but may vary as much in appearance as in size. With few exceptions, most true bulbs have a covering of white or coloured dry leaves called a tunic. In tunicated bulbs the fleshy leaves are rolled close together, as in hyacinths. In imbricated bulbs the leaves are thick and overlapping, as in all lilies.

The Corms are like true bulbs in that they have a basal plate from which the roots appear and one or two tunics quite similar in appearance to those of true bulbs. But corms are more or less round, flattish and solid. The swelling consists of the fleshy base of the stem which functions as the food store. On the surface of the corm are one or two buds from which a plant will grow. Among the most familiar plants stemming from corms are crocus and gladiolus.

The Tubers differ from both bulbs and corms in that they have no basal plates or tunics. While varying in size and appearance they usually resemble an irregular sphere with flattened ends. They consist either of part of a swollen stem or part of a swollen root sometimes called a tuberous root, the first bearing latent buds from which the flowers emerge and the latter making growth from buds congregated round the collar or base of the stem. Dahlias and ranunculi are typical examples.

The Rhizomes are thinner and more elongated in shape than tubers and are actually underground stems with buds, as is evidenced in the anemone.

PROPAGATION

One of the big bonuses in gardening with this group of flowering plants is that, although the growth and development of a plant varies according to its particular kind of underground storage organ, all propagate themselves in one way or another, the majority literally producing new stock for the amateur gardener.

Dahlias do not grow in the same way as hyacinths. We have already seen that a bulb is a complete plant with a perfectly formed if embryonic flower and all other necessary organs plus its own food supply. As soon as exterior conditions are right the stem begins to emerge and grows very rapidly, the plant, in most cases, needing only a few weeks to complete its growth above ground.

Unfavourable conditions, however, may prevent the plant from making its debut above ground. This will not damage the bulb for it will continue its life underground, transferring its food store and perpetuating itself either by producing a secondary lateral bulb or by forming fresh scales inside its tunic. So although a bulb may sometimes hesitate to develop into a flower for a year it will eventually grow and flower.

A bulb is capable of remaining in a dormant state for a definite period of time, depending upon the particular mix of temperature and humidity. But it cannot survive indefinitely. When bulbs are preserved above ground for a considerable length of time they will, in most cases, shrivel away. But some are capable despite withering to form a fresh bulb or corm which grows without the assistance of roots or foliage, drawing sustenance from the mother-bulb, which shrivels away as soon as it has transferred its food reserves. Bulb growers in Holland have learned to take advantage of the situation and by determining the exact conditions and period of time necessary for this process have been able in a number of cases to create artificial seasons, alter the growing cycle and produce flowers at will.

Before emerging through the soil bulbs put out roots, sometimes an incredible number of them. Hyacinths, for example, may produce over a score of roots as much as several feet in length to obtain firm anchorage and water. Only when the roots are properly formed will the plant begin to grow above ground, sending up stem, leaves and flower. When the flowers fade the leaves take over, producing nourishment for transmission to the bulb. This is the reason why gardeners should never remove any of the bulb's foliage once it has flowered but allow it to die off naturally. For it is in the vital weeks after flowering that the leaves make their contribution to the following year's bloom.

The particular methods of propagation vary according to the kind of bulb and exterior conditions. The flowers of bulbs are, of course, capable of producing seeds but with few exceptions most bulbs also possess another means of reproduction of more practical advantage to the amateur gardener.

Although there are, admittedly, a few bulbs which can only be increased from seeds, the raising of bulbs from seeds should be left to the specialist or the most enthusiastic of amateurs. It is, frankly, the most difficult way of obtaining new stock. The seed of many bulbs does not come true; that is the seedlings raised have characteristics which differ from their parents. The problem of cross-fertilisation must be taken into account too, and raising bulbs from seeds is a lengthy and rather risky undertaking as well.

Nearly all bulbs multiply, producing new stock for the gardener sooner or later. Some bulbs in effect divide and produce offsets or growths which form at or near the base of the parent. You can see for yourself how, as a narcissus bulb grows bigger year by year, it fragments into two to four smaller bulbs of sufficient size to flower the following year. With tulips and certain other bulbs, however, the mother-bulb disappears but not before producing two or three little bulbs capable of flowering the next year.

And there are other types of bulbs and corms which form many tiny bulbils or cormlets which will flower two to four years later. Some lilies and iris form bulbils and gladioli and some crocus form underground cormlets.

In some cases all that needs to be done by the gardener is allow the bulbs to form natural expanding colonies. In other cases the clumps can be dug up, the bulbs separated according to size, and then be replanted. Rhizomes and tuberous roots may be treated in the same way, so each eye will, with care, produce another plant.

Still other bulbs, like many lilies, will produce aerial bulbils in leaf axils. These are pea-sized but perfectly formed miniature bulbs, which fall away from the mother plant soon after flowering. In favourable conditions they begin to grow and become bulbs capable of flowering in a year or two. And still other bulbs, some tulips and lilies among them, produce stolons, elongated tubular growths at the end of which a tiny bulb forms. These too will in time become flowering bulbs.

CULTIVATION

Although the natural reproduction of bulbs provides continuation of colour and beauty in the garden it is from the selection of new bulbs each planting season for fresh applications, new colour schemes and different breath-taking effects that the gardener derives a real sense of achievement and consequently the greatest enjoyment and satisfaction.

When grown away from their native homes, even in pots or bowls indoors, bulbs will adapt themselves to quite different soils and conditions than those to which they are subjected in their natural habitats. In Britain and North America it is impossible to provide for most bulbs conditions similar to those they are accustomed to in the wild. But an appreciation of the conditions under which bulbs grow in nature is of help in understanding their needs in cultivation. No one garden is likely to provide ideal conditions for all bulbs and different species may do better in one part of a garden than in another. Faced with such a vast choice of bulbs from various parts of the world, the amateur gardener may understandably feel baffled for consideration must be given to the size, design and aspect of the particular garden in selecting bulbs best suited to these conditions.

The scope of applications is covered in Chapters 2 and 3 and the detailed information on the various genera, their species and horticultural varieties under the respective headings will further assist gardeners in selection and application. The remainder of this chapter is devoted to explaining the principles which are the basis of successful cultivation.

Buying Bulbs. It pays to buy the best. Always avoid so-called 'bargain' offers which almost inevitably land you with worthless rubbish. Choose good-sized, good quality bulbs from a reliable and established retailer in ample time for planting. Tunics should be intact but some peeling, particularly in tulips, is natural and in no way harmful. A good bulb is heavy for its size, firm to the touch, plump and free from scars.

The size of most bulbs has been standardised. Before sale they are measured in centimetres and, with the exception of narcissi, classified according to their circumference. Few retailers, however, offer bulbs by this official classification. When size is indicated at all, most retailers use such designations as 'exhibition', 'top', 'first', 'No 1' or 'good flowering' size. The gardener who buys the largest bulbs available cannot go wrong but this is not always necessary. The largest hyacinth bulbs are best for indoor cultivation but 'second' or 'bedding' size hyacinths are adequate for garden plantings. And 'double nose' narcissi produce better bloom than round 'single nose' bulbs.

By buying Dutch bulbs you can be assured of good-sized, top quality

1 *above:* (*left*) Triumph tulip Garden Party and Darwin Hybrid tulip Dover in a mixed bed

2 (*right*) Double narcissus Texas and Double Early tulip Willemsoord in a border planting

3 (*centre*) Fritillaria imperialis and greigii hybrid tulips highlight a garden pool

4 *below:* (*left*) Kaufmanniana tulip Heart's Delight and chionodoxa luciliae blend beautifully together

5 (*right*) Hyacinth Perle Brillante, narcissus Music Hall and tulip Feu Superbe at the base of garden steps

6 *above:* (*left*) Hyacinth Bismarck, narcissus February Gold and tulip Merry Widow planted among paving stones

7 (*right*) A natural home at the base of a tree for muscari armeniacum Blue Spike

8 (*centre*) Hyacinth Lady Derby bring a pink glow to a terrace tub

9 *below:* (*left*) Hyacinth Perle Brillante in a colourful window box planting

10 (*right*) Hyacinths L'Innocence and Anne Marie bid visitors welcome

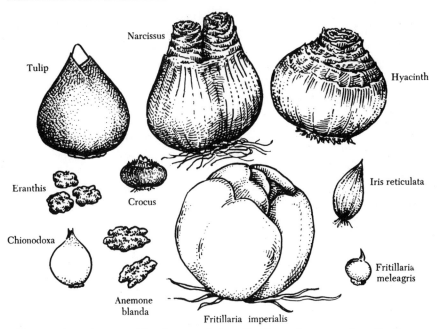

Comparative bulb sizes. The shape and size of bulbs varies as much as the flowers they produce. Generally the size of the flower will be in direct proportion to the size of the bulb, the larger the bulb the larger the resulting flowers. In the case of the narcissus shown, the bulb is 'double-nosed', indicating that two flowers will emerge from this single bulb.

bulbs for the Dutch Government permits export only of those bulbs big enough to produce full-sized flowers the first year. And all bulbs exported from Holland have passed rigid examinations and are certified to be healthy and free of all plant pests and diseases.

Handling Bulbs. Having purchased good bulbs they should be handled with care. Parcels or containers, indeed each bag of bulbs, should be opened at once. It may not be convenient to plant them immediately but this should not be put off for too long. Narcissi, in particular, should be planted early. Tunicated bulbs should be kept in open bags or spread out in flat boxes and stored in a cool, dark, airy place until planting time. Scaly bulbs like lilies and all bulbs with fleshy roots should never be exposed for long, for being without tunics they wither easily. They should be planted on arrival but if this is impossible they should be put in damp peat or sand in flat boxes and stored in a cool place.

Soil Preparation. Although bulbs will grow in virtually any garden soil that is well drained, with few exceptions they prefer lightish, porous soil containing a generous measure of organic matter. Peat or leaf-mould added to any garden soil is beneficial and absolutely necessary in the case of clay or heavy compact soils. Bulbs should always be planted in ground that has been well dug for many strike surprisingly deep roots.

Fertilisers. Most bulbs do not require fertilisers in their first year although, like all plants, all bulbs respond to fertile soil. Some species are greedy feeders, like lilies, dahlias and gladioli, and appreciate additional quantities of humus worked into the soil. Fresh manure should not be used with any bulbs for contact with the underground parts can be disastrous. Only well decomposed manure should be dug into the soil, and even then kept from direct contact with bulbs.

Slow-acting fertilisers other than manure are recommended for feeding bulbs. Bone meal is one of the best and easily obtainable, and five to six pounds per hundred square feet is an adequate annual application. A regular 5–10–5 fertiliser as used in vegetable gardens is also suitable. These can be dug into the soil before planting or replanting or applied as a top dressing to bulbs in situ at any time after flowering and before top growth appears again the following season. Watering with liquid manure once or twice during the vegetative season will help leaf formation. Most bulbs prefer neutral or slightly acid soil. Some lilies are the only ones which require lime-free soil. Hyacinths, however, need chalky soil to survive.

Planting. There is nothing difficult about planting bulbs but it is the most important operation in bulb-growing. When planting quantities of bulbs in beds or in large clumps, the simplest way is to remove the soil to the required depth, set the bulbs securely in the ground and then cover them up with the soil that has been removed. Most bulbs are planted individually, a trowel being the handiest tool, by setting them at the correct depth, according to their species, in well-dug ground. Some species of bulbs may also be planted in lawns or rough grass. A special bulb-planting tool may be used for this or an ordinary spade can be employed to remove a piece of turf with soil, which can be replaced when the bulb has been set in the ground.

The precise depth at which each bulb should be planted varies according to the nature of the ground, the size of the bulb and the height of the

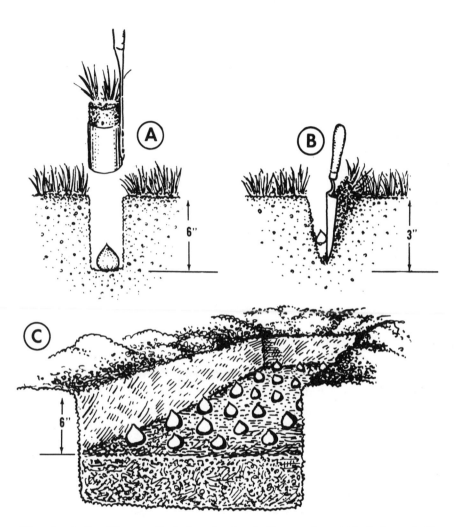

Planting bulbs. Three methods for planting bulbs are shown. (i) Using a bulb-planting tool, remove a core of earth to the proper depth, set the bulb in place and refill the hole.

(ii) The usual method for planting individual bulbs is to push the trowel into the soil to the required depth, pull the trowel towards you, insert the bulb and then refill the hole.

(iii) When a dozen or more bulbs are to be planted in one location, remove all of the soil to the proper depth with a spade, break up the soil below, set the bulbs in place and cover with removed soil.

flowering stem. For example, bulbs should be planted more deeply in light, sandy soil than in heavy, stiff earth. As a general rule bulbs can be set with their tops about two to three times the diameter of the bulb below the soil level. In most cases it is the pointed end of the bulb which should face upwards. Always avoid pockets underneath the bulb. It is better to plant too deeply than too shallowly. Spacing can also vary considerably according to the effect a gardener wants to create.

Planting Times. There are three bulb-planting seasons. All spring-flowering bulbs, and these include those harbingers of spring which bloom in winter, should be planted in late summer to autumn. The roots of narcissi develop slowly and these bulbs should be planted as early as possible. The hardy autumn-flowering species should be planted in summer. Summer-flowering bulbs should be planted in spring, after there is no more danger of frost. Lilies are the hardiest of all summer-flowering species, however, and can be planted in the autumn. In areas where winters are severe it is wise to plant stem-rooting types in the spring.

Watering. All sites in which bulbs have been planted should be watered immediately after planting. All bulbs require plenty of moisture when actively growing and as much water as possible when they are coming into flower. Rainfall may not be sufficient for proper development. Summer-flowering bulbs frequently suffer in dry weather. Spring-flowering bulbs too, although less susceptible, should be watered thoroughly whenever necessary and care should be taken to keep water from the actual flowers.

Particular care must be taken after flowering, for it is between the falling of the petals and the withering of the leaves that the bulb stores the nourishment required for future flowering. This food is manufactured by the green leaves of the current season; therefore it is essential not only that sufficient green leaves to carry out this process be developed and retained but also that they be kept in good condition until their work is complete. When cutting flowers from bulbs it is vital that most leaves are left if the bulb is expected to produce flowers again. When bulbs are lifted before the leaves have ripened to provide space for other plants, they should be heeled into the ground elsewhere so that the leaves ripen normally. All bulbous plants should be fed, and watered when necessary, after flowering to keep them alive as long as possible.

Mulching, which involves covering the soil with a layer of peat or well-rotted organic matter to retain moisture, is mandatory for the successful cultivation of lilies and will benefit other summer-flowering bulbs too. It will also discourage weeds.

Mulches can be employed effectively for winter protection in areas where severe winters can be expected, although in general mulching is rarely required. Any type of mulch can be used—peat, salt hay, straw or dried leaves. Three to six inches of mulch should be applied only after the top couple of inches of soil are frozen. The purpose of winter protection is not to keep the bulbs warm but to minimise the hazards of alternate freezing and thawing which may lift and expose bulbs or break their roots.

Staking. Most bulbs have strong enough stems to support themselves. The taller bulbous plants, such as dahlias, gladioli and lilies, can be damaged by high winds and storms and it is a wise precaution to stake them to prevent accidents. Stakes in proportion to the plants they support should be erected when the bulbs are planted to obviate damage. As the plants grow the stems can be tied to the stakes, concealing the stakes as much as possible.

General Care. Bulbs, like all other plants, do not like being smothered in weeds or cluttered with debris. An untidy garden is in any case an eyesore. Gently loosening the soil round growing bulbs keeps down weeds and assists drainage but care should be taken that the hoe does not touch the bulbs. After flowering the stems should be cut off just below the flower for seed-formation draws on food reserves and weakens bulbs for future flowering. Fallen petals should be removed to prevent any risk of soil contamination. Even when leaves begin to turn yellow they should be retained until they have completely withered. When bulbs are grown in clumps on lawns, uncut islands should be left for the leaves to do their proper job. Rough grass should not be cut at all until the bulbs have completed their vegetative cycle.

Moving Bulbs. Most bulbs prefer not to be disturbed too often. The vast majority of the hardy spring-flowering bulbs can be left in their particular garden homes during the winter and, indeed, need not be moved for at least three or four years. When bulbs are flourishing in spots they like they tend to increase rapidly. Pleased as every gardener will be there is a real danger that congestion will affect proper growth. When overcrowded, bulbs remain small and the flowers degenerate and become fewer. When this occurs, the clumps should be dug up, the bulbs divided and replanted in fresh sites. This should be done during the bulb's dormant period, after the foliage has completely withered away.

There are always exceptions in the world of bulbs, however, and snowdrops, for example, must be lifted, divided and transplanted immediately after flowering. Moving growing bulbs should be done carefully, ensuring that clumps of soil are left adhering to the roots. They should be replanted in new situations immediately and be given plenty of water.

Most summer-flowering bulbs, being tender should be lifted after flowers have faded and foliage has died down for storage away from frost during the winter months. Again there are exceptions. Lilies are genuinely hardy bulbs and should not be disturbed. Anemones, montbretias and ranunculi can be left in situ with a protective mulch except in those areas with really severe winters.

Storing Bulbs. Dormant bulbs do not require much attention but on no account should they be piled on top of each other. Damp is fatal and bulbs should be stored in a single layer with space between each in flat boxes or on open slats to ensure good ventilation. All dead foliage and earth should be removed and storage places should be dry and cool but frost-free. Dahlia tubers appreciate being stored away in boxes of clean fresh peat.

Pests and Diseases. Bulbs are fortunately subject to fewer troubles of this kind than the majority of plants. The best insurance is to purchase healthy Dutch bulbs from reliable retailers. Few gardeners who do this are ever troubled by diseases, particularly when a high standard of garden cleanliness is maintained. All rotten or diseased material or dead and diseased plants should be cleared out as soon as spotted and burnt before they can spread infection.

Spring-flowering bulbs bloom so early in the year that it is still too cool for insects to be a nuisance. Summer-flowering bulbs have various potential insect pests and precautionary preventive measures are described for each kind of bulb under its respective heading.

Although quite rare the possibility of a bulb contracting a disease cannot be ruled out entirely. Any suspect bulbous plant should be immediately lifted and burned and a close watch kept on neighbouring bulbs for any signs of spreading infection. Should this occur lifting of the healthy bulbs, disinfecting them, and replanting them in an area not previously used for the same kind of bulbs will usually save them. The soil in which any infected plant has been sited should be sterilised before being used again.

The major pests are slugs and snails and fortunately these can be controlled by modern slug killers. Ants can sometimes cause trouble but they too can be controlled with several products now on the market.

Birds seldom give trouble but have been known to attack and ravage crocus flowers. Criss-crossed cotton thread is an effective if unsightly deterrent and gardeners may well prefer to purchase the bird repellents now available.

Mice can cause damage to bulbs in the garden and those that are stored. A cat will keep mice under control or there are modern poisons for destroying mice and rats which are not harmful to children or pets.

Gardeners should not dwell unduly on the possibilities of attacks by pests and diseases which can only detract from the enjoyment of bulbs. Purchase the best, provide good growing conditions, practice garden hygiene, take preventive measures where possible and when using garden chemicals carefully follow the manufacturer's instructions and your troubles will be minimal or non-existent.

Chapter Two

BULBS IN THE GARDEN

BULBS CAN be used at so many times in so many places and in so many ways that the modern labour-saving and leisure-oriented home environment is incomplete without them. Bulbs are to gardening today what 'convenience foods' are to home catering—quick results from a handy complete package when you want them with the least possible trouble. And the 'convenience factor' of bulbs far outstrips that of foods for their applications in comparison are almost infinite.

With a little imaginative selectivity every garden, whatever its size, shape or aspect, can be bright and beautiful, for only a few dozens of bulbs of various kinds will produce a pageant of colour in spring. This brilliant seasonal debut is what comes to the minds of most gardeners when they think of bulbs, for bulbs have long been the traditional heralds of spring. Yet spring is not the only 'natural' season for bulbs as the uninitiated seem to think, for by selecting a few dozens more of the many other kinds of bulbs available a succession of gay and exotic flowers can be enjoyed throughout the year.

A YEAR-ROUND BULB CALENDAR

Although nature tends to be fickle and each year introduces her seasons at slightly different times, often varying her favours from area to area even in relatively close proximity, the following calendar of bulb flowering times provides a useful general guide to the particular sequence of bulb bloom outdoors in Britain. As the sequence of bloom, with rare exceptions, is identical in North America, gardeners there can easily adjust these dates to the arrival of the seasons in compiling their own local bulb calendar.

January

Crocus ancyrensis
Eranthis cilicica, hyemalis (winter aconites)
Galanthus elwesii, nivalis, nivalis flore pleno (snowdrops)

February

Crocus biflorus, chrysanthus varieties, sieberi varieties
Iris bakeriana, danfordiae, reticulata hybrids
Leucojum vernum (Spring Snowflake)
Narcissus cyclamineus, cyclamineus February Gold and Peeping Tom, lobularis, minimus, obvallaris
Scilla tubergeniana
Tulipa biflora, pulchella violacea (Violet Queen)

March

Anemone blanda varieties
Chionodoxa gigantea, luciliae, luciliae Pink Giant, sardensis (Glory of the Snow)
Crocus tomasinianus varieties
Dutch crocus (large-flowered) varieties
Iris histrioides major
Muscari botryoides, botryoides album (Grape Hyacinths)
Narcissus bulbocodium citrinus, bulbocodium conspicuus, campernelli, cyclamineus March Sunshine, nanus, W. P. Milner
Puschkinia libanotica (scilloides), libanotica alba
Scilla bifolia, siberica, siberica alba, siberica Spring Beauty
Tulipa eichleri, praestans and varieties, turkestanica, Kaufmanniana hybrids

April

Anemone appenina, appenina alba, de Caen varieties, St. Bavo mixtures, St. Brigid varieties (autumn-planted)
Brodiaea uniflora (Spring Star Flower)
Erythronium dens-canis mixtures, revolutum hybrids, tuolumnense
Fritillaria imperialis varieties, meleagris varieties
Hyacinthus

Iris tuberosa (Hermodactylus tuberosus)

Muscari armeniacum (Early Giant), armeniacum Blue Spike

Narcissus canaliculatus, triandrus albus (Angel's Tears), triandrus varieties, trumpets, large and small-cupped, doubles, jonquils, tazetta, poeticus varieties

Ornithogalum nutans

Tulipa aucheriana, chrysantha, clusiana, kolpakowskiana, tarda, tubergeniana, urumiensis, Fosteriana hybrids, Greigii hybrids, Single Early, Double Early, Mendel, Triumph and Darwin Hybrid varieties

May

Allium aflatunense, karataviense, rosenbachianum

Camassia cusickii, esculenta

Leucojum aestivum, aestivum Gravetye (Summer Snowflake)

Lilium pumilum (tenuifolium), pumilum Golden Gleam

Muscari plumosum (comosum), tubergenianum

Narcissus albus plenus odoratus, Silver Chimes

Ornithogalum umbellatum (Star of Bethlehem)

Scilla campanulata (Endymion hispanicus), nutans (Endymion non-scriptus)

Sparaxis

Tulipa acuminata, batalinii, linifolia, marjolettii, persica (celsiana), Darwin, Lily-flowered, Cottage, Rembrandt, Parrot and Double Late varieties

June

Anemone de Caen varieties, St. Brigid varieties (spring-planted)

Allium albopilosum, giganteum, moly, neopolitanum, ostrowskianum, roseum

Brodiaea lactea, laxa, Queen Fabiola

Camassia leichtlinii Caerulea

Dutch Iris varieties

Eremurus bungei, robustus, Ruiter hybrids, Shelford hybrids

Gladiolus nanus varieties

Ixia mixtures

Ixiolirion ledebourii (montanum), pallasii

Lilium Brandywine, candidum, Cinnabar, Destiny, Enchantment, hansonii, Harmony, longiflorum, longiflorum Holland's Glory,

Marhan, martagon, Orange Triumph, regale album, Tabasco, Tangelo, Vermilion Brilliant
Oxalis adenophylla
Ranunculus

July

Allium sphaerocephalum
Begonia
Brodiaea tubergenii
Canna
Gladiolus butterfly, large-flowered, primulinus
Ismene (Hymenocallis) calathina Advance, Festalis
Lilium amabile, Bellingham hybrids, Bright Star, Citronella, Fiesta hybrids, Fire King, Golden Splendour, Golden Sunburst, Joan Evans, Limelight, longiflorum Mount Everest, longiflorum White Queen, Maxwill, Olympic hybrids, pardalinum, pardalinum giganteum, Pink Perfection, regale, Royal Gold, sutchuenense
Montbretia (Tritonia) mixtures
Ornithogalum thyrsoides (chincherinchee)
Oxalis deppei, deppei alba
Sprekelia formossisima
Tigridia (Ferraria)
Zephyranthes robusta (Habranthus robustus)

August

Acidanthera murielae
Colchicum autumnale, autumnale major (byzantinum)
Crocus speciosus, zonatus (kotschyanus)
Dahlia
Freesia (outdoor)
Galtonia candicans
Lilium auratum, henryi, speciosum, speciosum album, speciosum Grand Commander, speciosum Lucie Wilson, speciosum roseum, tigrinum, tigrinum flaviflorum, tigrinum splendens

September

Colchicum autumnale minor, autumnale album, Waterlily
Crocus pulchellus, speciosus albus

Lilium speciosum rubrum, speciosum Uchida, tigrinum flore pleno,
   tigrinum Fortunei giganteum
Zephryanthes candida

October

Colchicum The Giant, Lilac Wonder
Nerine bowdenii, bowdenii Pink Triumph
Sternbergia lutea

November

Sternbergia lutea

December

Crocus laevigatus

It should be noted that a number of summer-flowering bulbs, particularly gladioli and dahlias, go on flowering until the first frosts.

GARDEN DISPLAY

Because the basic requirements of bulbs are so easily met gardeners can
concentrate on the enjoyable side of gardening—planning and achieving
attractive displays and delightful colour combinations of flowers. This is
especially easy with bulbs because their diversity and adaptability
provide such wide scope.

It is the characteristics or qualities of any plant—flowering time,
size, habit and colour—that we should look to for clues as to the situations in which it looks best, the most appropriate planting locations. And
I have found over the years that it is almost invariably better to grow
the plants suited to the particular conditions of one's garden than to
attempt to modify substantially the conditions to suit particular plants.
This does not mean, however, that we should not continually strive to
improve conditions by enriching our soil, correcting inadequate drainage
and ensuring that our gardens retain good access to light by trimming
trees and keeping shrubs under control.

Choice is then made easier; it comes down to considering when and
where flowers are to bloom, and then selecting those which best lend
themselves to given situations. Of course, choice of one type or one
variety of bulb flower over another sensibly and simply boils down to
planting what one likes.

Few of us are endowed with a natural aptitude for design but it is a facility we can all acquire. I am convinced that genuinely effective garden displays and eye-catching colour combinations are the result of thoughtful forward planning. This involves becoming acquainted with the qualities of plants, observing their behaviour in one's own and other people's gardens and encouraging the desire both to learn by mistakes and to continue experimenting with new species and varieties.

Beginners will find it helpful to sketch on paper rough large-scale planting plans for every garden situation that presents a problem, incorporating firstly the sites of any subjects already permanently established and then when siting bulbs to note simultaneously their respective characteristics. As knowledge and experience is acquired paper work will become unnecessary and planning can be carried out by conjuring up mental images of the results of plantings.

The vast majority of gardeners are in for a pleasant surprise for the range of applications is exceeded only by the choice of bulbs available for each application. Most genera of bulbs, in fact, provide us with species of varying characteristics for different applications. And it is the rare individual species or horticultural variety that cannot be deployed in a number of ways. The specific applications to which they can be put forms an integral part of the descriptions of all plants in this book. This chapter seeks to give gardeners maximum assistance in planning and an at-a-glance indicator of scope by defining and explaining the various applications and listing under each all genera of bulbs from which plants can be selected.

Bulbs in Beds. Bulbs, particularly spring-flowering bulbs, are still widely used in parks and public gardens for bedding for there is no other group of plants which is quite so effective in providing masses of early brilliant colour. The diminishing size of private gardens in the face of soaring land values and the increased population densities per acre of modern times, however, has made heavy inroads into the long-time popularity of planting bulbs in vast formal beds in private gardens. The concept of the private garden is gradually changing too with both greater informality in lay-out and the wider use of the garden as a leisure area. The days of planting out masses of fragrant hyacinths or flamboyant tulips in huge and elaborate symmetrical patterns in private gardens has all but disappeared.

Today bulbs can and are being used for bedding in new ways. Small

Page 48 (*above*) Formal beds of hyacinths at the Keukenhof; (*below*) informal beds of daffodils at the Keukenhof

Page 10 (*above*) Muscari armeniacum Interplanted effectively with trumpet daffodils; (*below left*) double early tulips are ideal for bedding; (*below right*) a mixed border planting of N. Carlton, T. fosteriana Red Emperor, T. kaufmanniana Goudstuk and N. Unsurpassable backed by shrubs

formal beds of bulbs are ideal for enclosed or segmented gardens and can produce tremendous impact when used to enhance architectural features of a house, to 'dress' retaining walls, to call attention to raised terraces, to highlight a pool, to 'soften' different levels of lawn, to give lustre to a group of evergreens, or to brighten long lengths of hedge.

Even with the present trend towards labour-saving woodland or wild gardens, particularly in rural areas, there is usually a transitional area between the house and the woodland garden where bedding schemes can be employed most effectively. Beds need not be completely formal and can be linked to irregularly placed paving stones or sections of low hedge or wall.

Gardeners living in industrial areas where pollution tends to contribute a layer of grime to permanent plantings will find temporary beds of bulbs particularly useful in keeping gardens fresh-looking.

'Sitting out' or dining areas, perhaps partially concealed by wooden trellises or perforated concrete walling from the remainder of the garden, offer fresh scope for smaller decorative beds of bulbs. Rose beds can be transformed from the dull areas they are before the roses burst into bloom by underplantings of spring-flowering bulbs like hyacinths, tulips, crocuses, chionodoxa or grape hyacinths which give an early blaze of colour.

The wider use of summer-flowering bulbs for bedding is coming in too as more gardeners discover the exotic beauty of grouped acidanthera, tigridia, galtonia and lilies to augment the more familiar dahlias and gladioli.

Bulbs, whatever their particular season of flowering, need not be planted in solid blocks of a single colour. Two or more varieties of the same kind of bulb in contrasting or harmonising colours may be used together, such as pink and white hyacinths, mauve and yellow tulips, or indeed, a lively mixture of half a dozen varieties of the same class of tulips.

More than one kind of bulb can be used in a single bed, for example, daffodils and grape hyacinths or anemones and ranunculi, or off-beat combinations like acidanthera and galtonia. As the combinations become more complex, however, the gardener has to exercise more care. A single variety of any kind of bulb in a bed is foolproof, but it is easy to make mistakes when different kinds of bulbs or even different varieties of the same class of bulbs are used together. The single variety bed is hardly a creative challenge and consequently the mixed bed has wider

11 (*above*) Tulip Bellona, hyacinth Jan Bos, narcissus Golden Harvest and crocus Pickwick dispel winter gloom

12 (*right*) Hyacinth Blue Jacket and narcissus Gold Medal herald the approach of spring

13 *below:* (*left*) Prepared tulip Christmas Marvel is aptly named

14 (*right*) Narcissus Cragford can also be had in flower for Christmas

15 *above: (left)* Crocus purpureus grandiflorus, narcissus Van Sion and scilla tubergeniana add colour to any windowsill

16 (*right*) Tulipa kaufmanniana Johan Strauss and Triumph tulip Paris make interesting indoor companions

17 (*centre*) Crocus chrysanthus Goldilocks is an effective home brightener

18 *below: (left)* Tulip Paul Richter, narcissus Gold Medal and crocus Remembrance create a mini-garden indoors

19 (*right*) Parrot tulip Karel Doorman and iris reticulata are unusual indoor plants

20 *above:* (*left*) A simple but effective triangular arrangement of tulips. daffodils and Dutch iris

21 (*right*) A Christmas arrangement of Dutch iris

22 (*centre*) A basketful of beauty with tulips and daffodils

23 *below:* (*left*) Elegance with Dutch iris

24 (*right*) Unusual living bookends

25 Fresh flowers add sparkle to traditional gifts

appeal. When choosing bulbs for such plantings it is vital to select kinds intended to provide planned colour combinations that will bloom together and are appropriate in height.

Bulbs need not be used alone in beds. Gorgeous effects can be achieved by employing bulbs in combinations with non-bulbous plants, such as alyssum, arabis, aubrietia, daisies, forget-me-nots, heliotrope, lobelia, pansies, phlox, polyanthus, salpiglossis, violas and wallflowers. Many subtle or alternatively daring colour associations can be worked out from season to season and year to year.

The preparation of beds should be thorough. Soil should be well dug and allowed to settle for a week or two before planting. Digging in of well-rotted manure or compost will benefit most beds and an application of bone meal mixed in at the rate of a quarter to a half pound per square yard is helpful too. If bulbs are to be mixed with other subjects, such as wallflowers, these are best planted before the bulbs. It is appreciated that few gardeners can afford the space to devote beds exclusively to bulbs, even if summer-flowering bulbs follow a planned succession of spring-flowering bulbs. If beds are to be used at other times for other plants, bulbs can be lifted before their foliage ripens provided they are heeled in to wither away normally in an odd corner of the garden.

In planting bulbs in beds do remember that, like all flowers which look only one way when in bloom, bulbs like narcissi and gladioli are better sited in beds against a wall or fence or with a background of shrubs than in beds which are viewed from all sides.

Some bulbs, like acidantheras, hyacinths or the more recently introduced outdoor freesias, produce scented flowers and will be particularly rewarding when planted in beds close to the house, terrace or 'sitting out' area.

Gardeners can draw upon the following genera of bulbs for species and varieties suitable for planting in beds:

Acidanthera	Colchicum	Gladiolus	Narcissus
Allium	Crocus	Hyacinthus	Ornithogalum
Anemone	Dahlia	Iris	Ranunculus
Begonia	Freesia	Ixia	Scilla
Camassia	Fritillaria	Ixiolirion	Tigridia
Canna	Galanthus	Lilium	Tulipa
Chionodoxa	Galtonia	Muscari	

Bulbs in Borders. Most of the principles applicable to the use of bulbs in beds apply to the use of bulbs in borders, although there is a greater choice and wider flexibility in planting. The background and contrast which can be provided by shrubs in a mixed shrub, bulb and herbaceous plant border can be delightful. The use of perennials, biennials and annuals of various kinds informally with bulbs makes possible a continuing succession of flower in one border with less movement of bulbs and other plants. Minor replanting is necessary from time to time, of course, but major replanting becomes mandatory only after intervals of about five years.

Informal mixed borders may be established close to the house, may extend in sweeping curves along the drive, a wooded copse, a stream or even a drainage ditch, and may be sited against a background of shrubs or against a wall, hedge or fence.

Bulbs of various flowering heights can be selected for the front of the border and for all points to the very back. Even narrow borders under a wall or in front of a sun-house will provide superb sites for shorter-stemmed bulbs that appreciate extra warmth.

Bulbs planted in well-dug borders should always be grouped irregularly rather than in geometric patterns. When selecting bulbs for grouping the number needed for each area may be relatively small if their flowers are large and relatively large if their flowers are small. Normally the bigger the border the bigger the groups of bulbs should be. In the average border medium-sized bulbs like tulips, daffodils and hyacinths are most effective if planted in groups or clusters of a dozen or more together while smaller subjects such as crocuses, snowdrops and winter aconites should be sited in plantings of at least 3–4 dozen. Often tall, large-flowered bulbs like crown imperials (fritillaria imperialis), galtonias or lilies can be planted in groups of only half dozen or so for striking impact in a mixed border.

Bulbs such as crocuses, chionodoxas, narcissi, montbretias and others that multiply rapidly to form spreading colonies should be planted in border areas allowing room for expansion and where they need not be disturbed.

Locate bulbs with long coarse or leafy foliage behind perennials that will grow up and hide yellowing leaves after the flowers have faded. If annuals are used to provide colour after bulbs allow enough space between or near the bulbs to permit filling in with annual seedlings.

Remember too that many bulbs prefer sun but that a surprising number will flourish in partial shade. Plants should never be jammed into a border but lovely displays can be achieved by combining bulbs with lower-growing ground covers.

The gardener who keeps records of flowering dates, subjects that blend effectively or provide striking contrast and other pertinent data will find the information most useful for improving existing borders or planning new ones. Consideration of colour and form is as important as size in achieving maximum results in mixed borders.

Not only more kinds of bulbs but more species and varieties of them are suited to border plantings. Gardeners can choose widely from the following genera:

Acidanthera	Dahlia	Hyacinthus	Narcissus
Allium	Eranthis	Iris	Ornithogalum
Anemone	Eremurus	Ismene	Oxalis
Begonia	Erythronium	Ixia	Puschkinia
Brodiaea	Freesia	Ixiolirion	Ranunculus
Camassia	Fritillaria	Leucojum	Scilla
Chionodoxa	Galanthus	Lilium	Sternbergia
Colchicum	Galtonia	Montbretia	Tigridia
Crocus	Gladiolus	Muscari	Tulipa

Bulbs in Woodlands. A surprising number of gardeners, particularly those living in rural areas, have patches of open woodland or orchard near their homes, often forming an extension of the garden proper. They make wonderful homes especially for many prolific and easily spreading species of bulbs and can literally transform the outlook. Few bulbs will grow in heavy shade but in semi-shade or in open glades a wide range will flourish. It is possible to have lovely masses of colour for most of the year in open woodland that is not too dry but trees should be used largely as background with plantings sited away from those trees with surface roots or thick foliage.

For woodland planting, as for bed and border planting, it is wise to break up the ground first working in additional leaf-mould or peat in cases of heavy soil or in places where drainage is not all it should be. Bulbs should always be planted informally, in drifts or irregularly-shaped groups. Many of the smaller bulbs will thrive in rather thick clumps but some like fritillarias, certain lilies and species tulips should be allowed more breathing space. A surprising number of bulbs will grow

Page 58 (*above left*) T. kaufmanniana thrive in a sunny foundation planting;
(*above right*) transforming an odd corner with hyacinths and daffodils;
(*below left*) scilla siberica and greigii tulips planted between paving stones;
(*below right*) N. Rembrandt admirably set off garden steps

in competition with grass but most lilies, for example, prefer special soil preparation and a clear area for their roots.

Depending upon conditions the gardener can choose from these genera:

Anemone	Eremurus	Gladiolus	Montbretia
Colchicum	Fritillaria	Iris	Narcissus
Crocus	Galanthus	Lilium	Scilla
Eranthis	Galtonia		Tulipa

Naturalising Bulbs. The least demanding and, for many, the most attractive way of growing bulbs is by naturalisation. Naturalised bulbs are those grown under as near natural conditions as possible, both in terms of arrangement and location. The proven advantages of this method of bulb gardening are that vigorous and hardy bulbs happily located will fend for themselves and multiply rapidly over the years, creating enchanting garden pictures with a minimum of maintenance and expenditure.

Naturalised bulbs are those planted to appear as if they had emerged from natural offsets or seeds. The spacing rules are abandoned and the bulbs are simply scattered and planted at the normal depths where they fall. To enhance the effect plants that are not too developed horticulturally are employed, single flowers, on the whole, being more suitable than double flowers.

There is a large range of bulbs available for naturalisation. Selections may be made that are suitable for planting in lawns, on grassy banks or slopes, in meadowland, in shrubberies, under solitary trees or in copses, among rocks or in remote corners of the garden.

Naturalisation adds a new dimension to gardening, making maximum use of space and requiring a minimum of care. There is the initial planting but no seasonal round of lifting, drying off, cleaning, storing and subsequent replanting. Naturalised bulbs are not regularly weeded, although the most invasive subjects may require curbing, nor does a great deal of attention have to be devoted to such routine chores as cultivation and staking. The one essential requirement for the continuance of bulbs naturalised in lawns or grassland is that lawns and grass are not cut until the leaves of the bulbs have died down. Bulbs naturalised in lawns, therefore, are better sited on the periphery rather than in the centre, along sloping areas where a continuous short velvety effect is less important, or under trees or shrubs.

Most gardeners are familiar with narcissi naturalised in grass. The stronger varieties of trumpets and large-cupped daffodils are ideal for this purpose and many small-cupped varieties also do well when naturalised. Poeticus recurvus or old Pheasant's Eye is a fragrant subject for this method of bulb growing. There are miniature narcissi which flourish when naturalised including bulbocodium conspicuus or the Yellow Hooped Petticoat, triandrus albus or Angel's Tears, or the early cyclamineus varieties.

The average gardener doesn't have the space to naturalise narcissi in their thousands in vast meadows or woodlands but drifts ranging from a few dozen to a few hundred create lovely pictures as the years go by. Most suppliers offer special mixtures of narcissi for naturalisation at most economic prices.

Combine them with puschkinia, muscari or chionodoxa or naturalise them under flowering cherries, dogwoods and light trees of all kinds.

The large-flowered Dutch crocus and the earlier flowering silvery lilac Tomasinianus varieties will flower in great profusion in the lawn or orchard, at approaches to woodland or even right under that mighty oak.

When naturalising bulbs in dozens rather than in hundreds, it is advisable to relate them closely to an important shrub, evergreen or tree. Plant bright yellow winter aconites beneath the winter-bronzed foliage of a mahonia or site snowdrops in scattered groups in the shelter of evergreen shrubs. Use blue muscari under gay yellow forsythias or with japonicas. Colonies of blue or white chionodoxa are very effective near azaleas or beneath magnolias. Carpet the ground under Viburnum fragrans or cotoneasters with blue or white scillas, or try them beneath shrubs and trees that border lawns.

If there is a rather moist and partially shaded area camassias naturalised there will be most effective. The common bluebell multiplies rapidly when naturalised in wooded areas. Colonies of fritillaria meleagris with their chartreusy tones look delightful under the branches of cotoneasters or among rocks. Anemones produce endless colour in partially shaded conditions.

For the most part tulips are not suitable for naturalisation but some species, including clusiana, praestans and tarda, do very well when planted in this way. The whole group of Kaufmanniana varieties in a wide range of cheery colours will naturalise effectively.

Valuable for massing and naturalising are leucojum vernum or Spring Snowflakes and the dwarf kinds of ornithogalum can be planted

Page 61 (*above*) Turf is the natural habitat of daffodils and no bulbs naturalise as effectively as these; (*below left*) crocus can be easily naturalised, even under huge trees; (*below right*) Chionodoxa luciliae Pink Giant naturalised in a rockery

at random in shady positions near shrubs and hedges and be naturalised in places where few other bulbs will flourish.

Erythroniums naturalise well in sheltered positions and even lilies can be naturalised if their roots are looked after. Try some of the lovely mid-century group in grass in the wild garden where they can catch the morning sun. The well-known tiger lily will flower profusely when naturalised and for something special plant some magnificent white lilium longiflorum Mount Everest in woodland surrounds.

Autumn-flowering crocus can be naturalised and those handsome autumn-flowering colchicum, if planted in grass under tall trees in exposed parts of the garden, will flower profusely from year to year. The clear yellow crocus-like flowers of sternbergia lutea are most effective on grassy banks and, once established, bring lovely late autumn colour to the garden.

These are but a few ideas for naturalising bulbs. A good look round the garden will yield many more suitable sites. While naturalised bulbs require a minimum of care do treat them as valued permanent residents of the garden, remaining on location and supplying you with delight and enjoyment year after year. It is essential that the soil they are planted in is fertile and well-drained. Bulbs should be planted at the correct depths.

When planting small quantities of bulbs in lawns it is practical to lift sections of the turf, work over the soil mixing in a little humus and bone-meal, and then scatter the bulbs on top planting them where they fall before replacing the turf. If large numbers of bulbs are involved it is worth investing in a special bulb planting tool. Whenever a bulb planter is used, however, when placing bulbs at the bottom of holes make sure the soil is loose and in firm contact all round the bulbs. Fertiliser is not mandatory when planting bulbs this way in healthy turf for such turf is itself an indicator of reasonable soil conditions.

All naturalised bulbs will benefit from an annual application of bone meal or complete fertiliser whether in grass or not. Those naturalised in grassless places under trees or shrubs will also welcome an annual application of peat or leaf-mould.

Naturalised bulbs will go on for years, multiplying and creating new garden pictures. After a number of years they will, however, tend to become overcrowded. When the flowers become fewer and smaller then its time to lift the bulbs after their foliage has died down, separate and sort the bulbs according to size, and store the bigger ones for replanting at the appropriate time.

Bulbs suitable for naturalising can be selected from among the following genera:

Allium	Crocus	Leucojum	Puschkinia
Anemone	Eranthis	Lilium	Scilla
Camassia	Erythronium	Muscari	Sternbergia
Chionodoxa	Fritillaria	Narcissus	Tulipa
Colchicum	Galanthus	Ornithogalum	

Bulbs in the Rock Garden. Rock gardens are becoming more popular than ever with both British and North American gardeners because they provide focal points for charming displays as well as homes for a wide variety of plants in a comparatively small area. As few of us have natural outcroppings of rock in our gardens the vast majority of rockeries are artificial creations built of imported rocks and stone to simulate widely differing natural formations on a smaller scale. The different levels, contours and pockets and the frequent inclusion of a pool of one kind or another make ideal stages from which to present a series of intimate floral pictures, a succession of plant close-ups that can be admired and enjoyed at close range.

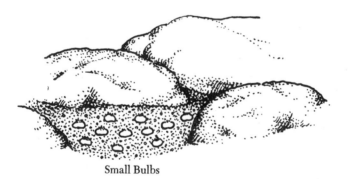

Small Bulbs

Rock pocket planting. With some of the smaller minor bulbs an entire clump can be planted in small pockets among the rocks in a rock garden.

Whether you have a large and elaborate rock garden with collections of Alpines and rare plants or a relatively small and simple area where a few rocks have been strategically sited in a bank or beside a sloping path the contribution which bulbs can make should not be overlooked.

Bulbs transform any rock garden into a year-round show place for it is not difficult to have bulbs flowering in the rock garden during every season and particularly early in the year and late in the autumn, outside the concentrated flowering times of most rock garden plants. And bulbs do not require the special soil conditions and cultural procedures demanded by so many traditional rock garden plants. They flourish in the open and often exposed situations of rockeries and revel in the good drainage essential to all rock gardens. Bulbs can be sited in any location in any size rockery where there is an adequate depth of soil; in full sun, partial shade, beside pools and even in rock crevices which permit their roots to reach down to good earth. They are perfect subjects to help the gardener achieve a natural setting, excellent foils in sheltered pockets in front of rocks as in difficult positions where more temperamental plants fail to thrive.

Of course it is primarily the shorter subjects that lend themselves to rock garden applications and the world of bulbs offers a tantalising choice of species remarkable not only for their miniature stature but for their prolific flowering, showiness of form and gay colours. They will hold their own in isolated positions where they can be left undisturbed to produce fresh floral pictures year after year or they can be grown in association with other plants.

As bulbs are without foliage for part of the year, they can be sited among plants that cover the ground when the bulbs are leafless. For example, the more vigorous species can be combined with creeping veronicas and thymes, through acaenas to lotus corniculatus and trailing hypericums.

Bulbs should be planted in naturalistic, informal groups in the rock garden in relation to their immediate surroundings and can be employed to contrast or harmonise with other subjects, to fill colour gaps, to draw attention to or highlight a contour or particular feature.

Many of the very early-flowering miscellaneous bulbs like winter aconites, snowdrops, crocus, dwarf iris and scilla to name but a few can provide colour long before most other rock-plants bloom. The wide choice of dwarf narcissi will give interest throughout the spring and what other group of plants will provide such flamboyant splashes of colour for so long a period as the wide range of species tulips.

There are various kinds of anemones and ornithogalum which will thrive in positions that are shaded for part of the day. Little puschkinia do not insist on full sun either. Various kinds of erythroniums do

Page 65 (*above*) Eranthis hyemalis flourish among rocks; (*below*) T. greigii
Rockery Master are aptly named

Page 66 (*above left*) Iris danfordiae are superb rockery subjects; (*above right*) iris reticulata and C. chrysanthus Cream Beauty at home in a rock garden; (*below left*) sparaxis welcome the shelter of rocks; (*below right*) spectacular early colour with T. kaufmanniana Vivaldi in the rockery

particularly well in ·those somewhat damp sheltered positions. Free-flowering chionodoxas are most impressive in scattered plantings while fritillaria meleagris and the equally unusual brodiaeas add distinction to any rock garden collection.

Dwarf alliums and gladioli along with ixias and oxalis contribute with other choice bulbs to summer colour and for the autumn there are sternbergia and crocus, the latter genus providing species that keep your rockery in colour right through the winter.

Many gardeners may consider it anathema to employ anything but dwarf subjects in a rockery. But there are larger bulbs that look as much at home among rocks as their smaller relations. I have seen outsize fritillaria imperialis with their large tufted heads reflected in a rock garden pool transform a rockery from the ordinary to the spectacular. I have often used those elegant lily-flowered tulips to give impact to a deep pocket among large rocks in my own rockery.

Choose imaginatively from among the following genera to add a new dimension and year-round colour and interest to your rock garden:

Allium	Erythronium	Leucojum	Puschkinia
Anemone	Fritillaria	Lilium	Ranunculus
Brodiaea	Galanthus	Muscari	Scilla
Chionodoxa	Iris	Narcissus	Sparaxis
Crocus	Ixia	Ornithogalum	Sternbergia
Eranthis	Ixiolirion	Oxalis	Tulipa

Bulbs for Outdoor Containers. Wherever one can gather together soil, drainage, light and air one can have a garden, even if it is a single tub on a couple of paving stones or a box on a window sill. Mini-gardening is of particular advantage to those deprived of orthodox gardens for mini-gardens can be established in courtyards, on balconies, roof-tops, outdoor-staircase landings, in or on retaining walls and even in such unusual places as basement area entrances to flats.

Mini-gardening is the answer to attractive terraces, patios, porches, paved or gravelled areas that are becoming so much a part of our home environment today whether in association with gardens or not. Growing bulbs in containers provides the unusual facility of mobility for flowering containers can be moved at will to wherever they may be wanted for decorative purposes. One can have them at the gate or front door, for example, and shift them conveniently to the terrace or sitting-out area when the weather permits entertaining guests outdoors.

Unexpected and novel effects can be achieved by growing bulbs in containers. One of the most charming mini-gardens I have ever seen was in a leaking dinghy, in which additional drainage holes were bored and brightly painted each spring, was sited on a quay at the bottom of a riverside garden.

Small drums of ten-gallon capacity can be halved, perforated and painted to line broad steps to a house or block of flats. Nail kegs and barrels of all sizes can be turned into gay mini-gardens. I have often seen long dis-used drinking troughs for horses resurrected and converted into most effective mini-gardens.

The increasing popularity of mini-gardening is reflected in the wide choice of different containers now on the market made of fibre-glass, plastics, ceramics, cast cement, asbestos, wood and other materials in the form of urns, tubs, troughs, buckets, boxes and even ornamental receptacles shaped specifically to fit over drain covers. These containers come in a host of sizes, styles and materials and can be selected to suit particular surroundings. Suitably placed containers can give character to any dwelling with or without a garden.

Drainage is vital in mini-gardening. Some broken crocks or stones should always be placed at the bottom of all types of containers. Drainage holes at fairly frequent intervals over the base should be about an inch in diameter and these must be kept free and open. The best plan is to use an inch layer of roughage, such as decayed leaves, fibrous peat or even a thin layer of turf with the grass side downward over the crocks or stones. This will retain moisture and prevent soil from clogging the drainage holes after watering.

If ordinary garden soil is used in containers, avoid heavy soils and clay and ensure that it has a reasonable texture. I invariably mix peat in with my garden soil for containers and very liberally. And while mixing I also add a good four to six ounces of bone meal per bushel.

Town gardeners may find it hard to come by garden soil and the simple answer here is to use a good potting compost. When filling boxes or other containers ensure that the soil or compost is pressed down firmly but not packed. Bulbs are planted at the same depths as in the garden so no container should be less than eight inches deep. After planting, the soil or compost should be level and at least an inch from the rim of the container to allow for watering.

Although containers are left outdoors and normally receive the same rainfall as the garden they may be sited partially under cover or so close to a wall that sufficient rain does not reach them. Or they may be in exposed positions where winds may tend to dry them out rapidly. Do not neglect watering whenever the soil or compost appears to be rather dry.

Almost any plants from dwarf evergreens and shrubs to bedding plants and seedlings will flourish in well-tended mini-gardens. The size of plants should be related both to the size of the container and the surroundings. Mini-gardens can go on through the year with clever interplanting, or a succession of mobile containers for winter, spring, summer and autumn-flowering can be planned.

Bulbs are, however, the mini-gardener's best investment. They are dependable and rewarding, thriving in containers with little attention and producing bloom prolifically whether in full sun or partial shade or in sheltered or exposed situations. Bulbs not only provide colour in containers at any time of the year but different kinds and species can be selected to compliment each other or to contrast with other plants.

For boxes at windows and on balconies it is advisable to choose bulbs with short or medium-height stems as winds can play havoc with tall-stemmed plants in exposed positions and staking in boxes is not particularly attractive. I like to devote boxes to a single kind of plant and there is no doubt that hyacinths are my favourite because they are perfect in form from any angle, require no staking, and are heavily perfumed. But I devote other boxes to dwarf narcissi, species tulips and dwarf iris; still others to combinations of narcissi and grape hyacinths or scillas; while my drain covers are camouflaged for three to four months each year with boxes of crocuses.

Tubs, urns and other larger containers give wider scope because of their greater depth, and taller-stemmed narcissi and the whole range of garden tulips look more in proportion in such containers. Many lilies in the 2–3ft height range make ideal container plants for summer spectacle and I have used bedding dahlias for long-lasting splashes of colour in large terrace tubs.

Bulbs are normally planted directly into containers but gardeners will find extremely useful the practice of growing additional bulbs for containers in pots sunk in the soil in an odd corner of the garden. These can be transplanted into containers when required to fill flowering gaps, provide a succession of colour, or, for example, to give added eye-appeal to a large container permanently housing a dwarf evergreen or other shrub.

When planting containers of any kind bulbs can be planted much closer together than in the garden for an almost solid mass of colour. For a really concentrated display of tulips or daffodils the perfect method is to plant bulbs at two layers in a deep tub. The bottom layer is planted first and the bulbs covered with soil or compost to just below their tips. The second or top layer is then planted between the tips of the lower layer of bulbs, ensuring that bulbs are not placed directly over each other, and covered over in the normal way.

Tulip and Chionodoxa

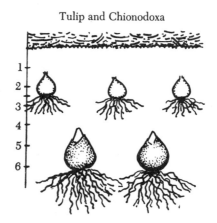

Planting combination. With 'double decker' bulb planting it is possible to achieve a greater concentration of bloom, either in the garden or in containers. The deeper bulbs should be planted first.

Containers with bulbs need never look untidy for once the bulbs have flowered they can be lifted from the container and heeled into an odd corner of the garden to allow their leaves to die down naturally. The containers can be put into immediate use again with bedding plants.

Choose from among the following genera, remembering to select species and varieties with flowering heights proportionate to the size of containers:

Anemone	Crocus	Iris	Narcissus
Begonia	Dahlia (dwarf)	Leucojum	Ranunculus
Chionodoxa	Galanthus	Lilium	Scilla
Colchicum	Hyacinthus	Muscari	Sternbergia
	Tulipa		

Bulbs in the Alpine House. Gardeners with an alpine house can enjoy delightful effects and excellent shelf display in the early months of the

26 (*right*) Typical Dutch bulb fields at Lisse

27 (*below*) Blooms are removed before fading in the bulb fields to ensure plump quality bulbs for the gardener

28 (*left*) The massive blooms of Darwin Hybrid Apeldoorn prove a scene-stealer at the fabulous Keukenhof Gardens at Lisse

29 *below:* (*left*) Spectacle and scent satiate the senses everywhere in the 62 acres that constitute the 'shop-window' of the Dutch bulb industry

30 (*right*) Constantly changing panoramas capture the eye round every corner in the Keukenhof Gardens

31 (*above*) Hyacinths are 'perfect' flowers as Anne Marie, City of Haarlem, Ostara, Pink Pearl and another Anne Marie testify

32 (*centre*) Hyacinth Carnegie

33 *below: (left)* String of Pink Pearls

34 (*right*) Hyacinth Perle Brillante

35 *above:* (*left*) Hyacinth Marconi

36 (*right*) Hyacinth Perle Brillante at the base of garden steps

37 (*centre*) Hyacinth Bismarck contrasts with narcissus Unsurpassable beside a boulder

38 *below:* (*left*) Hyacinth Blue Jacket and pansies in a raised foundation planting

39 (*right*) Hyacinth Anne Marie spectacularly tops a wall

year from January through April and again in the autumn with miniature bulb flowers grown in pots or pans with drainage holes. The well-
insulated and generally frost-free alpine house will bring bulbs grown
under its protection into flower earlier than in the garden.

The majority of bulbs can be grown successfully in any good potting
compost provided the pots and pans are ensured of good drainage by a
layer of crocks or stones at the bottom. Regular watering is also essential.
Pots and pans of bulbs must not be allowed to dry out, although less
water will be required in cold weather. The pots and pans of bulbs can
be sunk partially or to their rims into sand on alpine house shelves and,
if the sand is kept moist by occasional watering, will not require such
frequent watering.

Another important factor in growing bulbs in alpine houses is ample
ventilation. The alpine house should never be allowed to become too
warm, and must be completely ventilated as soon as the outside temperature rises above freezing point. In mild weather ventilators should
also be left open at night.

After flowering the bulbs must be kept growing until their foliage dies
down naturally. For their less attractive dormant period pots and pans
of bulbs can be plunged in a cold frame or in a sheltered part of the garden.
Repotting will be necessary only every second or third year but when not
repotted the top soil should be removed and replaced by fresh soil in
which some bone meal has been mixed.

The choice of bulbs for the alpine house is quite large and miniatures
from the following genera can be selected with confidence:

Anemone	Fritillaria	Iris	Tulipa
Crocus	Galanthus	Narcissus	

Bulbs in the Greenhouse. There are various types of greenhouses—cold,
cool, warm and hot—but the gardener need not stretch his or her pocket
book beyond the cool greenhouse as far as most bulbs are concerned.
The cool greenhouse is one with sufficient heat to keep out the frost and
maintain a minimum temperature of 40–45° F (5–7° C). This small
amount of heat makes a great difference to the bulbs which can be grown.
The most important thing to remember when growing bulbs under glass
is that slow, steady growing conditions produce the sturdy plants and
fine full blooms that bring such satisfaction.

Many spring-flowering bulbs can be brought into early flower in the
cool greenhouse and few of them want or need more than gentle forcing

while quite a number of the more tender bulbs and corms that brighten our summer gardens will flourish in a minimum temperature of 45° F (7° C).

Bulbs for the cool greenhouse must be potted at the correct time to achieve the correct growing rhythm and specific cultural instructions for each kind of bulb is included in their descriptions later in this book. The best soil to use is a mixture of equal parts of loam, peat and sand but it should be fresh and moist. Alternatively John Innes Potting Compost No 1 or its equivalent can be used although hippeastrum prefer a somewhat richer mixture. Use clean old pots or soak new pots thoroughly in water for a week. Pots, pans or boxes must have adequate drainage and should be deep enough to enable bulbs to root freely. Most start off plunged in cold frames or under a 6in covering of ashes or peat outdoors, only being introduced to the cool greenhouse when growth is well underway. It is of vital importance that proper root development takes place before the bulbs are moved into the greenhouse.

Pots of bulbs will usually require more ventilation than most other greenhouse plants, they must be watered carefully and some will require shading while others can be introduced to full light immediately. Most, however, are in no way difficult to grow under glass and both specially prepared bulbs and ordinary bulbs can be used, which means that some varieties of hyacinths, narcissi and tulips can be brought into flower for Christmas.

A large number of choice bulbs from the following genera can be grown in the cool greenhouse:

Freesia	Ixia	Nerine	Sprekelia
Hippeastrum	Lilium	Oxalis	Tigridia
Hyacinthus	Montbretia	Ranunculus	Tulipa
Iris	Muscari	Scilla	Vallota
Ismene	Narcissus	Sparaxis	Zantedeschia
	Zephyranthes		

Chapter Three

BULBS IN THE HOME

THERE IS a growing trend for flowers in the home today as modern architecture and modern decor make our houses and flats lighter and brighter. More and more flowers in the home are becoming an integral part of our way of life; increasingly regarded as a necessity rather than a luxury, a means of bringing fresh beauty, colour and cheer into our every-day environment, a reflection of our talents and an expression of our personality.

Flowers are no longer just for special occasions, for witness the growing fashion for sun-rooms filled with plants and double-glazed flower-windows as well as the fantastic expansion of flower arranging as a hobby.

When thinking of flowers in the home we cannot help but be aware of the invaluable dual contribution of bulbs to our enjoyment—as indoor plants and as cut flowers. This chapter covers both aspects.

INDOOR GARDENING WITH BULBS

Nothing is more rewarding than forcing bulbs into bloom ahead of season and watching them develop from bud to full flower. Virtually anyone, with or without a garden, young or old, vigorous or ailing, indeed, even the handicapped, can participate in and enjoy this fascinating pastime. Bulbs forced indoors bloom during the cold winter months, just when flowers can do so much to add gay display to the home. Some such as hyacinths and certain narcissi are delightfully fragrant.

Hyacinths are the easiest but many other kinds of bulb can be forced into flower—early tulips, narcissi, crocuses, muscari, iris, scilla and others listed at the end of this section. But this does not mean that every species and variety of each kind can be used. All those that can have pertinent indoor forcing information included in their descriptions later in this book. The selection of bulbs for forcing is wide enough that there should be no difficulty in obtaining varieties from regular bulb suppliers.

Plant in Good Time. Order and plant your indoor bulbs in good time. Buy only good quality top size Dutch bulbs for indoor forcing. For very early bloom—from mid-November through the Christmas season—you will find that the Dutch bulb growers market what are called 'specially prepared' bulbs and offer a number of varieties of hyacinths, narcissi and tulips. These are specially cultivated and treated for the purpose of inducing early performance. Basically these bulbs are harvested very early and then stored for specific periods under strict temperature controls so that they bloom at a different season from their natural cycle. This process is highly technical and complicated, requiring great skill and patience, and is not for amateurs. After being harvested hyacinths are treated with heat, whereas narcissi and tulips are cold-stored. Prepared bulbs naturally are a bit more expensive than ordinary bulbs and planting of them should not be unduly delayed.

Many ordinary bulbs are capable of very rapid growth indoors when exposed to a high temperature, together with suitable humidity and lighting conditions but they cannot be expected to flower as early as prepared bulbs, although the artificial conditions of the home will bring them into bloom long before their natural outdoor flowering time. By planting both prepared and ordinary bulbs the flowering season indoors is lengthened.

Because individual pots or bowls of forced bulbs flower for about ten days to two weeks they should be brought into flower in planned succession to ensure continuous bloom. Any amateur can have bulbs in bloom from mid-November into late spring. This is done by purchasing both 'early' and 'late' varieties and making a succession of weekly or fortnightly plantings, through September, October and November. Bulbs reserved for later plantings should be stored in a cool, airy place in open bags.

How to Plant. There are several ways to grow bulbs indoors. One method is to use ordinary clay or plastic flower pots with drainage holes, in which case good garden top soil, a prepared potting compost or a hand-made mixture of three parts good loam, one part peat and one part sharp sand can be used. Old pots should be cleaned inside and out and dried before use, and new clay pots thoroughly soaked for twenty-four hours in a bucketful of water. No manures or fertilisers are necessary.

Prepare each pot for planting by placing at least three clean crocks, hollow downwards, over the drainage hole. Cover these with some peat or decayed leaves to keep the soil or compost from washing down and clogging the drainage. When planting the soil or compost should be cool and moist but not wet. Fill the pot to a suitable level and press it down lightly with the fingers. Do not, however, firm or pack the soil or compost beneath the bulbs or the downward pressure of the developing roots will lift the bulbs.

Then place the bulbs in position, setting them closely together but not so that they touch each other or the sides of the pot. The more bulbs planted in a pot the gayer the result will be and I usually plant mine no more than a pencil-width apart. Unless small bulbs are planted tightly they make an insignificant show. When positioning bulbs set them gently into the growing medium without hard pressure. The tips of the bulbs should be just below the level of the rim of the pot. More soil or compost should be added and this time pressed firm with the fingertips to anchor the bulbs. The noses of the bulbs will thus remain exposed and there will be an inch of room between the soil and the pot for watering. The potted bulbs should be well watered immediately after planting.

Another method is to use fibre in bowls, urns, pans or ornamental containers at least 5–6in deep without drainage holes. This is the simplest, cleanest method for flat dwellers or those without a garden. Bags of bulb fibre can be obtained from local suppliers along with your bulbs.

The technique of planting in bulb fibre is somewhat different. Bulb fibre must be thoroughly soaked, preferably overnight, and then squeezed out so that it is cool and moist but not wet when planting the bulbs. Fill the container with fibre and press it down firmly to within an inch of the rim. With the fingers scoop out a hole and plant one bulb. Press fibre firmly around it leaving the tip of the bulb exposed and repeat this process until the container is filled. With large containers capable of taking many bulbs I find it more convenient to place less fibre inside initially, setting out all bulbs at the correct depth before firming them into position with more fibre.

At this point I should like to stress that whether you plant in pots

Page 80 (*above*) Planting daffodils in bowls with fibre; (*below*) planting daffodils
in pebbles and water

Page 81 Four stages of growing hyacinths in glasses

with drainage holes or in watertight containers it is advisable to restrict
each receptacle to a single variety. It may seem safe to plant early or
late-flowering varieties of the same kind of bulb together but they will
seldom flower at exactly the same time.

If you want particular combinations of hyacinths or tulips, for example, it is best to plant bulbs individually in small pots and transplant
them complete with the compost round them into larger pots for the
desired effect. Different kinds of bulbs can be forced separately and later
brought together in mixed pots. I often grow a special supply of bulbs in
pots which I use later to put the finishing touch to window boxes and
balcony containers.

Some bulbs can also be grown in water. There are a number of types of
hyacinth glasses and plastic containers now available. The procedure is
simple. First drop a bit of charcoal in the clean glass or container to keep
the water sweet. Then fill the glass with water so that it almost but not
quite touches the base of the bulb where it rests on the specially lipped
glass or serrated container shelf. Rainwater is best but ordinary water
from the tap can be used in a tepid condition.

A number of early-flowering narcissi can be very successfully grown in
bowls of pebbles and water. The bulbs are set so that their lower half
only is below the surface of the pebbles. Water is then added until its
surface is just about level with the bases of bulbs. Vermiculite is sometimes used as a rooting medium but I cannot recommend it as it provides
no support for the bulbs when they become full-size plants.

Rooting. The secret of success in growing bulbs in pots or bowls is simply
to ensure that the newly planted bulbs have adequate time to develop
strong roots before they begin to grow upwards. Unless good root growth
is made under cool conditions before they are placed in forcing temperatures bulbs will not flower satisfactorily. Cool conditions mean a temperature above freezing but not greatly exceeding 45° F (7° C). The rooting
period varies somewhat between different types of bulbs and between
the specially prepared bulbs and ordinary bulbs but it generally takes
about 12 weeks before a proper root system develops and top growth
reaches two to three inches in height. This rooting development can take
place indoors or outdoors, but, with the odd exception, always in the dark.

For outdoor rooting plunge the well-watered planted containers in a
pit lined with ashes, sand or peat in a cool and shady position in the garden.
The soil from the pit is used to cover the bulbs. Ornamental bowls can be

Page 83 Pots must always be large enough to give hyacinth roots plenty of room to spread

wrapped in newspaper to protect them; the covering will soon soften up, permitting the bulb growth to penetrate.

Alternatively your containers can be placed on a bed of sand, ashes or peat on the surface. Then dig a trench round the position and use the soil from the trench to cover the containers. Whatever method is employed six inches of covering is essential to protect the bulbs from frost. The covering soil should be porous so if your soil is heavy add peat or use all peat with a top layer of soil. In areas of prolonged intense cold an extra mulch of leaves, straw or peat over the plunge is helpful.

For indoor rooting simply store your containers in a cool, frost-free and well-ventilated place. Because so many of us now keep our houses comfortably warm in winter cupboards are no longer suitable places to root indoor bulbs. A warm atmosphere prompts leaf growth before enough roots are made. Therefore, the floor of the garage or shed or a cool cellar or unheated store room are better places, the light being kept from the bulbs by a covering of thick paper.

You can tell that the root system is properly developed by the fact that the flower bud is well out of the neck of the bulb and growth is about two inches high. Bulbs grown in water or in pebbles and water must, with the odd exception, also be stored in a cool, dark place for the root formation period. With these you can literally see the masses of long white roots that have been formed.

After the appropriate rooting period, when the buds are well out of the neck of the bulbs and thrusting the rudimentary leaves apart, the pots or bowls can be brought into the house and gradually introduced to warmth and light.

Watering is most important. When in the garden plunge or when rooting in cellar or garage the compost or fibre must not be allowed to dry out. Water must be applied liberally when the flower buds begin to show colour and liberal watering should continue until the flowers are fully open. Only then can less water be given to make the blooms last longer.

Indoor Care. It usually takes three to four weeks from the time bulbs are brought into the house to reach the full-flower stage. When first moved the growth will be pale and containers should be placed in half-light for a week or so until growth assumes a healthy green appearance. Containers should be gradually introduced to heat too. Too much heat too soon results in pale-looking foliage, general weakness and poor quality bloom.

A night temperature of 50°–57° F (10°–14° C) with a daytime rise to 60°–64° F (16°–18° C) is ideal for most bulbs.

For really successful blooms keep your pots and bowls away from gas and electric fires, radiators or hot air vents. While they will enjoy a sunny windowsill during the day keep them away from windows at night in case of severe frost.

You will notice that your indoor bulbs will automatically reach for the light. To prevent a one-sided look to a bowl or pot, turn the container every time you check on the need for water. And do keep your indoor bulbs out of draughts.

Light working of the compost in pots of bulbs will not only prevent the formation of a hard top crust but will also ensure good drainage. Even bulb fibre appreciates a light stirring.

Gardeners can, of course, grow foliage among their bulbs, like saxifrage, sedum or grass. These can be sown round the pot immediately it is removed from the plunge or indoor store. Moss, which can be obtained from florists, can also be used to decorate pots of bulbs. It should be placed loosely over the compost and kept damp.

Taller bulbous plants like daffodils, tulips and the heavy trusses of hyacinths should be staked early before the growths have an opportunity to sag. Light twiggy branches, thin canes or aluminium plant supports, anodized green, are not unsightly if unobtrusively positioned.

Once flowers have faded, the deadheads should be consigned to the dustbin. Indoor bulbs will continue blooming for a surprisingly long time, particularly if pots and bowls in bloom are kept out of direct midday sunlight and removed from centrally heated rooms to a cool but not cold place overnight.

Keep a watchful eye on your indoor bulbs, not only checking for water supply and turning containers to maintain symmetry, but for 'drawing up' through lack of light or excessive heat. A few minutes attention regularly is not much to ask and is amply repaid. The novice will soon get the hang of growing bulbs indoors and discover how simple it really is.

After Flowering. House cultivation does not exhaust bulbs in the same way as commercial hot-house forcing but bulbs that have flowered beautifully indoors should not be expected to flower indoors a second year. After bulbs have finished blooming indoors, put them in a cool place and water them about once a week while the foliage is ripening. As soon as garden soil is workable in spring the bulbs can be turned out of their pots or bowls with as little disturbance as possible and planted anywhere you like in the garden.

Alternatively, the bulbs can be removed from their containers once the foliage has died down completely and be dried off but not baked in the sun. When dry enough they should be gently cleaned and stored in a cool, frost-free and well-ventilated place until the time comes to plant them in the garden in the Autumn.

Bulbs grown in water or water and pebbles will be completely drained of vitality and should be discarded. Those grown in bulb fibre will take longer to recover than those grown in soil or potting compost and blooms the next season will hardly be of show standard, even when dressings of bone meal are added to garden soil. I usually transplant my indoor bulbs in an odd corner of my garden to give me an additional supply of cut flowers.

Choosing Bulbs for Forcing. Do remember that top quality bulbs produce finer flowers and that second sizes, which are suitable for outdoor planting, are less likely to provide satisfactory results indoors. And when choosing bulbs for forcing select species and varieties that are known to be especially suitable for this purpose. This is particularly important in the case of bulbs that are to be forced into bloom well ahead of their normal flowering time outdoors. Most bulb catalogues indicate the best forcing varieties but many of the smaller local suppliers do not. This book specifically recommends species and varieties for indoor forcing from among the following genera:

Chionodoxa	Galanthus	Muscari	Sprekelia
Colchicum	Hippeastrum	Narcissus	Tulipa
Crocus	Hyacinthus	Nerine	Vallota
Erythronium	Iris	Puschkinia	Zantedeschia
Freesia	Ixia	Scilla	
Fritillaria	Lilium	Sparaxis	

BULBS AS CUT FLOWERS

A vast array of bulbs produce flowers which are ideal for floral arrangements, with their sturdy stems, long-lasting blooms and buds that open beautifully in water. They are particularly valuable for cutting because their flowers follow one after another from late winter into spring and summer and well into the autumn.

The small early kinds, such as snowdrops, glories-of-the-snow, grape hyacinths and scillas, which most of us never consider as cut flowers but which make delightful intimate arrangements, can be gathered from generous garden plantings without being missed. Narcissi too, can often be picked from naturalised plantings without noticeable loss of display.

But for a constant supply of cut flowers for indoor decoration without sacrificing garden display and perhaps generating heated family arguments, a special cutting garden is the best solution. There is no need to give over a substantial area of your garden to cut flowers. A small plot will yield quantities of cut flowers if properly planned. Part of the vegetable garden may be utilised for a cutting garden or some sunny spot beside the garage or garden shed may well prove practical. The main subsidiary advantage of a cutting garden is that at least twice as many flowers planted in rows can be grown with no more effort and attention than when they are planted in informal borders.

I am not suggesting that a cutting garden be devoted exclusively to bulbs any more than I would imply that only bulbs should be grown elsewhere. Bulb flowers mix well with other flowers and foliage in the garden and in the home. Indeed, the most labour-saving and space-saving cutting garden is one with a section devoted to annuals and biennials and another reserved for perennials, each providing a home for certain bulbs.

With your annuals and biennials you should plant summer-flowering bulbs like gladioli, freesias, dahlias and other bulbous and tuberous plants which are lifted at the end of the growing season and replanted again the following spring.

With your perennials you can site all those bulbs, like narcissi, tulips and lilies, that remain in the ground year after year.

Where space allows, plant in rows for quick and easy surface hoeing or cultivating during the growing season. But where space is limited you can plant bulbs quite closely together in beds about four feet wide. This means hand weeding, of course, but weeding can be minimised by mulching with a few inches of peat.

Bulbs do not necessarily require special exclusive areas of the cutting garden. Lilies, for example, prefer shade on their roots and will bloom more prolifically when interplanted with low-growing perennials which retain their foliage in the summer. Narcissi and other early-flowering bulbs whose foliage withers away by early summer can be interplanted with perennials that do not make much foliage until late spring.

Interplanting is often a practical proposition in the annual section of the cutting garden too. My last succession plantings of gladioli are sited between rows of early annuals before their flowers are used to give me a second contribution of bloom from the same area. When sowing my earliest annuals I leave room between the rows for dahlia tubers. By the time my dahlias require maximum space I have already picked the flowers of my early annuals.

Soil Conditions. The soil in a cutting garden should be kept especially friable and rich for prime cut flowers. It should have good drainage and be of adequate depth. Whenever feasible I turn over both the topsoil and undersoil, burying generous quantities of well-decayed manure or compost. Mulching with peat twice a year not only keeps down weeds but helps maintain a fine tilth and I invariably work in bone meal before planting bulbs and other flowers. Where bulbs and perennials are *in situ* in the cutting garden I give an annual dressing of ordinary general purpose fertiliser, particularly in areas where I have planted bulbs that have been forced indoors.

Cultivation and Cutting. Looking after bulbs in a cutting garden is little different from the attention they require when grown elsewhere. Watering is important, particularly in dry spells when they are in leaf both before and after flowering. I have adopted the habit of adding liquid manure to the water as soon as flowering spikes appear and continue weekly applications until the buds show colour. This makes for finer blooms and better stems.

Cutting gardens can become disaster areas if taller stemmed plants are not properly staked. Crooked flower stems are a problem in flower arranging and this can be prevented by timely staking. When staking bulbs it is wise to erect stakes at the time of planting for it is all too easy to drive stakes through bulbs at a later stage of development.

All of us like to have some foliage with flowers in an arrangement and the natural foliage of the flowers we use is particularly effective. But the removal of leaves while still green does affect the ability of the bulb to manufacture the food it needs to store for the following year's performance. If you cut leafy stems as long as possible, cutting them virtually at ground level, then the bulbs will not bloom the following year and may even die. I must confess to doing this occasionally with tulips, Dutch iris and gladioli but only when I am planning to substitute different varieties. On these occasions I lift the bulbs themselves and discard them.

Normally when cutting bulb flowers you should take as little foliage as possible and never more than a sixth of the total leaf area if you want flowers from the same bulb the following year.

Stems that are without leaves, like those of narcissi, can safely be cut to within an inch or so of ground level. Nearly all bulbs should be cut in bud, more specifically when their buds begin to open. Bulbs with a number of flowers per stem, like lilies and gladioli, should be cut when the first few buds open; the others will open in water. There are exceptions, of course, like May-flowering tulips, which should not be cut until the flowers are about three-quarters of their ultimate size. If cut too early these blooms will remain relatively small.

The best time for cutting bulb flowers is early morning, when the dew is still on them. The next best time is late evening. It is unwise to pull up or break off stems. They should be cut with a sharp knife or scissors and placed immediately in two to three inches of tepid water in a clean bucket. Always give them ample time to absorb all the water they want by keeping the bucket of cut flowers in a cool dark place for at least six hours and if convenient overnight before arranging.

Flower Arranging. The secret of successful flower arranging is simply to let yourself go and thoroughly enjoy the pleasure of working with the most beautiful materials nature provides. Arranging flowers is one of the most enjoyable and rewarding methods of self-expression. You don't have to be an artist or an expert to create satisfying compositions (see page 53). Flower arranging brings a fresh interest in colours textures and forms and stimulates a new appreciation of light, shade, depth and quality. Indeed, it helps develop a more critical eye towards the interior decor of the home for you will invariably consider surroundings first and arrange your flowers to fit in with or enhance them.

Of course, there are easy and more effective ways of doing anything but successful flower arranging in the home does not require mastering the rigid rules and regulations of flower shows and competitions. Just please yourself, have fun with flowers, and your family and friends too will share in your pleasure.

Your own common sense will tell you not to site arrangements in direct sunlight or near heating appliances, in draughts or in danger spots where the floral container can easily be knocked over. Trial and error will quickly demonstrate that plain backgrounds are more suitable than fussy patterned ones; that flowers can be used to pick up colours and textures of backgrounds; and that light colours, for example, will show up best against dark panelled walls.

The proportion of container to flowers will become self-evident; too many flowers jammed into any container will look 'wrong' and tall-stemmed flowers in a miniature receptacle will obviously look 'ridiculous'.

You won't need a lot of expensive gear or equipment for flower arranging. Most basic materials are already in the home. The first essential is containers. These include ordinary vases and bowls designed for flowers but it is surprising what you will be able to find about the house to augment your supply. Almost any receptacle that holds water can be used for flowers, from coal scuttles and umbrella stands, through large glass ash trays and silver entré dishes, to china tea pots and pewter mugs. The most important thing about containers is to ensure that they are clean, and a thorough washing after use and before putting them away (polythene bags obviate the dust problem) is advisable.

For cutting good quality scissors are a must and they should not be too large. A sharp knife will be particularly useful for cutting and slitting the stems of foliage gathered from the garden or purchased from the florist, and pinking shears are handy for cutting ribbon. A pair of pliers will prove handy for cutting wire.

There are various methods for holding flowers in position in an arrangement, the most familiar being the different sized weighted pinholders and heavy glass bases with holes for floral stems. Ordinary two-inch mesh wire netting or plastic covered wire mesh can be cut into suitable squares and crumpled to hold flowers in a container. Very convenient and inexpensive are blocks of foam base, sold under various brand names by florists. These blocks of porous material can be cut to fit virtually any container and when soaked will take stems easily and hold them firmly in place.

Floral tape, available in green or white, will anchor pinholders that tend to slither, hold wire mesh in place, fasten those green, cone-like tin holders to a cane or stick to give additional height to an arrangement, and cover the stems of flowers you may wear. Although expensive, one roll will last a long time. Alternatively ordinary surgical tape can be used.

40 *above:* (*left*) Small cupped narcissus Barrett Browning

41 (*right*) Large cupped narcissus Sempre Avanti

42 (*centre*) Jonquil narcissus Trevithian

43 *below:* (*left*) White trumpet narcissus Mount Hood

44 (*right*) Double narcissus White Lion

45 *above:* (*left*) Yellow trumpet narcissus Golden Harvest

46 (*right*) Large cupped narcissus Yellow Sun

47 (*centre*) Large cupped narcissus Flower Record

48 *below:* (*left*) Small cupped narcissus Birma

49 (*right*) Bicolour trumpet narcissus Magnet

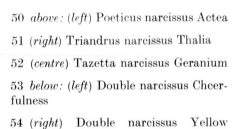

50 *above:* (*left*) Poeticus narcissus Actea

51 (*right*) Triandrus narcissus Thalia

52 (*centre*) Tazetta narcissus Geranium

53 *below:* (*left*) Double narcissus Cheerfulness

54 (*right*) Double narcissus Yellow
Cheerfulness

55 *above:* (*left*) Narcissus canaliculatus

56 (*right*) Narcissus cyclamineus

57 (*centre*) Miniature white trumpet narcissus W. P. Milner

58 *below:* (*left*) Narcissus bulbocodium conspicuus

59 (*right*) Poetaz narcissus Silver Chimes

There are many other accessories available from florists such as candle-cup holders and items like moss and ribbon to help conceal the mechanics of your flower arrangements. Still other accessories can be obtained free of charge from pieces of driftwood, twigs and pebbles to sea shells. Figurines and other ornaments as well as old picture frames and even fresh fruit and dried gourds can be used as accessories in floral arrangements.

Each flower should be handled carefully from the moment of cutting from garden or purchase until they die. I have already mentioned the importance of plunging cut flowers from the garden into a bucket containing several inches of tepid water immediately after cutting. When purchasing bulb flowers in bud from any retail outlet always untie them at once and before plunging them into a bucket cut a fraction off the bottom of stems to ensure that they can drink freely.

Most bulb flowers have sturdy stems but occasionally the flowers we purchase or receive as gifts, particularly tulips, arrive at our homes in a limp condition. To stiffen and straighten the stems all that is necessary, after cutting a bit off the ends, is to wrap the tulips firmly in newspaper before standing them for some hours in water. Do remember that daffodils or narcissi exude a milky white substance that can affect the vase life of other spring flowers. The remedy is simple—condition your daffodils in a separate bucket of water before using them in a mixed arrangement.

There are many so-called 'tricks' for preserving cut flowers, such as adding a crushed aspirin, honey, sugar, charcoal or a penny to the water. Frankly, none of these or indeed commercial cut flower preservatives add substantially to the vase life of flowers. The only way to get the most from cut flowers is to properly condition them before arranging and ensure that they have a constant supply of room-temperature water. It is not necessary to remove the flowers from an arrangement every night, cut a bit more off their stems, and plunge them into a bucket of water standing in a cool place overnight. This means re-arranging the flowers every day and excessive handling. Of course, containers with arrangements will benefit from being placed in an unheated or cool room overnight but the flowers themselves need not be touched. All you need do is top up the container with tepid water every day.

Because flower arranging is really a personal expression it is difficult to lay down a precise guide as to how flowers should be arranged. But these hints will make flower arranging easier.

Create your arrangement in your mind's eye first, taking into consideration the five basic elements of every flower arrangement—the flowers, the container, the location of the arrangement, the mechanics of keeping the flowers in place and alive, and the actual arranging or putting together of the flowers, container and accessories.

Start with the flowers, studying them carefully. Satisfy yourself that you know the shape, texture and colour of the blooms. Inspect the stems to determine how sturdy they are and whether they require any support. Examine the arrangement of the natural foliage, whether the leaves grow out of the stem or from the ground. Will you need additional foliage of other kinds? Recall to mind how your flowers actually grow.

Choose a container of the right size, shape and colour to give a balanced appearance and to tone or contrast with your flowers. Build up a collection of containers gradually. Although virtually anything that will hold an inch or so of water can be called into service, including baskets and wood or leather containers lined with tin or aluminium foil, do avoid anything that looks obviously contrived.

Where your arrangement is to be placed should influence its size and shape, even the colours of the flowers and container. It is far easier to make an arrangement for a specific place than to create an arrangement and then hunt for a suitable location for it. Consider all the places in your house where flowers might be used—the entrance hall, bedroom, kitchen, guest room, the dining or buffet table, the coffee or end table, the chest and corner cupboard, the floor, window seat, stair landing, the mantelpiece, bookcase, desk—you will find countless homes for flowers.

Placed in front of a mirror the back of an arrangement is as important as the front. On a bookcase or mantelpiece the arrangement is usually above eye level and is viewed from the front and both sides. On a low coffee table it will be seen all around. Whether it is placed against a plain white painted wall, patterned wallpaper, an oil painting, a natural stone wall, a panelled wall of pine or mahogany or dark hessian-covered wall will inevitably influence your choice of flowers and container as well as the quality of the arrangement.

Ensure that your pinholder, wire mesh or foam base is firmly placed in the container. Pinholders and holed glass bases are excellent for shallow containers while crumpled wire mesh and foam base can be cut to fit small, medium, large and oddly-shaped containers. Avoid using wire mesh in transparent glass where it shows and will distract from your

Page 97 (*above left*) Shallow containers are ideal for daffodils; (*above right*) small cupped narcissi lend themselves to diminutive arrangements; (*below* left) virtually anything that holds water can be used in floral arrangements; (*below right*) pot-et-fleur. combining growing plants and cut flowers. is becoming ever more popular

arrangement. Every flower and stem of foliage should be firmly anchored where it is placed.

Arranging flowers with water in containers is easier because the water provides better balance from the start. Fill the containers, except shallow ones which require far less water, about three-quarters of the way before arranging flowers and top them up at the end.

Flowers and foliage will conceal most if not all of your mechanics but you can also use moss, pebbles, ribbon, shells, fir cones and various baubles and ornaments.

If you find it difficult to start an arrangement, try using the basic shape of a triangle, placing three flowers in key positions and go on from there. The main stem should normally be at least one-and-a-half times as long as the container's greatest dimension. As stems of equal length in an arrangement deprive you of scope, do not hesitate to cut flower stems to different lengths. Stems placed so that they radiate from a central point make more effective arrangements than stems that cross one another above the mouth of the container.

Every flower wants 'breathing space', a chance to look its best; consequently no flower should be allowed to hide another. And when arranging buds remember to allow enough room for their expansion into full flower.

Floral colours don't clash, which means you can mix colours as much as you like. But flowers massed in blocks of colours are always more effective than flowers of different colours scattered through an arrangement. Colour can be used for harmony or contrast with 'heavier' colours reserved for the base and centre of any design.

Balance flowers and foliage according to size and shape, utilising their graceful, natural lines. Foliage, floral stems, candles and a wide range of accessories can be used to either fill in a design or set it off.

You don't need masses of flowers for all arrangements, often bold impact can be achieved with only a few blooms imaginatively arranged. Experiment with creating and locating flower arrangements. Try arranging each kind of flower separately to gain a genuine appreciation of its attributes. Work with single colours, then two or three and then wider mixtures for a better understanding of form, colour combinations, and textures. In short, practice to please yourself and enjoy having fresh flowers about you right through the year.

By growing a range of bulbs in a cutting garden you can have beautiful flowers on hand for floral arrangements for all but a few months of the year. For a host of species and varieties especially suitable as cut flowers refer to the descriptions in this book under the following genera:

Acidanthera*	Eremurus	Iris*	Narcissus*
Allium	Freesia*	Ixia	Ornithogalum*
Anemone	Galanthus	Ixiolirion	Ranunculus
Brodiaea*	Galtonia	Leucojum	Scilla
Camassia	Gladiolus	Lilium*	Sparaxis
Chionodoxa	Hippeastrum	Montbretia	Tulipa*
Dahlia	Hyacinthus*	Muscari	

(* Contain scented species)

Chapter Four

ORIGINS AND HISTORY

ALL BULBS were once wild flowers and formed part of earth's earliest plant life. Because they flourished in lands where civilisation attained an early foothold they played a role in the earliest gardens known to man. Such records as exist substantiate this conclusion.

An Egyptian papyrus of about 1800BC indicates that priests cultivated colchicums and scillas for use in medicine. There are records that the pharaohs had anemones in their gardens and that lilies and narcissi were used by their peoples in funeral tributes and in engravings on tombs.

The Madonna lily (Lilium candidum) was unmistakably portrayed on frescoes and jars discovered among the ruins of the Palace of Mirrors in Crete and considered to be nearly 4,000 years old. A bronze dagger found at Mycenae was inlaid with a pattern of gold lilies.

Solomon's garden contained lilies and crocuses and lilies were used as a motif on the columns of a temple he ordered built about 1000BC. Lilies are frequently mentioned in the Bible but possibly the original Hebrew and Greek terms were generic and described a number of known bulbous plants including lilies, irises and ornithogalums. Nevertheless, the Madonna lily is depicted in a number of Assyrian bas-reliefs uncovered at Nineveh, dating from about 700BC.

The Madonna lily was certainly also known to the ancient Greeks, for about 340BC the philosopher-botanist, Theophrastes, described it at some length. He also mentioned alliums, anemones, crocuses, gladioli, muscari, narcissi, ranunculi and scillas.

Somewhat later, Mithridates, King of Pontus, utilised the Madonna lily as an antidote to snake-bite.

The ambitious, foraging Romans were well acquainted with the lily, associated this flower with their gods and regarded it as the emblem of virginity. The epic poet, Virgil, (70–19BC) referred to the lily several times in his works.

About the first century AD the noted physician, Dioscorides Pedacius, in his treatise on the '*Materia Medica*', extolled the virtues of the Madonna lily as a basilicon or ointment. This particular ointment was made by pounding lily-flowers and mixing them with olive oil and was employed most successfully as a remedy for painful breasts caused by infant suckling. To this day some country people use lily oil to treat rough skin and burns.

Dioscorides also mentioned some of the bulbs described by Theophrastes and, in addition, included colchicums, hyacinths and ornithogalums. About the same period, that renowned Roman writer of natural history, Gaius Plinius Secundus or Pliny the Elder, mentioned four species of lilies, three of narcissi, as well as alliums, anemones, crocuses, gladioli, ornithogalums and scillas. And there are, of course, many fascinating Greek and Roman legends linking their gods with the origin of the lily, the hyacinth and the narcissus. Madonna lilies are said to have sprung from the earth where the milk of Juno, sister of Jupiter, spilt when Hercules, striving to obtain immortality, sucked so greedily that dribbles fell from his mouth to the ground.

A list of herbs grown in the imperial gardens of the Emperor Charlemagne, published in 812AD, included the Madonna lily. But during the dark ages that followed the fall of the Roman Empire, interest in gardening also declined. The monks, however, continued to maintain herb gardens in the monasteries and to cultivate flowers in them. One of them, Walfrid Strabo, even wrote in the ninth century, a poem called '*The Little Garden*', and so authored the earliest known medieval work on gardening. The earliest known treatise on gardening in English dates back to 1441 and lists no less than 97 plants growing in an English garden, among which were narcissi, lilies and crocuses.

It was the Crusades and the Renaissance that sparked a revival of interest in plants and gardens. Many people were travelling to distant lands and were discovering strange customs and plants. Interest first centred on the Mediterranean lands and those of Asia Minor and many plant specimens were lifted and brought back. Then the Americas were discovered and plants of various kinds were among the booty sent back to European homelands.

Gardens became fashionable in Europe. The Austrians, Dutch, English, French, Germans, Italians and Spanish alike vied with each other in the introduction of exotic plants to their gardens. The transportation of the times was slow and uncertain and many plants perished en route. It was undoubtedly because bulbs, with their dormant periods, better withstood the inevitable delays than most other plants, that accounts for so many kinds appearing in European gardens. Literally dozens, including crocuses, fritillarias, Martagon lilies, ranunculi and tulips were first introduced into England between 1550 and 1650.

Chronologically the story of the tulip begins in the sixteenth century but because it is the most popular of all bulbs today, involves such a fascinating tale and literally fostered the birth of the Dutch bulb industry, I beg the reader's indulgence in dealing with it in somewhat greater detail a little later in this chapter.

The ancient civilisations of the west as well as those of the east shared an interest in gardens and bulbs. Hernando Cortes, conqueror of Mexico, reporting back to Charles V in 1520, described the fabulous gardens of his hostage, Montezuma, in which dahlias flourished. A colour illustration of a dahlia is featured in the earliest known American book on plants, the *Badianus Manuscript*, an Aztec Herbal of the mid-sixteenth century.

The Incas who flourished in Peru for over 500 years until their defeat by Francisco Pizarro in 1532 cultivated a number of bulbous plants whose blooms were used in their nosegays.

With bulbs arriving from east and west the number of different kinds grown in European gardens expanded rapidly. The naturalist, John Tradescant, listing the plants he grew in his London garden in 1656, mentions many varieties of crocuses, fritillarias, hyacinths, narcissi, tulips and lilies as well as colchicums, anemones, alliums, leucojums, irises, ornithogalums, muscari and ranunculi amongst others.

The Dutch takeover of South Africa in the seventeenth century resulted in many more plants being introduced to Europe, the first among which were oxalis, freesias and gladioli. Colonists, of course, also brought their favourite garden plants from their country of origin to their new homes. By 1642 the Dutch had introduced anemones, fritillarias, lilies and tulips to New Amsterdam (New York).

In the wake of exploration and empire-building new interest was generated in plants and gardens. New plants of all kinds, including bulbs, were from the beginning of the seventeenth century collected systematically and became available to gardeners. The flow of new introductions has continued to this day.

John Bartram, regarded by many as the first great American botanist, sent American erythroniums and lilies to England and the Continent in the late 1730s. Before another half century had elapsed England was nurturing a new breed of professional plant hunters. The first of these, Francis Masson, was dispatched from Kew Gardens, London to South Africa to collect and send home both seeds and live plants. Among Masson's finds was ixia.

One William Kerr discovered in 1804 that the Chinese had been cultivating tiger lilies for over a thousand years and sent the first bulbs of lilium tigrinum to the western world. A Dutch surgeon, Dr. F. P. von Siebold, sent lilium speciosum and several other species to Holland from Japan in 1829. The most gorgeous lilies stem from the Far East and the introduction of lilium auratum, the golden-rayed lily of Japan, to England in 1862 by J. G. Veitch caused a sensation in horticultural circles. Lilium henryi was named after Augustine Henry who sent this species home from China not long afterwards.

An American plant hunter, who became known as 'Chinese' Wilson, sent the regal lily (Lilium regale) to the Arnold Arboretum in Massachusetts in 1911. It was not only professionals but amateurs from all walks of life and from many countries who contributed over the years to the range of living plants in our gardens. Propagators have ensured that the majority of these plants, and certainly all those with a distinctive character of their own, have continued to be available to gardeners. And skilled hybridisers, by carefully selecting and crossing wild species, have produced an almost unending array of new floral beauty queens.

THE TULIP STORY

The tulip is named from 'tulliband', the vulgar Turkish pronunciation of the Persian 'dulband' or 'turban', which the expanded bloom of the plant is thought to resemble. Although its history considerably post-dates that of the lily, the tulip belongs to the lily family and is native to Asia Minor, China, Persia, and Russia and is especially abundant in the Bokhara region of central Asia. It is possibly the most important of all genera of bulbs and has certainly baffled botanists, for until some thirty-five years ago there was general disagreement over the number of species in this interesting genus. Today we know that there are upwards of seventy species but the number of these in commercial cultivation is relatively small.

The exact date of the tulip's first appearance as a garden flower is unknown. The earliest illustration of a tulip is thought to be that on a vase dated about 1600BC, found in the Palace of Minos at Knossos in Crete, but it is not known if the multi-flowered tulip depicted was cultivated in gardens. The classic Greek writers did not mention the tulip in their records of plants but the tulip was certainly widespread in Persia from a very early date. Omar Khayam mentioned it in literature before 1200 and the poet Hafiz lauded it as the 'lalé' in 1390, although Persian artists do not appear to have used it as a decorative motif until the sixteenth century.

It was the middle of the sixteenth century before the tulip came to Western Europe. It is probable that the 'red lilies' which the French traveller, Pierre Belon, reported as growing in every Turkish garden in 1546 were tulips, but his description of them was not definitive. Certainly the Turks were growing many kinds of tulips in their gardens by this period. The Great Mogul, Mohammed Baber, who founded the Mohammedan empire in India in 1526, was not only a warrior but a gardener of some distinction. He collected various species of tulips on his marches and before he died in 1530 he visited the tulip fields of Samarkand and planted tulips, including a rose-scented species, in the many gardens he created both in Turkey and India. The gardens of Sultan Sulemein's harem were filled with tulips which he made a symbol of feminine grace.

In 1554, a Flemish diplomat, Augier Ghislen de Busbecq, was sent by the Emperor Ferdinand I of Austria as ambassador to Sulemein the Magnificent. On his way from Adrianople to Constantinople he saw in gardens a strange and brilliantly coloured flower which he said the Turks called 'tulipam'. His letters, containing the first mention of the tulip by a European, pointed out that the Turks were prepared to pay large sums for certain rare and gorgeously coloured varieties.

Not long afterwards Busbecq sent back bulbs and seeds of tulips to Vienna where they bloomed in the Imperial Gardens under the supervision of a herbalist named Carolus Clusius (Charles de l'Ecluse) who later became Professor of Botany at Holland's Leiden University. These were among the earliest, if not the earliest imports of tulips into Europe.

At about the same time, a consignment of bulbs from Turkey reportedly arrived in Augsburg for the gardens of a prominent banker called Herwart, and these bulbs first bloomed in 1559. The noted Zurich botanist, Conrad Gesner, rushed to Augsburg to inspect the new flower and published a description of it under the title '*Tulipa turcarum*' in 1561. Meanwhile the first known illustration of a tulip was published by Petrus Andrea Matthiolus in 1559–60 but he failed to describe or even mention his drawing in the text of his book. It was on Gesner's drawings and descriptions that the genus was later founded.

There is some dispute as to the date when tulips first reached Holland, some authorities claiming that the first tulip came into possession of an apothecary named Wallich Ziewirtz, in 1570–71 and others that tulips did not arrive in Holland until Clusius brought them there some two decades later.

What is certain is that when Clusius left Vienna in 1593 to take up his appointment at Leiden University, he took his entire collection of tulip bulbs with him and planted them in the rich, sandy soil of his new country. They were not wild species but garden forms, some with differences in the shape of the cup, just as they were being cultivated in Turkish gardens at the time.

The Dutch became enamoured with tulips, for everyone wanted to have specimens in their gardens. Clusius, however, appreciating their rarity, asked very high prices, and by doing so became very unpopular. Some sources state he was able to sell his bulbs but others allege his prices were so high that those who craved tulips had to resort to theft. One version of this tale credits an unknown thief with digging up most of Clusius' tulips on a moonless night and making a fortune by selling the stolen bulbs on a black market.

There is no doubt, however, that by 1600 the foundations of the Dutch bulb industry were laid. Tulips began to appear all over Holland, including many new varieties which were the result of haphazard cross-breeding.

Early in the seventeenth century the Thirty Years' War broke out and the Dutch began to grow wealthy. The tulip became an item for speculation and prices sky-rocketed. Growers became more numerous, hurriedly multiplying and cross-breeding the flowers to get new colours and shapes. The more a flower was striped or blotched, the higher its value. Connoisseurs fought over the bulbs, offering higher and higher prices to become exclusive owners of unique varieties.

Rich merchants in Flanders, France and Germany were as anxious as the Dutch to buy tulip bulbs and pushed prices up still further. The ladies of Paris created the fashion of wearing tulips on their dresses, stimulating competition among their suitors to present them with flowers of the rarest and newest varieties.

By 1623, a single bulb of 'Semper Augustus', which had 'crimson stripes interspersed with blue-grey tones on a white ground', fetched the equivalent of several hundred pounds sterling. But worse was still to come and by 1626 the bulb trade degenerated, the growers lost control, the public lost their heads, and between 1634 and 1637 the fantastic gambling in tulip bulbs spread all over Holland and became tulipo-mania.

Speculators were merchants, tailors, artisans and indeed people of all classes, many of whom mortgaged their homes and bartered their possessions to acquire tulip bulbs. Bulb growers too joined the ranks of the speculators. Inns became places where bulbs were bought and sold, and often bulbs still in the ground or even seedlings that had not yet bloomed were involved. Bulbs often changed hands several times a day, not the actual bulbs but bulbs which only figured on paper, just as stocks and shares do on the stock exchanges of today.

The mania spread like wildfire. Soon bulbs were no longer priced singly, but by a very fine weight, the measure being an 'ace' or 'azen', equivalent to 1/21st of a decigramme or 1/448th of an ounce. We can get an indication of what this meant from the fact that a good flowering size bulb today weighs about 7,000 aces.

At one sale at Alkmaar, 48,000 aces of tulip bulbs, equivalent to the weight of about half a dozen modern tulip bulbs, yielded no less than 68,553 florins. The variety which fetched the most fantastic prices was 'Semper Augustus'. In 1636 one bulb of about 400 aces reached the price of 13,000 florins. Another bulb of the same variety, weighing only 193 aces, sold for the sum of 4,600 florins plus a coach with two dapple grey horses, the money to be paid immediately and the coach and horses to be delivered a month later. The bulb itself was to be delivered to the purchaser several months later.

At still another sale frenzied bidding forced the price of an 'Admiral Liefkens' of 400 aces to 4,400 florins while a 'Viceroy' of 410 aces fetched 3,000 florins and an 'Admiral van Enkhuizen' of 215 aces brought in 5,400 florins.

Records reveal that a single bulb of the 'Viceroy' variety, sold to a man without ready cash available, was purchased by bartering the following goods for it: 2 lasts of wheat, 4 lasts of rye, 4 fat oxen, 3 fat swine, 12 fat sheep, 2 hogsheads of wine, 4 tuns of beer, 1,000 pounds of cheese, 2 tons of butter, a silver tankard valued at 2,500 florins, plus a complete bed and various items of clothing.

Tulipomania rubbed off on England too, the first tulip having reached the country in 1582. By 1629 John Parkinson in his '*Pardisus*' listed no less than 140 varieties of tulips grown in England.

The mania continued in Holland for three years until in the winter of 1636–37 the Dutch Government finally cracked down with a decree halting speculation in tulip bulbs. There was endless litigation, a special commission to bring about agreements and untangle the mess, thousands of people were ruined, but the price of bulbs fell.

The tulip was temporarily in disfavour but demand soon grew again. Tulips became fashionable in France once more. In dealing with tulips in the first book on gardening to be published, '*La Floriste Français*' (1654), the author, de la Chesnée Monstereuil, stated that 'as man dominates animals, as the diamond dominates other stones, as the sun dominates the stars, so does the tulip dominate all other flowers.'

In fact tulips took a prominent place among the flowers planted in the most magnificent gardens throughout Europe and soon the finest artists were being commissioned to immortalise the beauty of the tulip.

The tulip varieties that caused the craze in the 1630s were what are now known as 'broken' tulips, really mutants or freaks of variegated colours. Modern botany did not get underway until 1753 with Linnaeus' binominal classification. All varieties of garden tulip as distinct from wild species were grouped together under the name 'tulipa gesneriana', after the botanist who first described the flower. Clusius had listed several kinds of tulip as early as 1573; an English catalogue dated 1792 lists 665 varieties and by 1874 one Dutch grower offered over 2,000 different varieties in his catalogue.

Up until recently there were officially no less than 23 different classes or categories of tulips but since 1969, when a more logical and simplified classification was introduced by the Royal General Bulbgrowers' Society of Holland, there are 15, comprising well over 4,000 registered varieties.

Although tulip breeding was carried out in France, Belgium and England as well as in Holland in the past, it was and is the Dutch who have raised most of the new varieties and originated the many new and spectacular hybrids. The bulk of the world's supply of tulips has always come from Holland where soil and climate are most suitable to their culture. The breeding of tulips is a story in itself and during the present century the science-oriented and experienced Dutch bulb industry has scored a significant succession of breakthroughs which have not only given the gardeners of the world new and exciting forms and colours but a much longer season of tulip bloom.

There are these who think that the Dutch are still involved in a kind of tulipomania, introducing more and more new varieties of tulips every year. But, in fact, no new variety is ever marketed to the public unless it is genuinely different from and an improvement on an established variety. And many varieties, indeed entire classes of tulips, are gradually taken out of commercial cultivation as new and better varieties supersede them in popularity.

What is important today is that the story of the tulip is not yet at an end; it is a continuing story that constantly brings fresh beauty and enjoyment. The tulip, a gift to the world from the Dutch for some 400 years, still has a brilliant future.

THE DUTCH BULB INDUSTRY

Although the Dutch bulb industry was founded on the tulip in the 1600s it has gradually expanded on sound and scientific lines to encompass the commercial cultivation of the widest range of bulbs in the world. Tulips, hyacinths and narcissi are the three main types of spring-flowering bulbs with gladioli as the main summer-flowering type. But scores more genera of bulbous and tuberous plants have become increasingly popular and literally hundreds of different species and thousands of different varieties of them are cultivated in quantity to supply the gardens and homes of the world.

Compared with most agricultural activities, the acreage under bulbs in Holland is small but some 8,000 growers manage on about 30,000 acres to produce over 4,000 million bulbs each year. This figure, of course, excludes the many millions of bulbs which are forced to produce cut flowers. Dutch gardens and homes are traditionally ablaze with bulb colour but the bulk of the Dutch bulbs grown every year are exported to over 100 countries around the globe.

Bulbs have always done extremely well in Holland. No emigrants gathered from every continent could have acclimatised themselves so well nor rewarded their hosts so satisfactorily. Many people are surprised to learn that bulbs are not grown in a single area of Holland.

It is the narrow strip of land creeping up the North Sea coastline that

Page 109 (*above*) Removing pollen from stamens for cross-pollination; (*below left*) microscopic research to determine possible presence of nematodes; (*below right*) soil research to check on parasites

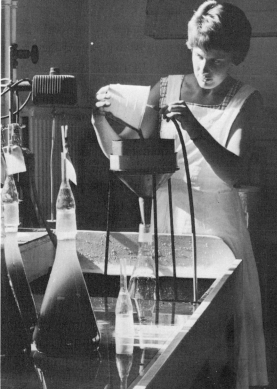

is so famous because its bulb production is concentrated into a mammoth patchwork quilt of brilliant colour and has consequently become one of the most popular tourist attractions in the world. This area extends north of the River Rhine along the western ridge of sand dunes from Leiden to Haarlem, forming a rough rectangle covering about 25 square miles (see page 71).

But it is the second area north of the North Sea Canal linking Ijmuiden and Amsterdam, including some of the polders of the Ijsselmeer and part of West Freisland, that actually produces the most bulbs. Its bulbfields are scattered, however, and are therefore less spectacular.

The remarkable development of the wild flowers, as all bulbs once were, by the Dutch is one of the most fascinating sagas of commercial enterprise. For this industry has brought much new beauty to the world. When the first bulbs from distant lands were brought to Holland and handed over to the early growers for experiment, their immediate response to care and attention led to the assumption that it was the sandy, well-drained soil of Holland which was the key to their success. We now know that this was only partly true, for bulbs grow in almost any kind of soil in virtually every type of climate, although this is largely due to the scientific culture and treatment of the bulbs before they are exported.

A proportion of the total acreage under bulbs is devoted to nursery work. It takes about seven years to produce from seed a bulb ready to flower. Even if the producer depends almost entirely on the bulblets which grow every year on or from the parent bulb, it still takes at least three years, according to the type and variety of bulb, for these progeny to become sufficiently large for sale.

Perhaps the most interesting aspect of the industry's story is the production of new varieties. Hundreds are evolved each year but only a relative handful ever reach the market. The professional flower breeder usually has two main aims—the improvement of existing varieties and the advancement of knowledge on the phenomena of cross-fertilisation.

The breeding of new varieties follows several more or less fixed rules and methods although most breeders have special techniques of their own. And what most of us regard as freaks of nature still produce the largest number of variations or new varieties.

To produce new floral beauty queens, the Dutch growers do not carry out haphazard pollination on the off-chance of getting something unique. They work out in detail exactly what characteristics they want the new blooms to have and then select the parent flowers with the

60 *above:* (*left*) Single Early tulip Princess Irene

61 (*right*) Double Early tulip Scarlet Cardinal

62 (*centre*) Triumph tulip Attilla

63 *below:* (*left*) Darwin Hybrid tulip Beauty of Apeldoorn

64 (*right*) Darwin tulip Gander

65 *above:* (*left*) Lily-flowered tulip West Point

66 (*right*) Cottage tulip Mrs John T. Scheepers

67 (*centre*) Fringed cottage tulip Burgundy Lace

68 *below:* (*left*) Viridiflora cottage tulip Artist

69 (*right*) Multi-flowering cottage tulip Georgette

70 *above:* (*left*) Parrot tulip Texas Flame

71 (*right*) Double Late tulip May Wonder

72. (*centre*) Tulipa kaufmanniana

73 *below:* (*left*) Tulipa fosteriana Red Emperor

74 (*right*) Tulipa greigii Red Riding Hood

75 *above:* (*left*) Tulipa acuminata

76 (*right*) Tulipa clusiana

77 (*centre*) Tulipa chrysantha

78 *below:* (*left*) Tulipa pulchella violacea

79 (*right*) Tulipa tarda

utmost care. The finest specimens are selected and marked during the actual flowering season and the bulbs then set aside, whilst after hybridisation (by which the pollen from one variety is artificially transferred to the pistil of another), the seeds are nursed like delicate children through their years of adolescence until they reach maturity. And even then only one seedling out of a million may yield a new variety worthy of commercial production.

While the bulb breeder seeks to develop exotic new varieties his chief work is to improve the quality of existing ones. He concentrates on healthier culture by means of selection because in the long run better quality gives the best satisfaction. Few amateur gardeners realise the trouble that is taken to ensure that even the most ordinary of varieties is not merely up to standard but has a vitality and resilience that makes it 'fool-proof' for the gardener.

The bulb breeder also caters to public demand or fashion in terms of colour, form, stem length and other attributes. The original Parrot tulips, for example, were weak of stem for the mammoth flower heads but breeders have been responsible for the development of the sturdy stems which now support the big flowers. In more recent years whole new classes of bulbs have been evolved by breeding achievements, as witness the appearance of the many kaufmanniana, greigii and fosteriana hybrids with new colours, new forms, even new leaves and an extended season of flower for the tulip genus as a whole.

The bulbs growers have in fact developed techniques to out-manoeuvre nature, as is evidenced by the hyacinths, tulips, narcissi, hippeastrums and other bulbs you can have in flower in your homes at Christmas, months before their normal flowering time.

Because bulb growing is a specialised industry, the number of workers engaged in it is not large by usual industrial standards. Some of the 8,000 growers, carrying on family traditions that go back for centuries, have large production plots, while others grow on a comparatively small scale. Altogether there are some 25,000 workers involved in bulb production, including field workers, breeders, inspectors, sorters, packers, transporters and clerks, and there are many training schemes to ensure for the industry a regular flow of skilled professional workers.

The bulb industry is a complicated one but is extremely well organised. Its record in developing social security services for its workers is matched only by its achievements in creating and maintaining the most modern production machinery.

Page 116 (*above left*) This special pattern of spading to about 36in is character-istic of the Dutch bulb fields; (*above right*) good drainage is essential in the cultivation of bulbs; (*below left*) frames or rollers are used to press furrows in the soil preparatory to planting; (*below right*) after bulbs are planted in furrows, the bed is covered with soil from the next bed to be planted

In terms of quality as well as quantity, the bulbs of Holland exceed any foreign production, partly because of climatic and historic conditions but partly also because the growers and workers between them have channelled growing into a real art.

The expansion of the industry was not achieved by clever salesmanship or adroit business methods but by unparalleled co-operation. Although the Dutch are individualists by nature, tulipomania taught them a lesson they have never forgotten. In building up the bulb business into a world-wide trade, competition was not abandoned but resources were nevertheless pooled to tackle the problems of pests and diseases and the complexities of production, distribution, research and promotion.

Chief of the organisations in bulbland is the Royal General Society for Bulb Culture which brings together all the growers. There are also separate associations for the growers of tulips, hyacinths, narcissi, lilies, dahlias, irises and gladioli. Not all the growers are exporters, however, and the exporters are organised in the Bulb Exporters Association, which has separate sections for the various marketing areas.

There are inspection services which work within these associations in close co-operation with Plant Disease Department of the Government to maintain health and quality standards. There are consultant and information services whose staff move through the bulbfields and pass on the results of research and experiments connected with all the problems the industry meets, from pests and packing through soil composition and water level to fertilisers.

There is a Union for Bulb Traders and the actual bulb trade is concentrated in the Bulb Exchange at Hillegom, where millions of bulbs are bought and sold without one being on view. Trust and confidence are the basis of this industry. Any disputes in the bulb industry do not go to ordinary law courts whose judges could not be expected to be familiar with the ramifications of the trade but to the industry's own Special Arbitration Court.

The industry is represented in other organisations such as the semi-governmental Commodity Board for Ornamental Plants, basically a marketing organisation.

Growers and exporters contribute by means of a compulsory levy to a common fund which is devoted to research and promotion. Science has played a major role in the advancement of the industry and since 1917 the industry has had its own Laboratory for Bulb Research at Lisse, which is financed jointly by the industry and the Government. Its

Page 118 (*above*) After bulbs are planted the fields are covered with straw, often transported by stretchers; (*below*) lifting hyacinth bulbs with a Lakeman lifter, after which the bulbs are put in baskets by hand

Page 119 (*above*) Moving lifted bulbs by canal boat; (*below left*) sizing hyacinths with a sizing board; (*below right*) consignments of bulbs packed in aerated cartons for export

achievements in combating pests and diseases, determining the conditions of growth and storage of bulbs, developing cultural methods to meet the wide range of climatic and seasonal conditions in different parts of the world, and ascertaining the best methods of shipping and handling bulbs are of practical benefit to professional horticulture and amateur gardening on an international plane.

Also operating internationally is the Associated Bulb Growers of Holland (known as the Netherlands Flower-bulb Institute in the United States and Canada) which was formed by the growers and exporters in 1925 to distribute information, advertise and promote Dutch bulbs. It is largely the comprehensive work of this organisation that is responsible for the annual export of some £50 million ($120 million) worth of Dutch bulbs.

The industry is noted for its exhibitions. First and foremost is the now famous 62-acre Keukenhof Gardens at Lisse (see page 48), the outdoor shop window of the industry, open each year from the beginning of April to mid-May in a continuous display of some ten million bulb flowers. Featuring some 80 different gardens in one beautiful landscaped setting the Keukenhof, located at the heart of the bulbfields, is the most colourful show on earth. There are 15 miles of paths with a succession of breath-taking views, fountains, lagoons, windmills, sculptures, restaurants and cafes, a post office with a special postmark, flower arrangement demonstrations, photography exhibitions, to say nothing of thousands of square feet of greenhouses filled with exotic blooms. One is devoted to those giant lily-like hippeastrums while another maintains a chequerboard display of some 700 varieties of tulips.

In front of the Bulb Exchange buildings at Hillegom is a demonstration garden called 'Treslong' revealing the application of bulbs in garden architecture. There are also covered exhibitions at different seasons, such as the West Friesian Flora at Bovenkarspel and the Liliade at Akersloot.

The Dutch operate what amounts to a national health service for bulbs. In fact no product is subjected to such intensive examination and inspection as the Dutch bulb. It is not generally known, for example, that certificates of health accompany every shipment of Dutch bulbs sent abroad. Gardeners everywhere can be assured that every Dutch bulb is a healthy, top quality specimen of flowering size.

Chapter Five

HYACINTHS

HYACINTHS HAVE everything—beautiful colours, delightful fragrance, magnificent heads of bloom, perfect form and sturdy stature. And they are so easy to grow in any well-drained soil anywhere outdoors except the wild garden in full sun or partial shade, interplanted with other subjects or on their own. They do equally well in pots, bowls or glasses indoors, flourish in greenhouses and make long-lasting cut flowers. From whichever angle they are viewed they cannot be faulted.

Although it is little more than 400 years since it was brought to Western Europe from Asia Minor to foster gradually a hyacinth cult that is enjoying a renaissance today, the hyacinth is a plant of great antiquity. In Greek mythology, Hyacinthus was the son of King Amyclas, and a youth of outstanding beauty, talent and skill. Loved among others by the Sun God, Apollo, and the god of the West Wind, Zephyrus, he was killed by the latter in a fit of jealousy and, the legend relates, Apollo, being unable to restore his life, made a flower grow from the blood of Hyacinthus.

Whether we place any credence in mythology or not, it is a striking coincidence that the genus Hyacinthus, a member of the lily family, is restricted to a single species, Hyacinthus orientalis, native to the Eastern Mediterranean countries. The wild form, no longer in cultivation, had a 10in stem carrying about 15 bell-shaped flowers, pale blue, purple or white, with a delicate scent, blooming in April. It is from the wild form that all the waxy, fat and stout horticultural varieties or florists' hyacinths of today descend.

It is believed that the Roman empire-builders cultivated the wild

form of hyacinth for its scent. Certainly they were described by Theophrastes and Virgil. The first recorded introduction of the wild form into
Western Europe was in 1562 when bulbs were imported into Padua,
Italy from Constantinople. A few years later the hyacinth was introduced into Holland, where it has been grown and improved upon ever
since, and from which fine bulbs have been exported to many other
countries. To this day the Dutch in the Haarlem-Leiden area are the
chief growers of horticultural hyacinths, which are known everywhere
as Dutch hyacinths.

The English herbalist, John Gerarde, grew hyacinths in his garden in
England as early as 1596. The first double-flowered hyacinths were
mentioned in 1612, and though much favoured in the eighteenth century,
are now rarely seen. By 1686 the Botanical Gardens at Leiden listed
35 blue, purple and white varieties, some single and others double. The
Dutch were so preoccupied with tulips through much of the seventeenth
century that hyacinths did not receive their full share of attention until
about 1700. Then interest arose, particularly in double-flowering
varieties, in the similarity and symmetry of the bells on the spikes and
in the purity of colours. By 1760 the number of varieties had risen to
upwards of a thousand and by the turn of the century to nearly 2,000.
Commenting on this incredible range 'with double and semi-double
flowers in white, red, blue and yellow, in scent without end,' the English
Curtis' *Botanical Magazine* in 1806 reported that 'acres are employed in
the environs of the city of Haarlem for the cultivation of these flowers;
from thence we receive annually the best bulbs.'

Although new varieties fetched quite high prices, hyacinths never
stimulated a craze like tulipomania. But certain novelties sold for as
much as £200 ($500) for hyacinths had become the flower of fashion
and remained so until the French Revolution. Madame de Pompadour
persuaded Louis XV to order extensive plantings of hyacinths in his
various palace gardens and hundreds of hyacinths were grown indoors
'on glasses'.

The French Revolution and then the Napoleonic Wars completely
changed the situation, for there were few wealthy people left. But
slowly the general public began to grow single hyacinths and soon catalogues were quoting prices for bulbs in hundred lots, indicating that
larger quantities were in demand. Victorian England revelled in mass
garden displays of hyacinths. Today large plantings are largely confined
to public parks, exhibition gardens and the bigger private gardens

but hyacinths are being used in many more and different ways in the gardens of the seventies and never have so many people grown them indoors.

Hyacinths are still grown in a strictly localised area between Haarlem and Leiden in Holland, in a soil that suits them admirably, consisting almost entirely of fine sand from the levelled dunes. The small fields are bisected by canals, which are so important in maintaining the absolutely controlled water level. This district is less than a foot above mean sea level. The soil lies at least 2ft deep.

There is no particular secret about growing hyacinths but the soil in which they are grown must be deep enough and really well drained. If you grow a hyacinth bulb in a glass with water you can see for yourself the remarkably long and extensive root system.

The commercial cultivation of hyacinths is exacting, involving precise temperature controls and virtually every process is carried out by hand rather than machine. Hyacinths also take a long time to grow from bulblets to saleable, flowering-sized bulbs. Bulblets are produced by scoring the bottoms of large bulbs in mid-summer with three deep knife crosses or by hollowing out the bottom in a cone-shape. These are set on wire-mesh tables in a shed with controlled temperature and humidity. Small bulblets gradually form on the wounds, sometimes as many as 80. Late in the autumn the bulbs are planted and in the following spring appear as clusters of grassy foliage with a few flowers. In July the bulbs, now dry, withered skins containing dozens of bulblets, are lifted. These are picked by hand and planted out in the autumn. The bulbs are lifted each year for several months of summer rest and treatment in the bulb sheds before being replanted again in the autumn. It takes all of three to four years to produce saleable bulbs from bulblets.

New varieties are obtained either from seed of good proven varieties that have been cross-pollinated or by propagating in the bulblet fashion those plants which have thrown a 'sport' or mutation. A 'sport' is simply a change in character (colour, form, substance, etc.) that differs from the true variety. The growers are interested only in one type of 'sport', namely bud mutation where only the colour has changed through some prank of nature, while the other original characteristics, such as strength of stem and time of bloom, remain the same. Since it takes as long as six or seven years for the black seeds to produce flowering-size bulbs, hybridising is a slow process. Even when a new variety is accepted for commercial production, it takes another fifteen years to propagate

Page 124 Scooping out the bottom of hyacinth bulbs which are then placed in ventilated crates and kept 2–3 months in a shed at a special temperature and humidity. During this time the new hyacinth bulbs grow in the hollow bottom

enough to offer them for export. So the introduction of new varieties is slow and very selective.

At the present time there are only about 150 registered varieties, of which relatively few are really popular. In recent years hyacinth breeding has tended to produce more massive uniform spikes and clearer, stronger colours, particularly among the reds. Despite competition from new varieties quite a number of 'old' varieties including L'Innocence, Orange Boven, Lady Derby, La Victoire, Bismarck, King of the Blues and Queen of the Blues have remained firm favourites for about a century.

HYACINTHS IN THE GARDEN

Because hyacinths are perfect from any angle they can be grown at any height in the garden, from the base of steps to the top of walls, and still spell grace and poetry. Hyacinths suit today's living conditions. With the big architectural swing to terraces, patios and 'leisure areas' home-owners are discovering that hyacinths cannot be excelled as subjects for tubs, urns and other containers. They have become the favourite flower for spring window boxes in private homes and flats as well as in public buildings, office buildings, hotels and restaurants. Because of their fragrance gardeners like to plant them close to the home, along the foundations of the house, in sunny corners between house and garage, at the base of steps or in containers on porches, terraces, balconies, outdoor staircase landings and even on flat roofs.

Plant hyacinths in groups of six to a dozen in front of dark evergreens, in the foreground of perennial borders, along a garden path or drive, in small groups in the rockery. Larger informal drifts or staggered rows, two or three bulbs wide, are charming in front of a stone wall, picket fence or hedge. Brighten up the sunny side of the garden shed with hyacinths, or use them at the base of flowering trees.

Hyacinths look elegant on their own but as their colours blend beautifully with other bulbs and plants they can be interplanted effectively with low-growing subjects like aubrietia, dwarf forget-me-nots or early-flowering pansies. Impressive displays can be created by interplanting hyacinths with narcissi, grape hyacinths or early-flowering tulips. The colour range of hyacinths is wider than most gardeners realise and the hyacinth is the only large-flowered genus to produce true blue blooms in spring.

Choose red, blue or mauve varieties to contrast with clumps of yellow or cream-coloured narcissi. White and blue hyacinths help to balance the brilliance of the many pinks and reds of azaleas. Cheerful yellow or orange hyacinths in curves between shrubs or in groups at the base of other shrubs are ideal. Rose and pink shades of hyacinths are magnificent beneath magnolias, flowering crabs or cherries or with blue grape hyacinths in a border.

For extraordinary colour contrasts plant various varieties of hyacinths with flamboyant fosteriana tulips or with those brilliant oriental greigii hybrids. And hyacinths can transform an area when planted with golden yellow or white alyssum or with primroses or wallflowers.

Although hyacinths will grow in any well-drained soil in good condition they prefer light rich soils. They like sunny positions and plenty of nourishment but fresh manure should never be used and fertilisers should not be allowed to come into contact with the bulbs. The bulbs can be planted in the garden and in outdoor containers from September through October, about 5–6in deep (from the top of the bulb) and 5–6in apart. But never plant hyacinths when the ground is wet and ensure that all containers have adequate drainage.

When planting do remember that different varieties flower at slightly different times in April; early, mid-season and late as indicated in the descriptive list at the end of this chapter. It is safest to plant only one variety per group but if you want multi-coloured display ensure that all varieties planted together bloom during the same period. By selecting varieties from the different flowering periods for different groups you can obtain a longer succession of hyacinth colour and fragrance.

For the garden and outdoor containers use 'bedding' grade bulbs. These are more economical than the 'exhibition' or 'top' grade bulbs used for indoor forcing. They are specially selected second-size bulbs, hand picked and healthy, and they will produce flower spikes almost as large as the top-size bulbs.

Hyacinths flourish throughout Britain and everywhere in North America except in the northern areas of Zone One. They have no spring-flowering rival in the warm climates of the United States for they are warm-climate bulbs. Some of the most beautiful hyacinths in the United States are grown in and around New Orleans. In the upper south hyacinths will continue to flower year after year. The flowers will decrease in size and produce fewer florets with age but fertilisation will help keep them up to standard longer. Hyacinths do extremely well in the middle and lower south too, although it will be necessary to replace the bulbs more frequently. Hyacinths can be spaced 5–6in apart wherever they are grown but research shows that the most effective planting depth in the upper and middle south is 6–8in while in the lower south of the United States 4–6in is better.

After your hyacinths have bloomed cut off the flower stalk but allow the foliage to ripen so that you will have good blooms the following year. The ripening foliage can be concealed with an overplanting of annuals or by loose-growing ground cover. If the space is required, however, lift the hyacinths carefully with a fork, heel them into an out-of-the-way spot until the foliage dies in six to eight weeks, then lift, sort, clean and store them in a cool, dry place until planting time in the autumn.

Hyacinths tend to degenerate more rapidly than other bulbs and hyacinths left in place should be given an autumn and spring feeding or top-dressing of well-rotted or dehydrated manure or other complete plant food, working it into the soil in October and early March. As the years go by the flowers will become more open and loosely arranged on the stalk. They are graceful and useful for flower arrangements.

Many gardeners prefer to lift hyacinth bulbs each year, replanting the old bulbs in a cutting garden or border and using new bulbs, perhaps of different varieties, in display areas. Hyacinths grown in window boxes and other outdoor containers should not be used for the same purpose a second year but be relegated to the cutting garden.

HYACINTHS INDOORS

Hyacinths have long been the great favourites for indoor gardening. Not only are they the easiest of all bulbs to cultivate indoors but they provide unparalleled colour and heady fragrance in the home from Christmas right through March.

For hyacinths in bloom in time for Christmas and New Year festivities, it is essential to buy 'prepared' bulbs. These are bulbs specially treated by the growers to advance their growing cycle and thus bloom earlier than the ordinary unprepared bulbs. Varieties prepared for Christmas flowering by the Dutch growers are indicated in the descriptive list at the end of this chapter but they are often retailed by colour rather than named variety.

The 'prepared' bulbs are cultivated in the same way as ordinary bulbs, except that they must be planted and plunged early in September and they require about ten weeks for root development. This means they can be brought into the light and warmth of the home about mid-November, when the buds will be well out of the neck of the bulbs.

When purchasing ordinary hyacinth bulbs for later flowering always buy the largest bulbs available. There are early varieties for forcing indoors from mid-January and late-flowering varieties for bringing to flower from mid-February. The ordinary bulbs will require 12–15 weeks in the garden plunge or cool, dark, frost-free indoor store before the buds emerge to a height of two inches or so out of the neck of the bulbs. By selecting both early and late-flowering varieties for succession planting through September and October you can easily extend your indoor hyacinth season.

Both prepared and ordinary hyacinth bulbs can be grown in soil or potting compost in pots with drainage holes, in bulb fibre in bowls without drainage holes or in hyacinth glasses in water. Pots and bowls should be at least 5in deep to give plenty of room for the roots, and while bulbs can be close together they should not touch each other or the sides of the container. Prepared and ordinary bulbs obviously cannot be planted in the same container, nor early and late varieties of ordinary bulbs. Indeed, I find it best to stick to one variety per container.

Pots and bowls can be placed in a garden plunge for the appropriate rooting period or kept in a cool, dark indoor store, in which case it may be necessary to give them water from time to time. They must, on no account, be permitted to dry out. It is better to delay bringing the containers into the light and heat than to start to force them before the roots are properly developed and the buds are well out of the neck of the bulbs.

When beginning to force the bulbs place the containers in subdued light for a few days. This will assist the flower stems to lengthen. Then the containers can be brought into full light. An even temperature of some 65° F (18° C) suits hyacinths best. They should be kept moist until the flowers are in full bloom (about a month) and I find that adding liquid manure to the water occasionally during this period keeps the foliage dwarf and assists the perfect colouring of the flowers. Once in bloom less water should be given to make the blooms last longer. Do keep growing bulbs away from heating appliances and turn them from time to time so each side of the plant gets good light and they grow evenly.

Should a bulb throw up two or more spikes or side shoots which are not wanted they may be cut off at the lowest point with no risk of damaging the main stem. If a second spike is thrown from the centre, however, it should be pulled out rather than cut.

After the bulbs have finished blooming, put the containers in a cool place, cut off the flowering stem and water less frequently while the foliage is ripening. The same bulb cannot be used for indoor cultivation again but can be planted in the cutting garden or border after the ground becomes workable in spring. The bulb will bloom again in a year or so with bells more loosely scattered on the spike.

Hyacinths can be grown in water in the various types of hyacinth glasses or plastic containers now available. First drop a bit of charcoal in the clean glass to keep the water sweet. Then fill the glass with water so that it almost but not quite touches the bottom of the bulb where it rests on the curve of the glass or the perforated shelf of the plastic container. Hyacinths grown in water must also be placed in a cool, dark, well-ventilated place for the root formation period. When the bud is well out of the neck of the bulb you can bring the glasses, now filled with white roots, into a living room to subdued light for a few days and then full light. The water level must be maintained both during storage and growth to full flower. Bulbs grown in water have to be discarded after flowering for hydroculture is an acute form of forcing, sapping all the nutriment from the bulbs.

HYACINTHS IN THE GREENHOUSE

No plants are more useful for very early greenhouse forcing than hyacinths. Both prepared and ordinary bulbs can be brought into flower in the greenhouse instead of in the house. When taken out of the plunge the foliage will be pale yellow and pots should be kept in shade, under the stagings for example, until foliage is a normal green, before placing on benches. Pots should be turned so that the flowers grow evenly and heavy blooms should be staked for if the spikes should collapse or bend it is difficult to straighten them again.

YOUR CHOICE OF HYACINTHS

There are nearly three dozen varieties of hyacinths easily obtainable in Britain and North America from local bulb merchants, garden centres or specialist nurserymen.

In this descriptive list the flowering time out of doors is designated by (1) early, (2) mid-season and (3) late.

All of these varieties may be grown indoors but those marked * are easy forcing varieties, specially suited to indoor culture. Pots of ordinary hyacinth bulbs marked E (early) may be brought in from the garden plunge or indoor store from the first week of January while those marked L (late) must not be brought in until mid or late February.

Those varieties marked (P) are also available as specially prepared bulbs for Christmas flowering indoors.

White

1 **Arentine Arendsen** white, long spike .... *E (P)
3 **Carnegie** white, broad compact spike (see page 73) .... *L (P)
1 **Colosseum** white .... *E (P)
2 **L'Innocence** ivory white, loosely set bells (see page 34) ... *E (P)
1 **Madame Krüger** white .... E

Yellow

3 **City of Haarlem** primrose yellow (see page 73) .... *L
2 **Yellow Hammer** creamy yellow .... *L (P)

Orange

1 **Orange Boven (Salmonetta)** salmon, loose spike .... *E

Pink

1 **Anne Marie (Ann Mary)** light pink (see page 73) .... *E (P)
3 **Crown Princess Margaretha** pink .... *L
2 **Lady Derby** rose pink (see page 34) .... *E (P)
3 **Marconi** deep pink (see page 74) L
1 **Pink Pearl** deep rose pink (see page 73) .... *E (P)
3 **Queen of the Pinks** bright rose pink .... *L
1 **Rosalie** (very early) pink, small bulb .... *E (P)

Red

1 **Amsterdam** cerise red .... *E (P)
1 **Eros** rose red .... *E
1 **Jan Bos** scarlet (see page 51) .... *E (P)
1 **La Victoire** brilliant carmine red, slender spike .... *E

80 *above:* (*left*) Allium roseum

81 (*right*) Allium neapolitanum

82 *below:* (*left*) Allium aflatunense

83 (*right*) Allium giganteum

84 *above:* (*left*) Anemone blanda

85 (*right*) Anemone St Brigid

86 (*centre*) Anemone St Bavo

87 *below:* (*left*) Brodiaea laxa

88 (*right*) Chionodoxa luciliae Pink Giant

89 *above:* (*left*) Colchicum Lilac Wonder

90 (*right*) Crocus zonatus

91 (*centre*) Crocus chrysanthus Blue Pearl

92 *below:* (*left*) Large flowering Dutch crocus

93 (*right*) Erythronium tuolumnense

94 *above:* Erythronium dens-canis

95 *(centre)* Fritillaria imperialis lutea maxima

96 *below:* *(left)* Galanthus nivalis

97 *(right)* Iris histrioides major

Blue

1	**Bismarck** lavender blue (see page 34)	*E (P)
2	**Blue Giant** sky blue, large bells	*E (P)
2	**Blue Jacket** fine dark blue (see page 51)	*L
2	**Delft Blue** bright porcelain blue	*E (P)
3	**King of the Blues** indigo blue	*L
1	**Marie** very dark blue	*E
2	**Myosotis** sky blue, large flowering	*L
2	**Ostara** dark blue	*E (P)
2	**Perle Brillante** pale ice blue, large bells (see page 34)	*E
2	**Queen of the Blues** light blue	L

Violet

3	**Amethyst** lilac violet	*L
2	**Lord Balfour** wine coloured violet	*L

White Roman hyacinths, which also stem from Hyacinthus orientalis, are also available for forcing into bloom by Christmas, in soil, fibre or on pebbles in water. Each bulb produces several dainty spikes of fragrant loosely set bells.

Collections of multiflora or multi-flowering hyacinths, ideal for forcing in pots and bowls for bloom in the later part of January in greenhouse or house are available in blue, pink, red, white and yellow. Several graceful little spikes emerge from each bulb.

Pre-packed hyacinths in containers with fibre or in glass or plastic for indoor cultivation without soil are also in widespread distribution, complete with instructions for cultivation.

Chapter Six

NARCISSI

THERE'S AN amusing story in Greek mythology about the youth Narcissus. As told by Ovid, Narcissus, son of Cephissus and Leirope, was led to believe that a long and happy life would be his provided he never gazed upon his own features. But Narcissus, in a moment of vanity, glanced at his reflection in the quiet water of a pool and, falling in love with his own image, soon pined away. From the earth where he died sprang a beautiful nodding flower which thereafter was called narcissus.

Others, however, assert the name narcissus has quite a different origin. Pliny held that the name came from the Greek word 'narce', from whence comes the word 'narcotic', in reference to the alleged perfume of the flower. In mythology these plants were consecrated to the Furies, who are said by the older writers to have employed the narcissus to first stupefy those whom they wished to punish. Other ancient writers also claimed that the scent of the flowers led to hallucinations.

Although actual cultivation of the plant is unconfirmed before about 1500, it was mentioned by Theophrastes 300 years before the birth of Christ. Homer was one who referred to its narcotic effect, Sophocles was clearly familiar with it, and the early Greeks used 'Persephone's flower' as a motif in various forms of art. The universal appeal of the flower is most effectively reflected in the following ancient description of its origin:

> Earth, by command of Zeus, and to please all-welcoming Pluto, caused narcissus to grow, as a lure for the lily-faced maiden. Wonderful was it in beauty. Amazement on all who beheld it fell, both mortal men and gods whose life is eternal.

The prophet Mohammed referred to bread as 'food for the body' but the narcissus as 'food for the spirit'.

Many homespun names have been applied to this fair flower. One old name in England was 'Lent lilies' which no doubt stemmed from the Lenten season when they came into bloom. Still another was 'Chalice flowers' because the corona of the flower resembles the shape of the chalice or cup used for holding sacramental wine.

For centuries this flower has been immortalised by poets, including Constable, Herrick, Masefield, Milton, Noyes, Shakespeare, Spenser, Tennyson and Wordsworth, who referred to them as 'daffodils' or 'daffadillies' or 'daffadowndillies'.

Confusion over the name has persisted for hundreds of years. It is interesting to note that well over three centuries ago the English botanist, John Parkinson, wrote:

Many idle and ignorant gardeners do call some of these daffodils narcissus, when as all know that know any Latin that narcissus is the same thing.

And Parkinson was quite right; the names, in fact, are interchangeable. Daffodil is the common name; narcissus is the botanical name. In America the term 'jonquil' is often used, many people employing it to describe a trumpet daffodil. More correctly, a jonquil is a sweetly scented, rich yellow species of narcissus having slender round stems and rush-like leaves, or hybrids derived from the species.

Botanically, the narcissus or daffodil is a member of the amaryllis family. The narcissus grows wild only in the northern hemisphere but its habitat is widespread, ranging from the British Isles through France and Switzerland to Spain and Portugal. Some grow in North Africa and in central Europe but only one species, the bunch-flowered tazetta, has penetrated into Asia, as far as Japan. With one or two exceptions, such as tazettas, which include Grand Soleil d'Or and Paperwhite grandiflora, daffodils are hardy. They are the most tolerant of plants and will grow in virtually any situation except dense shade or badly drained soil. They are the earliest of our important garden flowers with a flowering season extending from February to May outdoors. They can remain in flower for three weeks or more and if cut in bud for indoor decoration will last in water for a week or so. Grown in pots or bowls indoors they begin to bloom as early as Christmas.

Modern daffodils stem from about the middle of the nineteenth century when breeding experiments developed significantly in both England and Holland. Breeding work on a professional plane followed in Ireland, the United States, Australia and New Zealand but today it is the Dutch who collect and commercially cultivate those varieties that give the gardeners of the seventies such an excellent and economic choice for their gardens and homes. Of course, breeding has and is being done by many amateurs as well. A new breed is obtained from a single bulb, and as long as the number of bulbs available is deliberately restricted they are bound to be expensive. But the Dutch bulb growers, in a few years, can produce narcissi in large quantities from a single bulb. And this is reflected in the prices you pay.

The daffodil, like the hyacinth, has a flower bud already formed inside the bulb. But it is possible for more than one flower to be inside a daffodil bulb. It is for this reason that daffodils are the only bulbs not classified for size in terms of circumference of the bulbs, but are sold as 'round' or 'double nosed' bulbs. The latter have two distinct points on the top, which indicates that two flowering stems will emerge, and such a bulb is, in effect, two bulbs fused together.

The bulbs of the different species and varieties vary greatly in size and shape. Those of the smallest of the species are no larger than a pea, while some of the trumpet and large-cupped varieties have bulbs measuring 5–6in in circumference. In shape they vary from the typical round onion form to an elongated pear shape. The tunics of the bulbs even differ according to the species from which the various varieties sprang. There are rough dull tunics, gleaming dark brown tunics, glossy golden brown tunics, and creamy tunics.

Although breeding of narcissi began in earnest only about 150 years or so ago, as early as 1548 there were at least 24 species and cultivated forms being grown. By 1620 their number had swollen to over 100, by 1907 to over 1,400 varieties, and by 1948 the classified list and international register published by the Royal Horticultural Society of London included no less than 8,000 names. The current list has grown to over 10,000 and today the interest in breeding and the introduction of new forms and colours is world-wide.

The narcissus genus is a large one and has always proved a problem, even for botanists. It has been reclassified a number of times, the latest classification in 1969, dividing the genus into 12 divisions. The amateur need not be concerned with the continuing botanical debates for this group of plants is still in the process of formation but it is useful to know something of the different divisions and be able to recognise the many different kinds now available. To do this it is essential to know a little about the botany of the flower. The 12 divisions of daffodils are separated primarily on the basis of the shape of the flower and the relation in size between the various parts of the flower.

There are two major parts to the daffodil flower. The back row of six petals is called the 'perianth'. Attached to this row of petals is another row, often growing together and resembling a tube. This is the 'corona' or 'cup'.

Often the back-row petals are referred to as 'perianth parts' and the entire ring as the 'perianth'. So the words perianth and petals really mean the same thing. This is also true of the 'cup'. With certain divisions and varieties, especially those in which this part of the flower is most noticeable, it is called the 'cup'. With others the botanical term 'corona' is used. Both, however, mean the same thing. To add to the confusion the term 'trumpet' is also used. Again, this is the 'cup' or 'corona', the term 'trumpet' being employed to describe those divisions of daffodils in which the 'cup' is long and resembles a trumpet.

While the perianth varies in size, shape and colour to some extent the corona takes many shapes and colours and varies considerably in length. There are even different types of edges, some sharp-cut, others serrated or rolled. Most varieties have one flower to a stem, but jonquil and triandrus hybrids often have two to six while the tazettas produce as many as eight or more small flowers per stem. The scent of this flower varies as much as its form and colour. In some, like the jonquil, poeticus and tazetta hybrids, it is strong; in others, like the trumpets, hardly discernible; and in still others, like the cyclamineus and triandrus hybrids, completely absent.

The descriptive list of recommended available species and varieties at the end of this chapter gives, along with flowering times and applications, the division in which the flowers have been registered, as most catalogues and retail shops now list the varieties under their respective divisions or at least give an indication of the types of flowers.

OFFICIAL CLASSIFICATION

To help gardeners find their way among the host of daffodils the official classification is given here in full. With the exception of divisions 10, 11

Page 140 (*above left*) N. Rembrandt; (*above right*) N. Geranium; (*below left*) N. White Lion; (*below right*) N. Thalia

and 12, each division embraces flowers of garden origin only. Three definitions heading the classification are:

(1) 'Coloured' means yellow or some colour other than white.

(2) 'White' means white or whitish.

(3) The length of a perianth segment is the extreme length measured on the inside from its junction with the corona along the midrib to the extreme tip, and the length of the corona is the extreme length measured from its junction with the perianth to the end of its farthest extension when the edge is flattened out.

Division 1—Trumpet narcissi
Distinguishing characteristics: One flower per stem; trumpet or corona as long or longer than the perianth segments.

(a) Perianth coloured; corona coloured, not paler than the perianth.

(b) Perianth white; corona coloured.

(c) Perianth white; corona white, not paler than the perianth.

(d) Any colour combination not falling into (a), (b) or (c).

Division 2—Large-cupped narcissi
Distinguishing characteristics: one flower per stem; cup or corona more than one-third, but less than equal to the length of the perianth segments.

(a), (b), (c), (d), as in Division 1.

Division 3—Small-cupped narcissi
Distinguishing characteristics: one flower per stem; cup or corona not more than one-third the length of the perianth segments.

(a), (b), (c), (d), as in Division 1.

Division 4—Double narcissi
Distinguishing characteristics: Double flowers.

Division 5—Triandrus narcissi
Distinguishing characteristics: characteristics of the triandrus species clearly evident, ie 1–6 flowers per stem, generally white; bowl-shaped cup.

(a) Cup or corona not less than two-thirds the length of the perianth segments.

(b) Cup or corona less than two-thirds the length of the perianth segments.

Division 6—Cyclamineus narcissi
Distinguishing characteristics: characteristics of the cyclamineus species clearly evident, ie one flower per stem, generally inclined or drooping. Perianth is yellow, the segments recurved backwards. The trumpet is thin, with a wavy fringed edge.

(a), (b), as in Division 5.

Division 7—Jonquilla narcissi
Distinguishing characteristics: characteristics of jonquilla group clearly evident, ie 2–6 flowers per stem, yellow, scented.

(a), (b), as in Division 5.

Division 8—Tazetta narcissi
Distinguishing characteristics: characteristics of tazetta (syn. poetaz) group clearly evident, ie 4–8 flowers per stem, scented. Perianth generally white. Cup generally yellow and much shorter than oval perianth segments.

Division 9—Poeticus narcissi
Distinguishing characteristics: characteristics of poeticus group clearly evident without admixture of any other, ie usually one flower per stem, scented. Perianth usually white. Cup short and shallow, yellow with wavy edge bordered red.

Division 10—Species and wild forms and wild hybrids
All species and wild, or reputedly wild forms and hybrids.

Division 11—Split-corona narcissi
Distinguishing characteristics: corona split for at least one-third of its length. This division was introduced in 1969, a number of varieties with split coronas having been registered since 1950.

Division 12—Miscellaneous narcissi
All narcissi not falling into any of the other divisions.

DAFFODILS IN THE GARDEN

Daffodils are amazingly adaptable, easy to grow, require very little attention, and flourish in just about any soil in any garden location. Put

them in sun or partial shade, near water or rock ledge, clustered in rough
grass, or under trees—they thrive everywhere. They look at home
wherever they are sited on their own or with other flowers.

Although the official classification does not segregate the miniatures
of the genus from the large-flowered, it is convenient from the garden
application point of view for gardeners to do so mentally. For the miniatures, on the whole, flower earlier than their larger sisters and have their
own distinctive range of applications.

The species daffodils of divisions 10 and 12 and the cyclamineus
hybrids of division 6 are generally short in stature and are the first to
flower from February into March, with certain exceptions. They are
quickly followed by the trumpets of division 1 and the large-cupped
narcissi of division 2. Before mid-April the small-cupped daffodils of
division 3, the doubles of division 4, and the delightful triandrus
hybrids, some miniature all burst into bloom. The sweetly scented
jonquils of division 7, again with some shorter-stemmed varieties, the
fragrant multi-flowered tazetta varieties of division 8, and the starry-
eyed perfumed poeticus varieties of division 9 are at their best from
mid-April into May. And if you look carefully through various divisions you'll find some daffodils that don't come into their own until May
is underway.

I have included stem heights in my recommended list of narcissi as
a guide to stature but it should be remembered that daffodils grown in
partial shade will tend to have slightly longer stems than those grown
in full sun and, of course, will flower for somewhat longer periods.
Short stems are not necessarily indicative of small flowers.

The miniatures are superb in rockeries and mingle well with creeping
rock plants and other subjects. They can be planted with cover subjects
of many kinds to provide a longer succession of bloom. The little daffodils
add a new dimension to windowboxes, to tubs, urns and other containers
and will bring cheerful early colour to terraces, walls and even between
paving stones. They, of course, do not require staking, however exposed
their planting sites.

They can be employed *en masse* in foundation plantings, are ideal for
edging and when planted in groups or clusters bring the front of any bed
or border alive earlier in the season. Most make long-lasting cut flowers,
perfect for intimate arrangements. Some of the earliest provide attractive
contrast for early-flowering species tulips.

Because they are closer to nature I find a number of them the best of the genus for naturalising, particularly bulbocodium conspicuus and cylamineus.

Quite a number of the larger daffodils have the stamina to compete with grass in lawns and rough grass in uncultivated ground. Scattered about as if they were growing wild suits many varieties among the trumpets, large-cupped and small-cupped divisions. In fact, there is no better way to plant daffodils than to naturalise them.

Sunny spots in flower borders are fine for daffodils too, particularly strong-growing trumpets, large-cupped and small-cupped, doubles and tazetta varieties. But full sun all day should be avoided. If buildings, hedges or trees or shrubs cast shade on the ground part of the day, no harm accrues. In fact, the bright clear colours of many varieties, such as those having pink or orange or red cups, last longer and stay fresher in the garden if the sunlight is filtered through tree or shrub branches.

Daffodils are particularly effective when the bulbs are planted in clusters. The number of bulbs placed in any one group will vary, depending upon the size of the garden and the way the bulbs are being used. No less than five bulbs should be included in every group, all of one variety.

Daffodils make ideal fillers between shrubs. Broad-leaved evergreens and others like azaleas provide for daffodil blooms a rich green background. These adaptable plants can make a lovely carpet of bloom under choice flowering trees and even deciduous trees.

There are many problem spots around the grounds where conventional plants cannot be grown, but daffodils will flourish almost anywhere.

Since varieties will flower at different times over a three month period or so, many colourful combinations with other garden flowers can be planned. Lavender-blue grape hyacinths can be clustered in front of golden daffodils, or sprinkled through an open mass of pure white daffodils. The sparkling colours of tulips contrast sharply with the soft yellows and whites of daffodils. Scillas are fine companions for daffodils in borders or naturalised under trees. Many perennials and bedding plants which bloom at daffodil time blend with them, including violets, forget-me-nots, pansies, primroses and assorted rock garden plants. And I particularly like planting white trumpets and tinted large-cupped and small-cupped varieties in conjunction with pastel coloured hyacinths.

Outdoor Cultivation. The important thing to remember about daffodil culture is early planting. Bulbs should be set out from late August to the end of September and certainly not later than October for they tend to throw fresh roots very soon after flowering and therefore rest for only a short period. They make little top growth in autumn and even if shoots appear in winter thaws there is no cause for concern, for daffodils withstand exposure to cold.

Bulbs of the larger daffodils should be planted so that they have a covering of between 5–6in of soil. Cover miniatures with 2–4in of soil depending upon the size of the bulb, height of stem and size of flower.

Spacing depends upon application. In beds, borders, and foundation plantings, indeed everywhere where daffodils are planted in groups or clusters, bulbs are best spaced about 6in apart, although the smaller bulbs of miniatures can be planted about 4in from each other. In containers, from which daffodil bulbs are generally lifted, closer planting is quite in order. When naturalising daffodils the bulbs are scattered at random but it is sensible to establish a minimum spacing of about 6–8in.

Daffodils multiply rapidly and can be left undisturbed in any garden planting for three to four years. Lifting is only necessary when clumps thicken to the extent that roots become intertwined and plantings show signs of overcrowding. These signs are large numbers of leaves in relation to blooms and clear evidence of 'blindness' among the plants. When replanting use only the larger bulbs, reserving the offsets for the cutting garden, and set them a good 6in apart.

Daffodils thrive throughout Britain and everywhere in North America, although gardeners in the lower south and southwest of the United States must exercise some care in choosing types and varieties. Daffodils with white and pink coloration usually do not do very well. Neither do varieties with double flowers perform as they do in the middle and upper south. Fortunately other varieties flourish in Zone Five and can be depended upon to produce glorious bloom year after year. These include varieties in the tazetta class, the triandrus hybrids and the fragrant jonquil varieties.

It is not really possible to give specific advice as to which varieties do best in Zone Five. Although most doubles fail to satisfy in many areas of the lower south they have been known to thrive in certain areas. Most bi-colours have this same record. The best advice I can give to gardeners in the warmer climates of the United States is to consult your local bulb supplier who has usually had years of experience. In the warmer climates, of course, daffodil bulbs should be pre-cooled before planting. Research reveals that best results are obtained if daffodils are planted 6–8in deep in the upper south, 6in deep in the middle south and 4–6in deep in the lower south. In the southwest a depth of about 6in is most suitable.

Fertiliser does little if anything to assist first season daffodil bloom, but will contribute to better flowering in succeeding years. As most daffodils are left undisturbed for years I recommend the use of bone meal or a commercial bulb fertiliser, mixed dry into the soil before bulbs are planted at the rate of 5 or 6lb to 100sq ft. Late in every subsequent winter generously sprinkle bone meal on the surface of planted sites, as an annual top dressing will maintain the quality of blooms.

Everything possible should be done to keep daffodils growing after flowering. Pick off old blossoms before the plant begins to produce seed pods. Foliage should never be cut before it ripens and it takes a month or more for the leaves to complete their vegetative cycle after the flower has faded. Grass in which daffodil bulbs have been naturalised should not be cut until the leaves have matured. In flower borders perennials and annuals can be used to conceal dying foliage. If fading leaves interfere with other later-flowering plants or appear unsightly they can be folded over several times and fastened with a rubber band or soft twine.

Daffodils like water and plantings should not be allowed to dry out. The ancestors of our garden daffodils came largely from mountainous areas where the bulbs had adequate drainage, combined, at the height of their growing season, with continuously moving underground water from the snows. This flooding gave them plenty of moisture at flowering time and when it stopped, as the foliage faded, the drier conditions helped ripen the bulbs for the following year.

DAFFODILS INDOORS

Thoughtfulness rather than skill is the attribute required for the successful cultivation of daffodils indoors. Provided you select the species and varieties best suited to forcing, as indicated in the descriptive list at the end of this chapter, they are not at all difficult to grow indoors and they will certainly bring spring colour into your home from Christmas well into the new year. They are also excellent greenhouse plants.

No other genus of bulbs provides such a range of different forms and colours for indoor cultivation. Both double-nosed and round bulbs can be used, and like hyacinths, daffodils can be grown in a standard soil mixture or potting compost in pots with drainage holes, in fibre in bowls or pans without drainage holes, and in water. Daffodil glasses do not exist, however, as the stem heights of most forcing varieties are too tall for this method. But a number of varieties, which I will list later, can be grown in water with pebbles.

Containers should be at least 5in deep as the bulbs make powerful roots and require plenty of room. Daffodil bulbs are planted in soil, compost or fibre in the same way as hyacinth bulbs, with noses showing and, although the bulbs can touch each other in a container, I like to space mine an inch or so apart to give ample room to the foliage. Once planted they must, of course, be watered thoroughly, to soak the soil underneath the bulbs.

Success or failure largely depends upon giving the bulbs sufficient time for root growth in the garden plunge or cool indoor store. The time required ranges from about 10–15 weeks. Indoor planting should begin in September and succession planting should end by early October.

If planted containers are kept in a cellar or other indoor store they will require watering from time to time. Usually, when roots show at the drainage hole in the bottom of a pot, and top growth is several inches high, the bulbs are ready to force. If planted in September the shoots of the earlier varieties will be about 4in high and ready to bring indoors to an unheated room or into the greenhouse in January. Daffodils like it cool and a temperature of 45–50° F (7–10° C) is sufficient for forcing until the flower buds are clearly visible. Then they are ready to go into a light window or be transferred from under the stagings to the greenhouse bench in full light, for flowering. At this time a 60° F (16° C) temperature is ideal. In the greenhouse give the bulbs a temperature of 55° F (13° C) at first, then 60° F (16° C). In temperatures much above this the plants tend to give up. Water freely and ensure adequate ventilation. Forcing into flower will take from 4–6 weeks. Just before the buds burst they should be sprayed lightly with water but once they are in bloom less water should be applied. Remove the foliage of sideshoots if these do not show a flower bud.

Forced daffodil bulbs cannot be used for forcing again and should be relegated to the cutting garden, where they can be given fertiliser, or discarded.

A number of varieties of daffodils are available as prepared bulbs (see list of recommendations) for Christmas flowering. Cultivation is the same as unprepared bulbs but timing is different. Prepared daffodil bulbs should be planted the first week of October and plunged in the garden or stored in a cool place indoors. Remove them from the plunge or store on 1 December, transferring to a room indoors with a temperature of 60° F (16° C) in subdued light. It is important to keep them in these conditions for four days. On 5 December remove the pots or bowls to a cooler room with an even temperature of 50–55° F (10–13° C) and give the plants full light. Water freely and they should be in flower for the Yuletide festivities.

Among the tazettas or bunch-flowered narcissi Grand Soleil d'Or and Paperwhite grandiflora, both of which are French-grown and not hardy enough for outdoor cultivation, can be grown easily in bowls of pebbles and water indoors for Christmas flowering. Another tazetta, Cragford, will flower for Christmas if grown in this way but Geranium and Laurens Koster are later flowering.

Bowl, dish or tray should be filled three parts full with small and medium-sized pebbles to anchor the roots of the bulbs. The container should be filled with water, and rainwater is best, well up to the base of the bulbs. The water should just touch the base of the bulbs and not float them. A small lump of charcoal will keep the water sweet.

Planting time for Christmas flowering is October and bowls should be placed in a cool place in the dark or dim light in a temperature no higher than 45° F (7° C). By the end of November, they can be removed to any airy room and placed on a windowsill where a temperature of 50–55° F (10–13° C) can be maintained. The later-flowering tazettas can be planted in pebbles and water up to mid-November and will take 8–10 weeks to root properly. All bulbs grown in water should be discarded after flowering.

YOUR CHOICE OF DAFFODILS

All of the many species and varieties of narcissi in the following descriptive list are highly recommended and are easily obtainable in Britain and North America.

The sequence of flowering out of doors is designated by (1) very early, (2) early, (3) medium early, and (4) late. Species and varieties for easy forcing indoors are designated by (a) for forcing from early January or (b) for forcing from late January or early February. Those available as prepared bulbs for Christmas flowering are indicated by (P).

Heights of flowering stems in inches are indicated by numerals in parentheses immediately following the names. Species and varieties suitable for naturalising are marked (N).

Division 1a (Yellow Trumpets)
2 **Dutch Master** (18) uniform soft yellow   b
3 **Gold Medal** (17) uniform golden yellow (see page 52)   b
2 **Golden Harvest** (17) golden yellow, huge trumpet (see page 92)   a (P)
3 **Explorer** (18) yellow   b
3 **Joseph MacLeod** (19) yellow, large flower   b
3 **King Alfred** (18) golden yellow   a
3 **Rembrandt** (18) deep golden yellow   b
3 **Unsurpassable** (19) golden yellow, large flower (see page 74)   b (N)

Division 1b (Bicolour Trumpets)
3 **Goblet** (16) white perianth, yellow trumpet   b
3 **Magnet** (17) white perianth, yellow trumpet (see page 92)   b
3 **Music Hall** (17) white perianth, yellow trumpet   b (N)
3 **Queen of Bicolours** (16) white perianth, canary yellow trumpet   b

Division 1c (White Trumpets)
3 **Mount Hood** (17) uniform white (see page 91)   b (N)
3 **Mrs. E. H. Krelage** (19) creamy white changing to pure white   b (N)
2 **W. P. Milner** (8) sulphur white (see page 94)   b

Division 2a (Large-cupped, perianth yellow, corona coloured)
3 **Carbineer** (18) deep orange cup   (N)
3 **Carlton** (17) uniform soft yellow, large cup   a (N)
2 **Fortune** (19) orange red cup   a
2 **Yellow Sun** (18) large golden yellow cup (see page 92)   a (P)

Division 2b (Large-cupped, perianth white, corona coloured)
3 **Flower Record** (15) yellow cup edged orange (see page 92)   b
4 **Mrs. R. O. Backhouse** (15) apricot pink cup   b (N)
3 **Sempre Avanti** (16) bright orange cup (see page 91)   (N)

Division 2c (Large-cupped, perianth white, corona white)
3 **Ice Follies** (16) pure white   a

Division 3a (Small-cupped, perianth yellow, corona coloured)
3 **Birma** (17) orange scarlet cup (see page 92)   b
3 **Edward Buxton** (19) deep orange cup   b (N)

Division 3b (Small-cupped, perianth white, corona coloured)
3 **Aflame** (16) red cup   b
3 **Barrett Browning** (17) brilliant red cup (see page 91)   a (P)
3 **Verger** (16) deep red cup   b (N)

Division 4 (Double Narcissi)
4 **Albus plenus odoratus** (14) snowy white gardenia-like
    scented flowers   (N)
3 **Bridal Crown** (17) three to four creamy yellow flowers
    produced in clusters   a
4 **Cheerfulness** (16) two to three sweetly scented creamy
    yellow flowers (see page 93)   b
3 **Inglescombe** (17) uniform pale yellow
4 **Mary Copeland** (14) outer petals creamy white, inner petals
    lemon yellow and orange
3 **Texas** (19) pale yellow with orange red centre (see page 33)   a (P)
3 **Van Sion** (14) golden yellow (see page 52)   b (N)
3 **White Lion** (18) white with creamy centre (see page 91)
4 **Yellow Cheerfulness** (19) primrose yellow (see page 93)   b

Division 5a (Triandrus Narcissi)
3 **Moonshine** (10) two to three nodding creamy white flowers
    per stem
2 **Shot Silk** (12) several silvery white flowers per stem, free
    flowering
3 **Thalia** (12) pure white (see page 93)   b

Division 6a (Cyclamineus Narcissi)
2 **February Gold** (12) clear yellow (see page 34)   a (N)
2 **March Sunshine** (10) yellow and orange   a (N)
2 **Peeping Tom** (14) rich golden yellow, long lasting   a (N) (P)

98 *above:* (*left*) Iris danfordiae

99 (*right*) Iris reticulata Cantab

100 (*centre*) Dutch iris Angel's Wings

101 *below:* (*left*) Ixia

102 (*right*) Leucojum vernum

103 *above:* (*left*) Tulipa praestans Fusilier, scilla siberica, muscari botryoides album

104 (*right*) Ornithogalum umbellatum

105 (*centre*) Oxalis adenophylla

106 *below:* (*left*) Scilla tubergeniana

107 (*right*) Scilla campanulata

108 (*left* to *right*) Butterfly, large-flowered and primulinus gladioli

109 (*left*) Lilium Fire King

110 *below:* (*left*) Lilium Harmony

111 (*right*) Lilium Enchantment

Division 7a (Jonquilla Narcissi)

2 **Golden Sceptre** (14) large deep golden yellow sweet scented flowers

Division 7b (Jonquilla Narcissi)

2 **Golden Perfection** (14) golden yellow
2 **Orange Queen** (10) deep golden orange scented flowers
2 **Trevithian** (15) lemon yellow perianth, clear yellow cup, sweetly scented (see page 91)

Division 8 (Tazetta or Poetaz Narcissi)

2 **Cragford** (14) white perianth, orange cup, four to six flowers per stem (see page 51)   a
4 **Geranium** (16) pure white perianth, deep orange cup, three to five flowers (see page 93)   b
Grand Soleil d'Or (16) yellow with orange cup, bunch-flowered, sweetly scented, for indoor cultivation only   a
3 **Laurens Koster** (15) white perianth, deep yellow cup, multi-flowered   b
Paperwhite grandiflora (16) pure white, bunch-flowered, sweetly scented, for indoor cultivation only   a
4 **Silver Chimes** (10) white perianth, creamy yellow cup, four to six flowers per stem (see page 94)

Division 9 (Poeticus Narcissi)

3 **Actea** (17) large pure white perianth, brilliant scarlet eye (see page 93)   b

Division 10 (Species, wild forms, wild hybrids)

2 **bulbocodium var. conspicuus** (syn. Yellow Hoop Petticoat) (6) golden yellow, rush-like foliage (see page 94)   a (N)
2 **bulbocodium var. citrinus** (6) soft lemon yellow
2 **campernelli double** (10) golden yellow, multi-flowering
2 **campernelli single** (10) golden yellow, multi-flowering, fragrant
4 **canaliculatus** (6) white perianth, golden yellow cup, three to four sweetly scented flowers per stem, narrow blue green foliage (see page 94)
2 **cyclamineus** (6) clear yellow, reflexed petals (see page 94)   a (N)

4 **jonquilla single** (12) golden yellow flowers, fragrant

1 **lobularis** (7) white perianth, yellow trumpet   (N)

1 **minimus** (3) smallest trumpet daffodil, yellow   a (N)

2 **nanus** (4) miniature yellow trumpet, larger than minimus   a

1 **obvallaris** (10) bright golden yellow tenby daffodil   (N)

2 **triandrus albus** (syn. Angel's Tears) (7) cluster of silvery
    white flowers   b

Chapter Seven

TULIPS

TULIPS, THOSE gay and showy kings of spring, offer infinite opportunities for creating colour effects in the garden and the home. No other genus of flowers provides us with such an artist's palette of colours and, at the same time, with so many different forms which bloom from February through May.

The primary attraction of tulips has probably always been colour. When Busbecq first reported his discovery of tulips in Turkey he wrote that 'scent in the tulipam is either lacking or very slight; they are admired for the beauty and variety of their colours'. Many of the tulips originally introduced into Holland from Turkey were not wild species but garden forms with 'broken' colours, ie the flowers were striped, splashed, streaked or blotched. It is now known that a virus infection was the cause of this. Modern bulb growers take all precautions to ensure that their stocks of named varieties do not become infected, but this was not so early in the tulip's history.

These 'broken' tulips became immensely popular, indeed fostered tulipomania, and continued to retain their popularity until the approach of the twentieth century. This breaking lent the tulip a special fascination for the breeder. Hybridising, whether of the random sort practiced centuries ago, or the carefully planned methods of today, has brought not only new colours but has modified the classic forms of the flower.

Although tulip breeding was carried out in the past in Belgium, England and France, as well as in Holland, in the present century it is the Dutch who have raised the many new varieties and have originated new types of hybrids. The first of the new types, the Mendels, were introduced early in this century and were the result of crossing the very early dwarf Duc van Tols with the later flowering Darwins. These vivid. self-coloured single-cupped tulips were the first of the mid-season garden tulips. They were followed in the 1930s by the Triumphs, developed by crossing Single Early tulips with Darwins. The Triumphs are not only sturdier tulips but they flower immediately after the Mendels and before the May-flowering tulips to further expand the tulip season.

It was not until the last decade of the nineteenth century that the botanist Regel travelled through Central Asia and described many of our finest species tulips, including greigii and kaufmanniana. The Dutch used these and another Central Asian species, fosteriana, more recently to achieve the greatest breakthrough ever in tulip breeding. These three species were crossed with existing varieties of tulips, especially among the Single Earlies and Darwins to increase their limited range of colour. Then the resulting hybrids were crossed and re-crossed among themselves and with other garden varieties to richen the mixture and develop new forms. The result is four new classes of hybrids—kaufmanniana, greigii, fosteriana and Darwin hybrids. Between them they provide a wider range of varieties of quite different and distinctive tulips, supply new colours, shapes and forms of flower as well as attractive development of leaves, and advance the blooming season in addition to introducing another mid-season class of garden tulips.

Many of the new named varieties of tulips originate from the spontaneous mutations or 'sports' that emerge from time to time in the tulip fields. There, the stocks are most carefully checked to ensure they are true to name, and the presence of a 'sport' is quickly spotted. This spontaneous mutation is not confined to any one type of tulip, and it can take the form of a change of colour or in the shape of the flower.

The fascinating aspect of the colour 'sports' is that apart from their colour the flowers are identical in shape to the original from which they developed. There is a white, flushed pink Double Early variety called 'Murillo' which has been particularly prone to colour sporting, and more than 500 mutations, of which many dozens are commercially cultivated today, have been found with white, yellow, purple, red, scarlet and many other colour variants, all of which are otherwise identical with 'Murillo'. Similarly the cochineal red Darwin variety 'Bartigon' has produced over three dozen 'sports' considered worthy of commercial cultivation. Another Darwin variety, 'William Copland', noted for its early-forcing quality and pale magenta colour, has produced at least a dozen 'sports'

Page 159 (*above left*) T. fosteriana Cantata; (*above right*) T. greigii Yellow Dawn; (*below left*) T. Orange Favourite; (*below right*) T. White Triumphator

in the rose and purple range, each retaining the original shape of flower and the forcing quality.

An example of the shape 'sport' is the parrot tulip in which the change takes the form of fringed or laciniated petal edges which are frequently accompanied by green stripes on the petals. New parrot varieties can only be obtained from 'sports', for they never transmit their strange shape to their seedlings.

The gardener can use knowledge of colour 'sports' in colour-scheme plantings. The flowers of all the different sports of 'Murillo', for example, will be uniform in every respect other than colour, thus ensuring the gardener of simultaneous flowering and standard height of stem.

The classification of tulips has long been a botanist's nightmare, for until the beginning of this century there was no coordination between the increasing number of raisers of new varieties, with different tulips often being given the same name, and there was no satisfactory system of differentiating between the various types of tulips. The first official classified list and international register of tulip names was published in 1915 by the Royal General Bulbgrowers' Society of Holland, based on the work of a number of leading Dutch and British tulip specialists. It is constantly being revised and the present (1971) version lists about 4,000 names in 15 divisions, basically according to flowering order and shape of flower. The first 11 divisions cover all the garden tulips and are divided into three sections—early flowering, mid-season flowering and late-flowering. The remaining four divisions cover the species tulips and their hybrids, again in flowering order except for the last division, gathering together 'other species and their varieties and hybrids', which flower from February into May.

The official classification, even quoted in full, is not all that meaningful to the amateur. I have, therefore, prepared a special chart utilising the official classification but incorporating considerable additional information to make it easier for gardeners to understand and appreciate what the tulip genus has to offer. Further detailed data is included later in this chapter with recommended varieties.

It will be apparent immediately that the tulip, a member of the lily family, is really a remarkable genus. Tulips come in all the colours of the rainbow and more, from white to almost black, from softest pink to deepest purple. They come in broken colours, self-colours, striped, streaked, shaded and tinged. They even come with touches of green in the blooms.

Page 161 *(above left)* T. Peach Blossom; *(above right)* T. Oxford; *(below left)* T. White City; *(below right)* T. Georgette

The flower is basically shaped like a cup or an egg, with six petals surrounding the reproductive parts, the anthers and ovary. But there is tremendous variation in the shape and size of flowers. Some are oval, some are shaped like turbans, others are square at the base, and still others resemble a whirl of flattened knitting needles. There are a number that are multi-flowering, producing several flowers on a single stem. Some tulips have tiny flowers while others produce blooms as large as the span of a man's hand. Some have stems only a few inches tall while others soar majestically to almost 3ft. The flowers last for at least a week, even in full sun, and, of course, the season of bloom is over three months long.

The tulip has a conical bulb with a sharp point widening to a bulging lower half, one side being slightly flattened. The bulb is sheathed in a thin, shining tunic that varies in colour from pale fawn through mahogany to deep walnut brown. The scales forming the bulb are attached to a basal root plate and are thicker and fewer in number than those of the hyacinth or daffodil bulb. The leaves are attached to the central flower stem so that none of the scales are connected with them as with hyacinths and daffodils. Propagation of the tulip is different too. The bulb is in effect annual, virtually vanishing by the end of the season leaving only its shrivelled skin attached to new bulbs. These will have grown during the season from the small buds at the base of the scales, one bud to each of the four or five scales. When the foliage has died down at the end of the season there will usually be one large flowering-size bulb and several smaller bulbs, the former repeating the cycle and the latter eventually growing into larger bulbs.

TULIPS IN THE GARDEN

As with daffodils and hyacinths the flower is in the tulip bulb when you purchase it and first season bloom is virtually guaranteed. Tulips prefer sunny, airy, well-drained positions sheltered from strong winds. They will thrive in partial shade, in which case they will flower slightly later and blooms will last somewhat longer. Tulips dislike wet soils and will not appreciate overly-rich soils, although good, friable soil will produce tulips at their best. I find that the smaller species tulips invariably do better in full sun. Spring rain usually supplies sufficient moisture for tulips but when necessary they should be watered to keep the ground from being parched.

Always plant tulips late in the season, which is from the end of October to mid-December or the first frost in Britain. Garden tulips should be planted 5–6in deep, measuring from the pointed tops of the bulbs to the soil's surface, and about 6in apart. Species or botanical tulips should be set about 4in deep except for the taller-stemmed fosterianas, greigiis and rarer species which should be planted like garden tulips. Most species tulips can be spaced about 4–5in apart, although fosterianas, because of their massive blooms, and foliage should have 6in between bulbs. The soil should be thoroughly soaked after planting to compress it and eliminate any air pockets.

Tulips provide gay colour everywhere in Britain and North America, although knowledge of the range well suited to warm climates is limited. Few flowers that can be grown in warm climates offer such rewards with so little effort as tulips. In the upper south the climate is favourable for repeat flowering for several years. The mid-south is the transition zone for tulips with many varieties repeat flowering in the northern section of this area. In the lower section, however, virtually all varieties require pre-cooling to flower even in the first year. In the deep south, the Gulf Coast and southwest, pre-cooling is mandatory and tulips must be treated as annuals as repeat bloom is rare. Treating tulips as annuals may seem expensive and wasteful but in fact is not. Bulbs are relatively inexpensive compared with the dividends of beauty they yield. Pre-cooling should be carried out in October and November so that the tulip bulbs can be planted in December or early January.

In the upper south experienced gardeners have indicated that planting tulips to a depth of 8in brings better results than the orthodox 6in planting depth. In the lower south where pre-cooling is essential and only one year's bloom results, shallow planting is better. Research in this area reveals that a 4in planting depth gives better results than deeper planting.

Except for a relatively few varieties most tulips do well in warm climates when bulbs are pre-cooled before planting. Some do better than others, but it is for the most part a matter of personal preference. The lists which follow do not include all the best varieties but represent a cross-section of those known to do well in warm climates. Some varieties have been excluded because distribution is limited or restricted. The beginner, however, can have confidence in all named below.

Triumph Tulips **Aureola, Blizzard, Edith Eddy, Elmus, Garden Party, Makassar.**

Lily-flowered Tulips **China Pink, Mariette, Queen of Sheba, Red Shine, White Triumphator.**

Darwin Hybrid Tulips **General Eisenhower, Holland's Glory, Red Matador, Spring Song.**

Cottage Tulips **Asta Nielsen, Balalaika, Burgundy Lace, Halcro, Maureen, Mrs. John T. Scheepers, Renown, Smiling Queen, White City** (Mount Erebus).

Darwin Tulips **Aristocrat, Cordell Hull, Demeter, Greuze, Mamassa, Niphetos, Pink Supreme, Queen of the Night, Sweet Harmony.**

Parrot Tulips **Black Parrot, Comet, Fantasy, Karel Doorman, Red Parrot, Texas Gold, White Parrot.**

Tulips are hardy bulbs and require no special care in winter, even in areas where winters are severe. In spring there is little to do except watering when necessary and fertilising older plantings. Fertiliser is not necessary for good flowering the first year but can help to maintain good bloom thereafter. Either bone meal or a complete fertiliser can be used.

Tulip flowers should be cut as they fade, preferably at the top of the stem, but, if desired, at its base. Leaves, however, should not be cut until they have died down completely. When cutting tulips for indoor arrangements the complete stem and flower can be taken, but never more than one leaf.

Tulips can be affected by a fungus disease called 'botrytis tulipae' or 'tulip fire'. It appears as soon as the first leaves emerge from the soil, the infected shoots become stunted and may shrivel up with a coating of furry grey mould. Should it occur, infected plants should be lifted and burned and neighbouring plants should be sprayed with Bordeaux mixture. Spraying usually prevents its spread and gardeners can keep their tulips healthy by maintaining a clean garden. Fallen petals should be picked up and ripened tulip foliage should be cut and burned. Tulips should not be planted again on infected sites until the soil has been sterilised and several years have elapsed.

If tulips have been planted in well-drained soil and are not subjected to wet or damp conditions they need not be lifted each year. With the help of fertiliser the bulbs will go on flowering for some years but flowers will tend to become smaller. Whenever I leave garden tulips in place for a few years I generally add new varieties each season for fresh display. Species tulips, except for those in naturalised plantings, I usually lift annually, both because I want to ensure brilliance of colour and size of bloom, and because I like to ring the changes and try different ones in different places.

Never lift tulips until the foliage is completely dead. Then dig up the bulbs, cutting off dead foliage, label carefully, and set aside for a week or two to dry off. The bulbs should then be rubbed clean and stored in a cool, well-ventilated place, preferably laid out in flat trays, and certainly not placed in closed bags or sealed boxes.

Although not all registered tulips are in commercial cultivation in Holland literally hundreds are and gardeners, wherever they live in Britain or America, will find a huge selection available. I have linked applications with descriptions of recommended species and varieties later in this chapter, but would like, at this stage, to make some general observations about the scope for tulips in the garden.

The early-flowering species tulips, particularly the dwarf varieties, can best be appreciated when planted where they can be seen close at hand or even glimpsed from the house. Plant kaufmanniana hybrids, for example, at focal points in the rockery, between light shrubs near the front door or corner of the garage, or scatter clusters of species bulbs through beds and borders in which perennials will not yet have started to grow when the bulbs bloom. All the dwarf species tulips as well as the shorter-stemmed Single Early and Double Early tulips can be used in windowboxes, tubs or urns, or for edging.

A small group of flamboyant fosteriana hybrids—remember the flowers are huge—will dominate a rock wall or shine across a front lawn if clustered in front of evergreen shrubs. They are also excellent for planting at the base of light trees, like cherries or crab-apples.

Use shorter-stemmed greigii hybrids in the rockery and taller-stemmed hybrids *en masse* in beds or borders. Remember that most of the rarer tulip species as well as kaufmanniana hybrids can be naturalised in grass.

All classes of garden tulips show up well in either formal or informal plantings. Planted in groups of a single colour, tulips lend sparkle and drama to a garden but never plant just one or two bulbs or a single row along a walk if a thin, forlorn look is to be avoided.

Many gardeners like to mass tulips formally in round, square,

Division	Height	Form	Colour	Comments	Flowering Time
Garden Tulips *Early*					
1. Single Early	10–15in	Single cup.	Red, orange, dark pink, yellow and white.	For bedding, edging and windowboxes.	From mid-April.
2. Double Early	10–12in	Cup filled with rows of petals.	Reds, pink, yellow, white, orange, self-coloured and variegated.	For mass plantings or edging.	From late April.
Mid-Season Mendel	16–24in	Large, single cups.	Vivid, self-coloured or edged with deeper or contrasting hue.	Especially for greenhouse forcing.	From late April.
4. Triumph	16–24in	Large, single cups.	All colours, some two-toned, satiny.	Greater range and sturdier than Mendels for beds and borders.	Immediately after Mendels.
5. Darwin Hybrids	22–28in	Large, single cups.	Noted for shades of red.	Handsome, huge flowers on strong stems.	From late April.
Late 6 Darwin	26–32in	Large cups, squared off at base and tops of petals.	All colours, mostly self-coloured, satiny textures.	Sturdy resistant to wind and rain.	From early May.
7. Lily-flowered	20–26in	Slender, urn-shaped with long curving petals turning outwards at tips.	Bright pinks, reds, roses, yellows, lilac, violet and white.	Graceful, elegant, long-lasting.	From early May.
8. Cottage	9–32in	Long, oval or egg-shaped.	Pastels and pastel blends, light hues of red, etc.	Graceful and sturdy, diverse, for bedding.	From early May.

Division	Height	Form	Colour	Comments	Flowering Time
Garden Tulips *Late* (Cont.) 9. Rembrandt	18–30in	Large, single cups.	Broken tulips, striped or marked.	Highly decorative for floral arrangements.	From about 5 May.
10. Parrot	20–26in	Large, open flowers with petals twisted, curled, deeply fringed.	White, pink, red, orange, violet, yellow, outside often tinged with green.	Showy for focal points.	From about 5 May.
11. Double Late	16–24in	Large cups filled with petals.	Shades of red, violet, yellow, white and two-tone.	Also called Paeony-flowered, sturdy.	From about 10 May.
Species 12. Kaufmanniana and hybrids	4–9in	Pointed buds, broad flat flowers.	Wide variety of colours many with leaves beautifully marked or striped.	Also called water-lily tulips. First to bloom.	From March.
13. Fosteriana and hybrids	8–16in	Single cups, very large.	Vermilion, hybrids in shades of red, orange, cream, white.	Flamboyant for focal points, tubs, urns, base of trees.	From early April.
14. Greigii and hybrids	9–20in	Very large, bi-coloured flowers.	Brilliant oriental colours, streaked and mottled foliage.	Strong stems, long-lasting flowers.	From mid-April.
15. Other Species	3–18in	Wild plant evident.	Wide range of colours.	Mostly dwarf stature.	From February to late May.

rectangular or diamond-shaped beds and after they have flowered, lift them, heel them into an unused corner of the garden, and use the beds again for later flowering plants. For formal beds of this type you will want maximum impact so it will be necessary to decide when you want colour. For April you can choose fosterianas, greigiis, Single Earlies, Double Earlies or Darwin hybrids. For early May plant Darwins, Cottage or Lily-flowered varieties and for still later colour choose from the off-beat Rembrandts, the gay Parrots or the lush Double Late tulips.

You can choose a single variety for your beds or select blending or contrasting colours for adjoining beds. As tulip colours do not clash, you can also mix varieties of the same division in the same bed but do check the flowering order and consider stem heights as well. You can also mix divisions, Cottage and Lily-flowered for example, provided the varieties flower about the same time and the stem heights are checked. Cottage tulip varieties are on the whole taller than Lily-flowered varieties so you will want your Lily-flowered tulips closer to the front of the bed.

Just as effective as beds is the not too narrow border. That foot-wide strip so common along driveways is never so gay as when tulips brighten it with colour. If the strip borders a fence or wall, you can use taller-stemmed tulips like Darwin hybrids, Darwins, Cottage or Parrot tulips. If the strip is bordered by lawn you'll find that the shorter-stemmed tulips like the Single and Double Earlies and the Double Lates are more effective.

Groups of tulips can also be used to edge a flower border, outline either side of a walk or path, or twinkle against a background of shrubs. Try interplanting Darwins or Triumphs among your roses, for example, to bring colour to the rose beds before the roses come into full leaf and flower. I use Darwin varieties in my rosebeds and to help conceal fading tulip foliage sow white alyssum between the bulbs.

By observing or calculating flowering times, tulips can be interplanted with many other bulbs and flowers. Short-stemmed early tulips look delightful with hyacinths. Or try brilliant fosteriana hybrids with pale blue muscari planted between them. White tulips look superb when set off by interplanted forget-me-nots and imaginative gardeners can create a host of attractive combinations. Late-flowering white narcissi look most effective, for example, grouped with bright self-coloured tulips flowering in late April.

Although most of my terrace tubs are devoted to hyacinths I can never resist each year planting one or two of them with tulips, ranging from multi-flowering species like praestans Fusilier through neon-like fosteriana hybrids to Double Early varieties.

I also like to spread groups of different varieties of tulips from various divisions through a deep and long mixed border so that from March to May there is a continuing scattered pattern of tulip colour.

Tulips are excellent for the cutting garden too. During the winter, of course, we buy tulips from the florist and those generally available are varieties from the Triumph, Darwin hybrid and Darwin divisions. Be different in your cutting garden and plant varieties from the Rembrandt, Lily-flowered and Cottage divisions, for example, not forgetting to include the odd viridiflora variety from the latter division.

TULIPS INDOORS

There is nothing particularly difficult about forcing tulips indoors for flower from Christmas onwards, provided gardeners do not attempt to rush matters and ensure that tulip bulbs are given ample opportunity to develop proper roots.

There are a few varieties of Single Early and Double Early tulips which may be successfully brought into flower for Christmas in the home or cool greenhouse. These are specially prepared bulbs (varieties available are given in the descriptive list following) which must be planted in pots or bowls before the middle of September and plunged in the coolest place in the garden. In the event of warm weather during this period the plunge should be watered sparingly but if the weather turns cold and wet it is advisable to cover the plunge with a sheet of material to prevent excess water from reaching the potted bulbs.

The pots should be brought into the house about 1 December and placed in the dark in a temperature of about 65° F (18° C). When the plants have grown another inch or two the containers can be transferred to a light room where a maximum temperature of 68° F (20° C) can be maintained.

The best time to pot all other tulips for indoor cultivation is from September to mid-October using fresh soil or loam mixed with sand or leaf-mould or a good potting compost. Tulips should never be potted in old potting material or soil from the garden in which tulips have been planted the year before. Smaller pots may be used but I recommend 6in diameter pots, taking eight to ten bulbs. Plant the bulbs with their flat sides to the container, so that half the bulb is exposed. The pots, after thorough watering, should be plunged or placed in a cool or shaded part of the garden and covered with some 6in of clean soil, in which the top growth is allowed to grow until it has attained a height of at least 3–4in. This will take 10–12 weeks. At this stage they may be brought indoors into a dark room at a temperature of not over 60° F (16° C) to allow the stems to lengthen. In greenhouses the pots should be kept under stagings.

After a fortnight to three weeks they may be removed to the light, but should be kept shaded from the sun. If necessary they can be covered with paper for a few days. Tulips should never be hurried for if allowed to grow slowly, the blooms will attain their normal size and colouring and last a long time. Avoid bottom heat and draughts and keep the containers well watered once you bring them indoors, although Darwins like being kept a little on the dry side. The highest temperature for tulips in their last stage is 68–70° F (20–21° C.)

Except for prepared bulbs tulips for indoor cultivation should not be brought into the home or greenhouse for forcing until mid-January. With succession planting you can have quite a number of different kinds of tulips flowering indoors for several months. The easiest tulips to force are varieties from the Single Early, Double Early, Mendel and Triumph divisions although there are a number of forcing varieties in the Darwin Hybrid, Darwin, Cottage and Parrot divisions. All the varieties suitable for forcing are so indicated in the descriptive list complete with the proper time for bringing them indoors.

YOUR CHOICE OF TULIPS

Gardeners in Britain and North America have an impressive array of tulips to choose from. I have tried, in the descriptive list, to assemble in one place for ready and easy reference as much pertinent information as possible. Tulips are listed in the order of the official classification. Flowering order in the garden is given before the names and is designated as (1) very early, (2) early, (3) medium early and (4) late. The appropriate times to bring indoors varieties suitable for forcing are indicated as (a) from the second week of January, (b) the last two weeks of January, (c) from the second week of February and (d) from the last week of February following the description. Tulips available as prepared bulbs are marked (P). The height of each variety is given in inches after the name.

112 *above:* (*left*) Lilium regale

113 (*right*) Lilium Royal Gold

114 *below:* (*left*) Lilium speciosum rubrum

115 (*right*) Lilium tigrinum

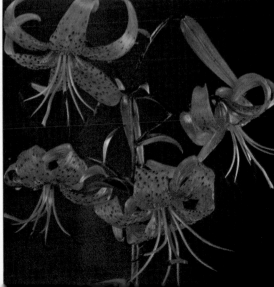

116 Whichever type or variety you choose dahlias are dazzling

117 *above:* (*left*) Acidanthera murieliae

118 (*right*) Anemone de Caen mixed

119 *below:* (*left*) Tuberous begonias

120 (*right*) Freesia mixed

121 *above:* (*left*) Montbretia

122 (*right*) Sprekelia formosissima

123 *below:* (*left*) Ismene festalis

124 (*right*) Ranunculus

Single Early Tulips. The earliest of the garden tulips are the Single Early varieties. They were derived from crosses between T. gesneriana, a 6–8in tall species with red or yellow bowl-shaped flowers from Asia Minor, and T. suaveolens, another early flowering 10in tall species with scented red and yellow flowers from Southern Russia. Single Early varieties are single-cupped in form with sturdy stems 10–15in in height. They come in striking shades of almost every known colour, some with scented flowers, and are more popular today than at any time in their 300-year garden history.

As they flower from mid-April, varying with the season and their variety, they are invaluable for massing in beds and borders to produce early dramatic splashes of colour in the garden. They finish flowering in time for sites to be cleared for planting summer bedding subjects. Because of their short stature and sturdy habit, Single Early tulips are excellent for edging and ideal for windowboxes and tubs. Most varieties are easily forced in pots or bowls indoors.

2 **Bellona** (15)   golden yellow, scented (see page 51)   b
2 **Brilliant Star** (12)   bright scarlet   a (P)
2 **Brilliant Star Maximus** (12)   improved Brilliant Star   a (P)
3 **Charles** (13)   scarlet, yellow base   c
2 **Christmas Gold** (14)   deep canary yellow   a (P)
3 **Christmas Marvel** (14)   cherry pink (see page 51)   a (P)
2 **Couleur Cardinal** (12)   purplish crimson   d
2 **De Wet** (13)   fiery orange, stippled orange scarlet, scented   c
3 **Dr. Plesman** (15)   orange red, scented   b
3 **Galway** (14)   orange red   c
2 **Ibis** (13)   deep rose   b
2 **Joffre** (10)   yellow, red nuances   a (P)
3 **Keizerskroon** (14)   scarlet, edged yellow   b
2 **Lucida** (14)   red, edged yellow   a
2 **Pink Beauty** (13)   pink shaded white   c
2 **Princess Irene** (12)   orange and purple (see page 111)   d
2 **Prince Carnival** (15)   yellow, flamed red, scented   c
2 **Prince of Austria** (15)   orange red, scented   c
3 **Ralph** (12)   deep lemon yellow   c

Double Early Tulips bloom a little later in April than Single Early tulips and are usually 10–12in in height. They have large, widely open double flowers, measuring up to 4in across, which, on the whole last longer than Single Early varieties.

First appearing about 1665, this attractive division of tulips boasts blooms that are self-coloured and variegated. Varieties are superb for mass plantings in beds and borders, where they do particularly well in sunny, partially sheltered positions. Their neat, even growth means they can be used most effectively for edging or in tubs or windowboxes. Most varieties are suitable for indoor cultivation.

3	**Carlton** (11) deep turkey red	c	
2	**Electra** (11) deep cherry red	c	
2	**Hoangho** (12) pure yellow	b	
2	**Hytuna** (12) buttercup yellow	b	
2	**Kareol** (12) deep buttercup yellow	b	
2	**Marechal Niel** (11) yellow and orange	c	
2	**Mr van der Hoef** (11) golden yellow	c	
2	**Monte Carlo** (12) sulphur yellow	c	
2	**Orange Nassau** (11) orange scarlet	c	
2	**Peach Blossom** (11) rosy pink	c	
3	**Scarlet Cardinal** (11) bright scarlet (see page 111)	a	(P)
2	**Schoonord** (11) pure white	c	
2	**Stockholm** (11) scarlet	b	
2	**Triumphator** (11) rosy red	c	
3	**Vuurbaak** (11) bright scarlet	c	
2	**Willemsoord** (11) carmine, edged white (see page 33)	c	
2	Mixed **Murillo sports** (11) mixed colours		

Larger bulb merchants and garden centres offer, along with rainbow mixtures of Single Early tulips, mixtures of Murillo sports of Double Early varieties at bulk prices for massing.

Mendel Tulips are one of the three divisions of mid-season flowering tulips which fill the gap between the early flowering and May-flowering divisions. They flower from the last week of April and a good two weeks before the Darwins appear in a normal season. Fewer varieties of Mendel tulips, first introduced in 1909, are available today than varieties of Triumph tulips, which to some extent have superseded them. Mendels are not as sturdy of habit as Triumphs, being the result of crosses between Duc van Tol tulips (these very early, brightly coloured 6in tall tulips were dropped from the official classification in 1969 and are now rarely cultivated) and Darwin tulips. They sport large, handsome single flowers in a broad range of colours on stems 16–24in tall.

Mendel tulips prefer somewhat sheltered positions in the garden. As they are self-coloured or edged with deeper or contrasting hues they look particularly elegant in clumps in beds or borders or beneath light trees. All varieties below are excellent for indoor forcing, from mid-January.

3 **Apricot Beauty** (16)   salmon rose, tinged red
3 **Athleet** (18)   pure white
3 **Golden Olga** (18)   purple rose edged yellow
3 **Krelage's Triumph** (24)   crimson red
3 **Olga** (18)   violet red, edged white
2 **Pink Trophy** (20)   pink, flushed rose
3 **Sulphur Triumph** (22)   primrose yellow
3 **Van der Eerden** (19)   glowing red

Triumph Tulips are available in a wide range of colours, many of them two-toned, on stiff and sturdy stems 16–24in tall and are weather resistant to all but the extremes of the late April and early May climate. They flower right after the Mendels. Derived from crosses between Single Early and Darwin varieties, they were first introduced in 1933 and have become increasingly popular ever since. They have large single-cup, heavy textured flowers, striped and margined, not to be found in other divisions of tulips. They are particularly valuable for exposed positions in beds, borders and other garden sites and make useful and graceful long-lasting cut flowers.

Triumph varieties are every bit as adaptable as Mendel varieties for forcing, but they should not be removed from the plunge and brought indoors until mid-February.

3 **Attila** (22)   light purple violet (see page 111)
3 **Aureola** (19)   bright red, edged golden yellow
3 **Bandoeng** (20)   mahogany red, flushed orange
3 **Bing Crosby** (21)   glowing scarlet
3 **Blenda** (20)   dark rose, white base
3 **Blizzard** (19)   creamy white
2 **Cassini** (16)   brownish red
3 **Crater** (18)   carmine red

3 **Danton** (19) deep carmine
4 **Denbola** (20) cercise red, edged yellow
3 **Dreaming Maid** (20) violet, edged white
3 **Edith Eddy** (20) carmine, edged white
3 **Emmy Peeck** (22) deep lilac rose
3 **Elmus** (21) cherry red, edged white
3 **Fidelio** (20) magenta, edged orange
3 **First Lady** (18) reddish violet, flushed purple
3 **Garden Party** (16) pure white, edged carmine (see page 33)
3 **Golden Eddy** (20) carmine, edged yellow
3 **Golden Melody** (24) buttercup yellow
3 **Hibernia** (16) white
3 **Kansas** (20) snow white
3 **Kees Nelis** (20) blood red, edged yellow
3 **K & M's Triumph** (25) orange scarlet
3 **Korneforos** (24) brilliant red
3 **La Suisse** (24) vermilion red, yellow base
3 **Levant** (20) lemon yellow
3 **Lucky Strike** (25) deep red, edged pale yellow
3 **Lustige Witwe** (**Merry Widow**) (24) glowing deep red, edged white (see page 34)
3 **Madame Spoor** (24) mahogany red, edged yellow
3 **Makassar** (22) dark canary yellow
3 **Meissner Porzellan** (25) rose and white
3 **Olaf** (20) scarlet
3 **Orange Wonder** (20) bronze orange, shaded scarlet
3 **Orient Express** (22) vermilion, tinged carmine
3 **Paris** (26) orange red, edged yellow (see page 52)
3 **Paul Richter** (25) geranium red (see page 52)
3 **Pax** (18) pure white
3 **Peerless Pink** (20) satiny pink
3 **Preludium** (19) rose with white base
3 **Prince Charles** (20) purple violet
3 **Princess Beatrix** (24) orange scarlet, edged yellow
3 **Reforma** (18) sulphur yellow
3 **Roland** (22) scarlet, edged ivory
3 **Rijnland** (24) crimson red, edged yellow
3 **Sulphur Glory** (22) sulphur yellow
3 **Thule** (24) red, edged yellow

2 **Tommy** (20)   brownish red
4 **Virtuoso** (19)   lilac rose
3 **Yellow Present** (20)   exterior creamy yellow, inside canary yellow

Gardeners can also obtain from larger suppliers mixtures of Triumph varieties of near or even height which flower at the same time in a blend of gay colours for mass plantings.

Darwin Hybrid Tulips represent perhaps the finest achievement in the history of the tulip. Obtained only recently chiefly from crosses between Darwin varieties and T. fosteriana, the most spectacular and possibly the largest flowered of all the species tulips and originating in Central Asia, the Darwin Hybrids are the newest of the garden tulip divisions, boasting the largest flowers yet produced. They are also noticeable for their brilliance of colour. Of superb stature with strong stems ranging from 22–28in in height, the giant flowers are massive single cups, particularly noted for satiny shades of red, and blooming about the end of April. They have already begun to 'sport'. Darwin Hybrids are a class apart and planted at focal points in the garden are automatic eye-catchers. They make long-lasting cut flowers. The few varieties available and suitable for forcing from the last two weeks of January are so marked.

2 **Apeldoorn** (24)   orange scarlet, black base (see page 72)   b
2 **Beauty of Apeldoorn** (24)   yellow   flushed   magenta,   edged
   golden yellow (see page 111)
2 **Dover** (26) poppy red, large flower (see page 33)
3 **Elizabeth Arden** (26)   dark salmon pink, flushed violet
2 **General Eisenhower** (26)   bright red, black base, edged yellow
2 **Golden Apeldoorn** (24)   golden yellow, black base
2 **Golden Springtime** (26)   pure yellow
2 **Gudoshnik** (26)   sulphur yellow, tinted red
3 **Holland's Glory** (24)   orange scarlet, black base
2 **Jewel of Spring** (26)   sulphur yellow, edged red   b
2 **Lefeber's Favourite** (24)   scarlet, yellow base
2 **London** (26)   vermilion flushed scarlet
3 **Oranjezon** (24)   bright orange
3 **Oxford** (24)   scarlet, yellow base
3 **Parade** (26)   scarlet, black base
4 **President Kennedy** (26)   buttercup yellow, spotted red

2 **Red Matador** (22)   carmine flushed scarlet

3 **Spring Song** (26)   bright red flushed salmon, white base

2 **Striped Apeldoorn** (24)   yellow, striped and flamed red

2 **Yellow Dover** (26)   buttercup yellow, black base

Larger suppliers offer choice mixtures of Darwin Hybrid varieties for mass planting.

Darwin Tulips. The best known of the tulip genus, the Darwins, made their debut in 1889 after permission had been obtained to name this splendid new type of tulip after the great naturalist, Charles Darwin. They were obtained by an amateur gardener, M. J. Lenglart of Lille, who selected them from old varieties in the Cottage division.

Darwin tulips are almost as important historically as the first few bulbs from Turkey to Western Europe. Not only have the Darwins proved to be fine tulips, but they have also demonstrated an exceptional capacity for being hybridised with other classes of tulips. From the Darwins have come the twentieth century divisions of Mendel, Rembrandt, Darwin Hybrid and Lily-flowered tulips.

Darwin tulips are superb in beds, borders, kitchen gardens or orchards as they have long sturdy stems 26–32in in height, which also make them superior cut flowers. The large single-cupped flowers are squared off at the base and tops of petals, come virtually in all colours, and have a distinctive satiny texture. All varieties are resistant to wind and rain, and can be grouped effectively among shrubs or evergreens or be interplanted between roses and other subjects. All varieties flower in early May, but some bloom earlier than others.

With the exception of Rose Copland, which may be forced from the end of January, other varieties marked are suitable for forcing from mid-February.

4 **Aristocrat** (30)   soft violet rose, edged white   c

4 **Bleu Aimable** (25)   lilac

3 **Cantor** (26)   coral pink, white base   c

4 **Clara Butt** (23)   salmon pink

4 **Cordell Hull** (26)   blood red, flaked white

2 **Demeter** (28)   plum purple   c

3 **Dix's Favourite** (27)   glowing red

3 **Flying Dutchman** (28)   vermilion scarlet

3 **Gander** (30)   pale magenta (see page 111)
3 **General Patton** (28)   deep lilac
4 **Golden Age** (26)   deep buttercup yellow, edged salmon   c
4 **Greuze** (28)   violet purple
3 **Lanseadel's Supreme** (27)   cherry red
4 **Magier (Magician)** (26)   white edged violet blue
3 **Mamasa** (22)   buttercup yellow   c
3 **Most Miles** (30)   currant red   c
4 **Niphetos** (29)   soft sulphur yellow   c
4 **Pandion** (25)   purple, edged white
4 **Pink Attraction** (24)   silvery violet rose
4 **Pink Supreme** (24)   rich deep pink merging to rose pink   c
4 **Prunus** (24)   rose pink   c
4 **Queen of the Bartigons** (25)   pure salmon pink   c
4 **Queen of Night** (30)   deep velvety maroon
3 **Rose Copland** (27)   pink   b
3 **Stylemaster** (28)   cochineal red
4 **Sunkist** (28)   deep yellow
4 **Sweet Harmony** (26)   lemon yellow, edged ivory white   c
3 **Vredehof** (27)   bluish violet
3 **Wim van Est** (30)   rosy red

Mixtures of Darwin varieties, especially blended and made up from named varieties flowering at the same time and producing a fine display of brilliant and constrasting colours can also be obtained from larger bulb merchants and suppliers.

Lily flowered Tulips are the most graceful and elegant of all the garden tulips. They create most striking pictures when planted in groups in beds or borders and add charm to any mixed plantings. I find the shorter stemmed varieties most effective in larger terrace containers. Beautifully reflexed and pointed petals form flowers of handsome beauty on tall, wiry stems some 20–26in tall. They contribute to distinctive flower arrangements, lasting long in water.

The resemblance of the blooms to lilies is responsible for their having been placed in a separate division. Lily-flowered tulips were introduced in 1914 and were derived from a cross between T. retroflexa, an old primrose species, and a Cottage tulip. T. retroflexa was itself introduced in 1863 after crossing T. acuminata, with its bright yellow or red pointed petals, with another form of T. gesneriana. The colours of Lily-flowered tulips are deep, rich and glowing and varieties flower about the end of April and early May, slightly earlier than the Darwins but about the same time as Darwin Hybrids.

3 **Aladdin** (20)   scarlet, edged yellow
3 **Captain Fryatt** (20)   garnet red
3 **China Pink** (22)   satin pink
3 **Dyanito** (22)   bright red
3 **Mariette** (24)   deep satin rose
3 **Maytime** (20)   reddish violet
3 **Queen of Sheba** (22)   red, edged orange
4 **Red Shine** (22)   deep red
3 **West Point** (20)   primrose yellow (see page 112)
3 **White Triumphator** (26)   pure white

Cottage Tulips also known as Single Late tulips, have more variation in form than any other division of garden tulips, particularly since recent reclassification incorporated a mixture which do not fit into other divisions. The flowers are single, generally large and egg-shaped, sometimes elongated, and resemble Darwins. But this division includes some multi-flowering varieties, each carrying 3–6 flower heads per stem, as well as viridiflora tulips with green as a base to the flowers.

Cottage tulips, so named because they were originally found in old cottage gardens of Britain and France, often have slender buds with long pointed petals. Distinct of habit and coming in pastels and pastel blends and in light hues of many colours, they are most effective when planted in bold masses. The viridiflora varieties are particularly popular with flower arrangers. Although normally tall of stem, the height of varieties in this division ranges from 9–32in, as most viridiflora varieties are shorter stemmed. A few varieties are suitable for forcing indoors from mid-February, but are not as strong and sturdy as the Darwins.

3 **Advance** (26)   light scarlet, tinted cerise
4 **Artist** (9)   salmon rose and green (viridiflora) (see page 112)
4 **Asta Nielsen** (28)   sulphur yellow   c
3 **Balalaika** (24)   turkey red
4 **Bingham** (26)   golden yellow
4 **Bond Street** (26)   yellow and orange   c

4 **Burgundy Lace** (26)   wine red with crystal-like fringe (see page 112)
4 **Claudette** (22)   ivory white, edged cerise rose (multiflowering)
4 **Dillenburg** (26)   salmon orange
3 **Frasquita** (28)   carmine, edged vermilion
4 **Georgette** (18)   celandine yellow, edged cerise rose (multiflowering)
(see page 112)
4 **Golden Artist** (9)   golden orange, striped green (viridiflora)
3 **Golden Harvest** (26)   lemon yellow   c
4 **Greenland** (24)   green, edged rose (viridiflora)
4 **Halcro** (28)   carmine red   c
4 **Henry Ford** (20)   carmine, spotted white   c
4 **Kingsblood** (28)   cherry red, edged scarlet
4 **Lincolnshire** (28)   vermilion
4 **Marshal Haig** (29)   scarlet, yellow base
4 **Maureen** (30)   marble white
4 **Mrs. John T. Scheepers** (28)   clear yellow (see page 112)   c
4 **Palestrina** (20)   salmon pink   c
4 **Princess Margaret Rose** (21)   yellow, edged orange red   c
4 **Renown** (30)   light carmine red   c
3 **Rosy Wings** (24)   apricot pink   c
4 **Sigrid Undset** (26)   creamy white, yellow base
4 **Smiling Queen** (30)   rosy red, edged silvery pink
4 **Vlammenspel (Fireside)** (30)   yellow, flamed blood red
3 **White City (Mount Erebus)** (28)   pure white

Multi-flowering Cottage varieties are in limited supply. Mixtures of Cottage tulips for mass plantings or for the cutting garden are available from larger suppliers at bulk prices.

Rembrandt Tulips. Tulip history reached its most notorious phase with 'broken' tulips for it was these magnificent specimens that sparked 'tulipomania' and fetched such fabulous prices. They can still be admired in old paintings and Rembrandt himself loved them as subjects. For many years 'broken' tulips were classified as Bizarres, Bijbloemen and Rembrandt tulips according to parentage and colour ground, but since 1969 they have been amalgamated into a single Rembrandt division. All are varieties striped or marked brown, bronze, black, red, pink or purple on red, white or yellow ground. Stem height ranges from 18–30in but they are not generally as vigorous as their parents in the Darwin, Cottage and old Breeder classes. All bloom in early May. Although lovely in clumps in the garden, they are mostly grown for cutting for indoor flower arrangements. As their popularity waned fewer and fewer varieties continued in commercial cultivation and today they are in limited supply.

4 **Absalon** (26)   coffee brown on yellow ground
3 **Black Boy** (20)   dark chocolate black on garnet brown
3 **Dainty Maid** (18)   magenta purple on white ground
4 **Insulinde** (23)   violet on yellow ground
3 **May Blossom** (18)   purple on creamy white ground
4 **Pierrette** (22)   pale violet, streaked blackish violet
3 **Victor Hugo** (18)   cherry rose on white ground

A few major suppliers may have collections of 'broken' tulips available.

Parrot Tulips made their debut in 1665 and were an immediate hit for the very large and beautiful flowers were strikingly fringed, scalloped, laciniated or possessed of wavy segments sometimes narrow and elongated. Originally the stems were rather weak for the heavy flowers but they are much improved today. Even so, Parrots are best planted in sheltered positions. Although grown primarily for cutting, groups of bulbs make a gorgeous splash of colour in the garden.

All varieties bloom in early May on 20–26in stems. The flowers come in a wide range of colours often tinged with green. The foliage is light green and provides a lovely contrast for the rich brilliancy of the blooms. All varieties are sports of tulips from other divisions and with the exception of their larger flowers and laciniated segments, retain many of the qualities of the varieties from which they originate. Several varieties can be forced indoors from mid-February.

4 **Black Parrot** (22)   purplish black   c
4 **Blue Parrot** (26)   bright violet
3 **Comet** (23)   orange red, edged yellow
3 **Erna Lindgreen** (26)   bright red
4 **Fantasy** (22)   soft rose streaked green   c
4 **Fire Bird** (25)   fiery red
3 **Karel Doorman** (20)   cherry red, edged golden yellow (see page
   52)   c

4 **Orange Favourite** (20)   orange with green blotches

4 **Red Champion** (24)   blood red

4 **Texas Flame** (22)   buttercup yellow, flamed carmine red, base green (see page 113)

4 **Texas Gold** (22)   deep yellow, narrow red edge   c

4 **White Parrot** (22)   pure white   c

Some larger suppliers offer mixtures of Parrot tulips.

Double Late Tulips are so like paeonies in flower form that they are often referred to as paeony-flowered tulips. They have large, fat, double flowers on sturdy and erect stems ranging from 16–24in in height. Breeders in Holland have devoted considerable time and skill to the production of new colours and the result has been the creation of extremely beautiful varieties, magnificent for bedding, for planting in groups in borders, for terrace containers and windowboxes or for interplanting with evergreens. Double Late tulips are splendid in flower arrangements and come in charming shades and two-tones. They flower from mid-May. When planting in the garden do site them in reasonably sheltered positions, for although the stems are strong they are susceptible to storm damage as the flowers are heavy.

2 **Bonanza** (18)   carmine red, edged yellow

3 **Eros** (22)   old rose, scented

3 **Gerbrand Kieft** (21)   purple, edged white

3 **May Wonder** (20)   clear rose, large flower (see page 113)

3 **Mount Tacoma** (19)   pure white, large flower

3 **Nizza** (20)   yellow with red stripes

3 **Orange Triumph** (20)   orange red, edged yellow

4 **Symphonia** (23)   cherry red

Species Tulips and their hybrids. The remaining divisions of tulips are devoted to varieties and hybrids of particular species and have been reduced in number from eight to four since 1969, since there are no hybrids of several species in commercial cultivation these days. The first three of the species divisions, kaufmanniana, fosteriana and greigii, have made spectacular advances in recent years and have assumed great importance in the garden.

Kaufmanniana, varieties and hybrids. The beautiful wild species tulip first discovered in the late nineteenth century in Turkestan by the German botanist, Eduard August von Regel, and introduced into Western Europe as the kaufmanniana or 'waterlily' tulip today has a host of offspring to bring the first real show of tulip colour to the garden. Dutch breeders have staged a literal revolution in tulip breeding by crossing this species with another wild species, T. greigii, as well as with traditional garden tulips. The resulting named varieties are very early-flowering, have new and subtle colour combinations, the unique shape of bloom which earned the kaufmanniana species the 'waterlily' nickname, and many have inherited from T. greigii beautifully mottled foliage so characteristic of that species.

The flowers are generally bi-coloured, the outside segments being deeper in tone than the inside. The long, narrow and pointed segments open out horizontally when the flower is in full bloom. The stems are short, all under 1ft, and this sturdy stature helps counter stormy spring weather (see page 113). The kaufmannianas quickly establish themselves and produce glorious bloom year after year. They are ideal for the rockery, borders, edging, terrace plantings in tubs or between paving stones, windowboxes, odd corners that need brightening, in pockets round shrubs, trees, steps, foundations or on walls. And kaufmannianas can be naturalised in grass.

1 **Alfred Cortot** (6) carmine red and deep scarlet, mottled leaves
2 **Daylight** (6) scarlet and yellow, mottled leaves
2 **Goudstuk** (**Goldpiece**) (6) inside golden yellow, exterior carmine edged yellow
2 **Heart's Delight** (8) inside pale rose, exterior carmine red, mottled leaves (see page 33)
2 **Johann Strauss** (8) inside white, exterior currant red edged sulphur, mottled leaves (see page 52)
2 **Shakespeare** (7) a blend of salmon, red and yellow
2 **Stresa** (10) inside golden yellow, exterior currant red edged yellow, mottled leaves
1 **The First** (6) inside ivory white, exterior white flushed red

Mixtures of kaufmanniana hybrids can be purchased from larger suppliers. Some also offer a 'Peacock' mixture, which is a very fine collection raised from kaufmanniana and greigii crosses.

Fosteriana, varieties and hybrids. Dutch breeders have taken a wild species tulip found on the mountain slopes of Bokhara and crossed it with kaufmanniana, Single Early and Darwin tulips to produce a fabulous new range of fosteriana varieties and hybrids. The fresh green foliage of the fosteriana species as well as flowers with glowing, neon-like colours have been transmitted to this new range, noted for its massive blooms and sturdy stems ranging from 8–18in in height. The fosteriana species is also one of the parents of the Darwin Hybrids and the flowers of the named fosteriana varieties are almost comparable in size. They flower in early April. Use them for dramatic, even startling effects in the garden. Plant them in focal spots in the rockery or border, at the base of light trees, in terrace or balcony urns, or employ them to spotlight drifts of muscari or early-flowering daffodils.

2 **Candela** (16)   soft golden yellow
2 **Cantata** (10)   vermilion red
2 **Easter Parade** (15)   pure yellow, flushed red
2 **Feu Superbe** (16)   bright red (see page 33)
2 **Galata** (15)   orange red
2 **Princeps** (10)   orange scarlet
2 **Purissima** (14)   pure white
2 **Red Emperor (Madame Lefeber)** (15)   vermilion red (see page 113)
2 **Yellow Empress** (16)   golden yellow
2 **Zombie** (14)   yellow flushed rose

Mixed fosteriana hybrids can also be obtained from larger suppliers.

Greigii, varieties and hybrids. Brilliant is the word for the greigiis now available to the gardeners of Britain and America. They are simply gorgeous with their huge, long-lasting oriental-coloured blooms and beautifully marked and mottled leaves. The mottling of leaves in the wild species discovered in the Chirchick valley of Turkestan has changed in some of the named varieties into broad, well-defined striping so that the leaves have marvellous decorative value, in addition to covering the soil in a way no other tulips do.

The greigiis of today (see page 113) are the result of crossing T. greigii with T. kaufmanniana as well as with traditional garden tulips. They grow 4–18in tall, have large cup-shaped flowers, some 5in in diameter or more. They add gay colour to the garden from about mid-April, in beds, borders, rockery and the base of walls. The shorter varieties are superb for terrace containers and windowboxes. All have good sturdy stems.

2 **Cape Cod** (8)　inside bronze yellow, exterior apricot edged yellow

3 **Golden Day** (16)　lemon yellow tinged red

3 **Margaret Herbst (Royal Splendour)** (16)　vermilion, yellow base

3 **Odessa** (12)　inside glowing vermilion, base purple brown, exterior glowing vermilion tinged violet

2 **Oriental Beauty** (14)　inside vermilion red, base deep brown, exterior carmine red

3 **Oriental Splendour** (20)　inside yellow, exterior carmine red edged yellow

2 **Pandour** (8)　pale yellow, flamed carmine red

2 **Perlina** (10)　inside glowing porcelain rose, exterior porcelain rose and lemon yellow

3 **Red Riding Hood** (5)　inside scarlet, base black, exterior carmine red (see page 113)

2 **Yellow Dawn** (15)　inside yellow, base purple red, exterior old rose edged yellow

2 **Zampa** (11)　primrose yellow, flushed red

Larger bulb suppliers offer mixtures of greigii hybrids for a long-lasting succession of brilliant colour.

Other species and their varieties and hybrids. The rare wild gems of the tulip clan are surprisingly inexpensive and of tremendous advantage to the gardener who seeks continuous colour and spectacle for by themselves they span the February to May tulip season and strike new notes of glory in the garden. With few exceptions they are dwarf in stature and again with few exceptions early flowering. They are ideal for the rockery, a boon to early spring windowboxes and tubs, superb for edging beds and borders, admirable for terrace gardening and most suitable for naturalising.

If anything they are hardier than garden tulips and as they originate in the Middle East and Asia, they do best in sunny positions. But partial shade will not harm them, only extend their flowering season. They can be left undisturbed to establish themselves and form ever-widening colonies over the years.

Your tulip season can begin as early as February if you plant

T. pulchella violacea or **Violet Queen** (see page 114), often called the 'crocus tulip' because of its violet-pink crocus-like flowers. Leaves are long and narrow, the 6in stems slender and the blooms long-lasting. Plant in sheltered positions and provide some winter protection for this poppet from Asia Minor.

In late February, **T. biflora,** which comes from the Caucasus, sends up on 4in branching stems several small star-like flowers, creamy white with a primrose yellow basal blotch and greenish pink outside petals. A species for collectors.

Multi-flowering like **T. biflora** is **T. turkestanica** from Turkestan. Each 6–8in stem bears up to 7 white flowers with a yellow basal mark, opening out like stars. It flowers in early March, and like **T. biflora,** is a most unusual contribution to the rockery.

The delightful 6in tall **T. praestans** from Central Asia also blooms in March with 2–4 orange-scarlet flowers per stem. Leaves are apple green with dark red edge. It is ideal in the rockery or alpine house. An exceptionally lovely form is **T. praestans Fusilier** (see page 152), with 4–6 brilliant flame scarlet flowers on each 6–8in stem rising out of luscious dark green leaves. Like **T. praestans Van Tubergen's variety,** which bears 3–5 orange scarlet flowers on stems of similar height, they create glowing garden portraits in clusters of a dozen bulbs under a light flowering tree.

Before the end of March too, the beautifully sculptured **T. eichleri** from the Transcaucasus bursts into flower. It has a large shining scarlet flower with slightly reflexed petals. The centre is coal black with a narrow band of yellow, and the battleship-grey foliage is unique among tulips. About 12in tall this species is excellent for windowboxes and terrace tubs and indeed, at any focal point in the garden.

T. chrysantha (see page 114), more correctly a form of **T. stellata** with somewhat larger flowers, blooms in April. Originating in Afghanistan it is only about 6in tall, the flowers are cherry rose margined yellow outside while the interior is pure buttercup yellow throughout. The foliage is long, straight and narrow. A decorative plant for the rockery.

From the steppes of Eastern Turkestan comes **T. kolpakowskiana** producing in April on each 6–8in stem, several golden yellow flowers shaded copper red on the outside. It is lovely in the rockery, but not always easy to establish.

One of the oldest known species, grown by Clusius since 1607, and widespread in Asia Minor, **T. clusiana** (see page 114) is also called the 'lady tulip' or 'peppermint stick tulip'. The small but dainty and grace-ful flowers bloom in April on slender 9in stems. The outer petals are cherry red while the inner petals of white have a violet base. They like warm, sheltered positions and a covering of 6in of soil.

The brightness of the flowers of **T. urumiensis** from Northern Persia is particularly appealing. The golden yellow heads with bronze reverse open in full sun, with the leaves in the form of a rosette creating a natural background. Only 4–7in tall this rare species flowers from mid-April.

During the second half of April, **T. tubergeniana** from the Bokhara region works wonders. Dutch breeders have produced a particularly lovely multi-flowering hybrid called **Keukenof** with scarlet flowers on 12in stems.

T. aucheriana from Persia is a charming 3in tall species with dainty orange pink flowers which open to a flat star. One of the tiniest of tulips it is free-flowering and sweetly scented, blooming in late April.

For charming clusters of up to 6 flowers standing out of long and prostrate foliage in late April, plant **T. tarda (dasystemen)** (see page 114), which is only 3in tall. The petals are alternately greenish purple and white with a green mid-rib and yellow base, the inside is golden yellow with pure white tips. In sunny positions these little gems are bright and cheerful and very effective in rockery, at border edges and between paving stones. They are particularly easy to establish and often carry on flowering into May.

The pale yellow flowers and creeping ribbon-like leaves of **T. batalinii** from Bokhara are at their best on 4–6in stems in May. It is most likely an albino form of **T. linifolia** which flowers at the same time and makes an excellent companion. The latter bears glossy scarlet cup-shaped flowers with a conspicuous black centre on 4–6in stems of red and its narrow ribbon-like leaves are also edged red. It looks superb on a sunny slope but it is not very vigorous.

There are a few taller species tulips, all flowering in May. **T. acuminata** (see page 114), often called the 'Horned tulip' or 'Turkish tulip' because of its long, thin spidery petals which are waved and curled, is 18in tall. The unique, surrealist blooms are yellow streaked with red. Hailing from Turkey, it is most unusual as a cut flower and makes tremendous impact in garden display if planted in clusters of a dozen or two. It should be treated like a garden tulip, planted 6in deep.

The stems of **T. marjoletti** also soar to 18in or more, bearing a pretty, elegant flower of creamy white faintly flushed pink. It flowers in the

125 Tigridia

126 Hippeastrum (Royal Dutch Amaryllis)

second half of May and makes a lovely cut flower. A member of the neo-tulipae group, it is native to the French Savoy.

The species tulip season ends in late May with **T. persica (celsiana)** which produces on slender 3–5in stems two or three fragrant flowers with bronzy exteriors and pale yellow interiors. Free-flowering and spreading rapidly with its flowers opening like stars, this unusual species, native to Spain and Morocco, can be best appreciated at the front of the rockery or border.

The species described above are among the easiest obtainable but supplies do vary. The bigger suppliers and specialist nurserymen will usually have at least a selection of these and other rare species.

Chapter Eight

REWARDS FROM 'LITTLE' BULBS, ALLIUM—GALANTHUS

BRITISH AND North American gardeners have never had such a wide choice of adaptable bulbs as they have today. There are, in addition to the kings and queens of the bulb world—the popular hyacinths, narcissi, tulips, gladioli, lilies and dahlias—nearly two score of princesses, mostly small in stature but producing big dividends in terms of colour, beauty, scent and spectacle, easily obtainable by the dozen or in hundreds at really inexpensive prices.

These various 'little', 'minor' or 'miscellaneous' bulbs in a vast host of species and varieties come from all parts of the world and are infinite in the range of garden glory they provide for the imaginative gardener for much of the year. To know where they grow naturally is often a help in choosing the proper soil and sites for them in your garden. Carefully cultivated, nurtured and improved by the experienced and science oriented Dutch bulb growers they quickly adapt themselves to both the smallest and largest of gardens adding new thrills of satisfaction and new dimensions of pleasure.

Most of them are fairly easy in their demands although a few require a little thought as to placement and care. The majority are hardy and once located where they are happy and can remain undisturbed they will increase rapidly and bring the reward of continuous blooming year after year.

Nearly all of these bulbs flourish in the rock garden or among odd rocks and stones which protect their delicate petals or small bells from the splashing mud of spring rains. Among rocks the gardener can usually control the type of soil more easily and provide the good drainage that all bulbs need. Others lend themselves to open woodland or a woodsy path, or to skirt the base of lightly shaded shrubs and flowering trees. Still others contribute spectacularly to beds and borders, create gay colour on slopes or under high, bare trees, or form great drifts in grass, orchards and meadowland. In short, the 'little' bulbs can be established in permanent homes in almost any area of the garden. Many make delightful and graceful cut flowers, many can be grown in outdoor containers, and quite a number can also be gently forced indoors.

This and the following chapter are devoted to all those 'little' bulbs which are planted in the autumn for bloom from late winter through spring and into the summer. They also include the relatively small number which are planted in late summer for autumn bloom, while Chapter 13 covers the 'minor' bulbs of more tender nature which must await spring for planting and high summer for flowering.

To keep track of your tiny treasures make a rough chart of your garden indicating just where you have planted each group of small bulbs. Many gardeners also carefully label each planting. This will forestall your grubbing them up accidently out of season as well as tell you what each kind is, important to know when you want to order more of those which especially appeal to you.

ALLIUM

Apart from the well-known edible species—garlic, onion, leek, shallot and chives—the allium genus, actually a member of the lily family, has a number of ornamental species that bring beauty to the garden over three months and versatility to the flower arranger, for alliums are ideal both for fresh and dried arrangements. The onion scent is not noticeable unless the leaves are bruised or when lifting the bulbs.

Although quite similar in form and flower, they provide infinite variety of colour and size for the gardener to choose from, from the purest white to the deepest purple as well as cream, yellow, pink, red and blue. The smallest allium is only a few inches tall while the tallest soar over 4ft and you can have alliums blooming freely in the garden from May into July.

Their lovely flowers are massed together in a ball which is solid or tasselled. These mostly hardy bulbs will thrive anywhere and go on endlessly. They flourish in well-drained ordinary soil, preferably on the sandy side, in full sun or partial shade. Most prefer lots of sun although **A. moly** does best in light shade. They are some of the easiest bulbs to grow. Just plant them in the autumn covering the bulbs two or three times their own depth. Smaller varieties can be planted 2in apart and taller ones about 6in apart. Then all you have to do is wait for the abundant flowers to appear. The bulbs need not be lifted and replanted until they become overcrowded and the flowers tend to become sparse. They will spread freely without special attention.

A. karataviense and **A. neapolitanum** can be grown in pots in a sunny greenhouse for late winter bloom. Use fertile and porous garden soil or a good potting compost. You will be able to get about 10 bulbs in a 5–6in pot. Plant in October and maintain a night temperature between 40–50° F (5–10° C). Water sparingly at first and freely when in active growth, gradually reducing the amount when the leaves begin to turn yellow. Liquid fertiliser can be applied regularly when watering from the time the pots are filled with roots until the flowers open.

All the following species are available:

A. aflatunense (see page 131), from Northern Persia, carries dense round heads of lovely lilac purple starry flowers in late May and early June and grows 2–3ft tall. It is a good variety for the border and a long-lasting cut flower.

A. albopilosum, from Turkestan, produces in June large heads, up to 10in in diameter, covered with star-shaped lilac flowers with a metallic sheen. The handsome, free-flowering plants, all of 2ft tall, look superb *en masse* in sunny locations and are favourites with flower arrangers.

A. giganteum (see page 131), from Central Asia, is enormous as its name implies, with a stem some 4ft tall, holding a magnificent ball-shaped mauve flower head, blooming in late June and early July. It welcomes a really sunny spot.

A. karataviense, first introduced from Turkestan in 1876, is a distinctive species with broad, flat and mottled green and purple leaves. The scapes are only 8in tall but they bear dense umbels of gorgeous lilac purple flowers up to 1ft in circumference from about mid-May and bloom profusely for a long time. Excellent in the rockery, they also do very well in pots.

A. moly, the 'golden garlic' from Southern Europe, is an old garden favourite and fine for naturalising as it spreads rapidly. It produces compact many-flowered umbels of bright yellow flowers in June on 1ft stems set off by broad, glaucous deep green leaves.

A. neapolitanum (see page 131), also 1ft tall, is distinguished by its mild sweet scent. From Southern Europe, it is grown extensively for cutting but is also splendid when naturalised and can be grown in pots under glass. It boasts big, beautiful white flowers grouped in loose umbels, blooming in June.

A. ostrowskianum, from Eastern Turkestan, is a pretty 10–12in dwarf species with fairly large heads of carmine pink flowers. Each bulb produces a mass of bloom in June and the plants spread rapidly.

A. rosenbachianum, from Bokhara, is a very large species with stems some 3ft tall and produces massive heads of purple rose flowers from mid-May into June. It is particularly striking when grouped near rhododendrons or interplanted with ornamental grasses.

A. roseum (see page 131), from Southern Europe, grows about 1ft tall, its slender stems surmounted in June by a lovely round 3–4in head of soft rose tinged with mauve. In warm positions in a large rockery it will spread freely.

A. sphaerocephalum, widely distributed in Europe and Asia Minor, is a good 2ft tall, with handsome flowering heads of reddish purple flowering in July.

ANEMONE

Although anemones, members of the ranunculus family, can also be planted in spring for superb summer show, if planted in late autumn they will produce rich glowing colour for several months of spring.

Very few flowering subjects can compete with the anemone for ease of cultivation, variety, colour, adaptability and long-lasting beauty. The range of colours, in fact, rival virtually all other flowers with the exception of tulips. From March to May is the time when so many different kinds of anemones provide lush colour in the rockery, border or in the grass. They combine well with other dwarf bulbs from species narcissus to species tulips in the rockery, and are lovely left undisturbed in an orchard or under light trees. Anemones are, of course, excellent cut flowers.

Suitable for cultivation throughout Britain and North America anemones are surprisingly effective in the warm climates of the United States when planted at the appropriate time. They are especially successful in the lower and middle south where they will flower profusely for all of 6 weeks. Planting time in the lower south is November and in the middle south it is October. In the upper south anemones should be planted late—in November, to prevent excessive growth before low temperatures arrive. Succession planting is feasible throughout the warm climates but most anemone plantings will flourish for one year only and new bulbs are necessary each year for high quality flowers.

Authorities differ on the origin of the name, but anemones are widely and appropriately regarded as 'windflowers', stemming from the Greek word for wind, 'anemos'. They are either tuberous or rhizomatous rooted, according to species. Gardeners can easily spot the difference between the wild species and the horticultural or florists' anemones.

A. appenina, the bright sky-blue anemone of the open woodlands of Southern Europe, has daisy-like single flowers on 6in stems and pale green leaves. They can be naturalised in rough grass, create lovely carpets of bright blue under the shade of trees, and are useful for shady sites in the rockery. There is also a white form, **A. appenina alba,** equally adaptable. Both flower in March–April.

A. blanda (see page 132), from Asia Minor, are those delicate but wonderfully hardy windflowers that produce small starry flowers in blue, pink and white, each made up of many rays of daisy-like petals in great abundance. The low, thrice-cut and pointed foliage provides a charming background for the cheerful blooms on 4–5in stems. They tend to flower a little ahead of appenina.

There is **blanda mixed** for effective colonies in borders, the rockery, darkish corners of the garden that need high-lighting or for naturalising. A number of named varieties are also available including the pure white **Bridesmaid,** the phlox purple **Pink Star** and the cyclamen purple **Rosea.**

Both these species should be planted in October or November about 2–3in deep in soil with plenty of humus and in large clumps or drifts, setting the fattish tubers about 4–6in apart. They develop large roots which increase by means of stolons. Lifting and replanting is necessary only when the plants become obviously crowded.

The large-flowered and ferny-leaved florists' or 'poppy' anemones are particularly showy, robust, free-flowering, brilliant in colour and, with 10–12in stems, especially valuable as cut flowers. The poppy anemones are hybrids and strains developed from **A. coronaria,** native to both Europe and Asia Minor. There are two types, the **de Caen** (see page 173) with large single, saucer-shaped blooms and the **St. Brigid** (see page 132) with charming semi-double flowers. The Dutch growers market splendid mixtures of each type.

The poppy anemones are hardy but in really cold climates prefer warm sheltered positions. Before planting soak the tubers or rhizomes in water overnight to swell them. This hastens growth, especially if soil is on the dry side. The irregularly shaped rhizomes or tubers are often referred to as claws and should be planted shallowly, no more than 2–3in deep ensuring that the buds, which look like small knobs surrounded with scales, are pointing upwards. Spacing should be at least 6in apart. For bloom from late March to May start planting in late November or December, with succession planting continuing until April. The later you plant the later the bulbs will flower. Winter protection by mulching will be appreciated in cold climates.

Poppy anemones can be grown in pots or flats or on benches in the greenhouse, provided it is sunny and airy and a night temperature of 40–50° F (5–10° C) can be maintained. Planting should take place as early in the autumn as the tubers or rhizomes become available and spacing should be 6in apart. Water moderately at first, freely when in full growth and add liquid manure to the water regularly from February onward.

Also available in Britain and America is the **St. Bavo** breed of anemone (see page 132), a vigorous and profusely flowering race, named after the patron saint of Haarlem, with large flowers coloured from pale pink to rose, salmon-scarlet and from lilac to warm mauve. You can buy them in fine special mixtures, and plant them like poppy anemones for glorious bloom on 12in stems from March to May.

BRODIAEA

Brodiaea is a genus in the lily family with severe name trouble for it is also known as breevoortia, dichelostemma, ipheon and triteleia. Most bulb merchants and bulb catalogues, however, refer to the genus which is native to Western North and South America as brodiaea or triteleia.

They are plants growing from corms and ranging in height from 6–24in. The flowers are borne in umbels like those of alliums and are bell-shaped. Flowering time ranges from March into July. The leaves, which appear in spring and disappear before the flowers bloom, are linear and rather grass-like.

Brodiaea are quite simple to grow. The small bulbs should be planted in September in good well-drained soil, preferably sandy, about 3in deep and quite close together in colonies. They do well in rock gardens, wild gardens and as pot plants and make excellent cut flowers.

For indoor cultivation plant several bulbs close together in well-drained pots or pans filled with sandy soil or potting compost with sand added in September. They can be grown in a sunny greenhouse or behind double glazing in the house when night temperatures of 39–46° F (4–8° C) until January and 40–50° F (5–10° C) thereafter can be maintained. Water sparsely at first, freely when in active growth, and reduce water when foliage begins to die. The flowers will bloom well ahead of those in the garden.

B. lactea, from the Western United States, boasts lovely white flushed lilac flowers arranged in umbels 2–4in in diameter on 18–24in stems. Flowering time is early June.

B. laxa (see page 132), native to California, has wide-mouthed tubular dark blue flowers on 18–20in stems and blooms in June–July.

Queen Fabiola, a recent medal-winning introduction, has gorgeous light-blue almost violet flowers in June–July.

B. tubergenii, a hybrid of B. laxa and B. peduncularis (also native to California), possesses very large umbels of light-blue flowers on 14–18in stems and is particularly valuable for cutting. It flowers in July.

B. uniflora, from Chile, hailed as the 'Spring Star Flower', is quite different from other species in the genus. It is star-shaped, violet blue and sweetly scented, flowering from April into May. Down the centre of each delicate petal runs a faint thin violet strip or line and orange stamens add to its charm. It flowers in such profusion on 6in stems that the blooms almost hide the grassy foliage. This species prefers sunny positions and light soil and increases rapidly by offshoots, making thick clumps in a short space of time. It is the easiest species to force indoors as well.

CAMASSIA

These beautiful North American members of the lily family are reminiscent of the European asphodel producing a profusion of starry flowers on graceful 2–3ft stems from May to July. The bulbs are mostly large and edible, indeed, long before the first colonists arrived in America the Indians used to gather the bulbs of some species and cook them for food. The name camassia comes from the Indian dialect word 'quamash'.

Camassia require no special treatment and grow vigorously, increasing if left undisturbed. They need lifting and dividing only about every third year. All species should be planted in autumn about 4in deep and

6–9in apart, in moist soil in sunny or semi-shaded conditions. They are excellent in borders, wild gardens and for cutting. They appreciate a mulch of leafmould or compost in the autumn and if the weather is dry during the spring growing season they should be watered freely.

C. cusickii, which is usually the first species to bloom in May, produces on 2ft spikes light-blue star-shaped flowers with pale-golden anthers above a rosette of broad glaucous foliage. This is an elegant species with the small flowers borne freely in loose racemes.

C. esculenta, also flowering as early as May, has graceful 18–24in spikes of showy rich dark-blue flowers and is particularly effective if planted in groups in a border or naturalised. From a distance groups of this species create the illusion of a blue haze.

C. leichtlinii Caerulea, flowering from June into July, has gorgeous flowers of brilliant aster blue on vigorous 3ft spikes. It will even flourish and spread if planted in clumps in grass.

CHIONODOXA

Chionodoxa were discovered only about a century ago high in the mountains of Asia Minor where they flowered in great sheets of blue backed by the melting snow. Thus this genus, a member of lily family, has come to be known as 'Glory of the Snow' and a hundred bulbs or so will produce the same glorious carpet of blue for you in your garden.

Chionodoxa seed themselves rapidly and also increase by offsets when naturalised in sunny locations. They are most effective too at the base of spring-flowering shrubs like yellow forsythia and creamy white magnolias. Plant some on a stone retaining wall, in terrace containers and in windowboxes too.

Their lovely sky-blue flowers are a most welcome sight in the March garden, appearing soon after snowdrops fade and along with the deeper-blue scillas which they somewhat resemble. Once seen together, however, you will never mistake them for the chionodoxa's cluster of blue flowers, each with its starry white centre, always faces up to the sky, while the early scillas nod their heads and are deeper blue.

The small, hardy pear-shaped bulbs should be planted in September or October about 2in deep and 2–3in apart in sunny locations. Those suitable for growing in pots and the home or cool greenhouse should be treated just like crocus (see page 205).

C. gigantea, from Turkey, with 10in stems has large flowers of gentian

Page 202 *(above left)* Allium aflatunense; *(above right)* Anemone blanda; *(below left)* Chionodoxa luciliae; *(below right)* Colchicum autumnale major

blue with an ice blue almost white small eye. The blooms are borne in a loose raceme and from a campanulate base open into a flat star like all other species. Flowering time is late March–early April. The leaves are deep green and strap-shaped.

C. luciliae (see page 33), from Asia Minor, is the best known and rated by most experts as the finest. There are more flowers per stem than C. gigantea, at least 6–12, and stems are but 4–6in tall. The broad linear leaves appear at the same time as the bright blue flowers with a clear white centre, in late March–early April. There is a pink form, **C. luciliae Pink Giant** (see page 202), with soft cattleya violet flowers on somewhat taller sturdy stems. Both can be gently forced indoors in pots.

C. sardensis, named after the plain of Sardis in Turkey where it was first found and not Sardinia, has porcelain-blue flowers, deeper blue than those of C. luciliae, with a small white eye. There are about 6 blooms in March on each loose raceme and stems, usually 2–3 in number as with all the species, range from 4–6in in height. And incidentally, all species last well in water, making delightful little arrangements in small bowls.

COLCHICUM

Often wrongly called 'autumn crocus' the species of this genus, a member of the lily family, are quite distinct in corm, flower and leaves. The corms are irregular and large, the crocus-like flower has 6 stamens compared with 3 of the crocus and the leaves, far from being fine, are large and broad.

Colchicums are most valuable autumn-flowering plants and too little appreciated by the majority of gardeners. Because the plants are quite naked of foliage at flowering time with leaves not appearing until spring, they have come to be known as 'naked ladies'. It's a good idea to keep this nickname in mind when planting colchicums so that the very effective tall foliage, often as high as 18in, does not interfere with spring-flowering subjects.

The name colchicum is said to come from Colchis, a district of Asia Minor, where many of the species are widespread. They are easy to grow, thriving in any well-drained soil, and despite the size of the corms need only a 2in covering of soil. They do well in full sun or partial shade, can be naturalised easily and are suited to wild gardens, the fringe of woodlands or around and under shrubs. But sited carefully in groups of 4–12, about 6–9in apart, they are also most attractive in borders. A host of flowers spring from each corm shortly after planting in late July or August. The foliage emerging in spring grows on until summer and when this dies down the corms can be lifted, the clusters separated and the corms replanted. This is not necessary, however, until the clumps become overcrowded.

Some species of colchicums have the surprising adaptability of being able to produce flowers without soil or water. The corms need only be placed in a saucer or on a sunny shelf, and they will form buds and flower perfectly. Each corm bears a number of flowers, up to 20 in succession if the corm is a very large one.

C. autumnale, native to Britain and known as the 'Meadow Saffron', is the common colchicum with lilac pink flowers. A number of varieties are well worth garden space.

C. autumnale major (byzantium), which flowers in late August– early September like the species, is 6in tall with a profusion of magnificent purple pink flowers with segments all of 2in long. This is the hardiest, strongest and most prolific of all colchicums, the best for growing in pots or dry on the windowsill. The spring leaves are about 10in tall.

C. autumnale minor, with smaller but abundant lilac flowers, almost star-shaped, is also 6in tall but blooms a little later.

The most recently introduced white form, **C. autumnale album** has small flowers as well but is very floriferous on 6in stems and a little later than the others to bloom.

There are a number of hybrids raised in Holland which are excellent for general garden purposes. All range in height from 6–8in, are useful as cut flowers, suitable for pot cultivation and also flower easily without soil or water. They flower from September into November, Lilac Wonder being the latest to bloom.

The Giant has very large dark lilac flowers with a white base and is fairly late flowering.

Lilac Wonder (see page 133), has lilac rose flowers, very late flowering.

Waterlily has enormous double mauve flowers with segments opening to the sun so that the blooms look like waterlilies. Flowering time is late September–early October.

CROCUS

Every autumn, through the winter and into spring up to the end of March the crocuses provide a prolific reward to the gardener who has allowed them to naturalise and spread over broad areas. They are also most valuable for rockeries, borders, among shrubs and in woodland areas as well as for windowboxes and outdoor containers. Many can be grown in pots or pans indoors or in the cool greenhouse. It is possible to start with a relatively small number and wind up with vast colonies. They prefer enriched soil and either sunny or lightly shaded sites. Plant autumn-flowering crocus in late July and August, winter and spring-flowering crocus in late August and September, 2–3in deep and 2–4in apart. Crocuses even do beautifully in most warm climates of the United States provided bulbs are pre-cooled and planted 2–3in deep in semi-shady areas. Never cut foliage before it dies naturally and fertilise established plantings lightly in autumn or early spring.

Indoor culture is simple. Use light rich soil or a good potting compost and plant 8–10 corms in a 5in pot or rather more in a larger pan in October. Set them 1–2in deep and $\frac{1}{2}$–1in apart. Plunge the pots outdoors in the garden or place in a cool cellar for about 8 weeks before bringing them indoors to a living room with a temperature of 50–55 °F (10–12° C). For a few days shade them from direct sun but when the shoots turn green they may be exposed to full light. Provide plenty of water. If kept watered until foliage dies naturally the corms may be planted in the garden to bloom once again, but corms cannot be used for forcing a second time.

Autumn-flowering crocus resemble their spring-flowering counter-parts, come in a wide range of attractive colours and are particularly interesting because of their striking styles, which divide into numerous stigmatic branches. The mixtures on sale are a particularly good buy for naturalisation but for continuous flowering choose named species.

C. speciosus, from Eastern Europe and Asia Minor, bursts into flower in late August–early September with gorgeous deep but bright blue goblet-like flowers with violet veinings and vivid orange stigmata on stems up to 4in tall. The blooms are purple violet inside. They spread freely from seeds and division.

The pure white form, **C. speciosus albus,** boasts rich red stigmata, is also free-flowering, and blooms from late September–October. It is most attractive when planted with **C. pulchellus,** from the Balkans, with lilac flowers, silvery blue at the base, and white anthers.

C. zonatus (kotschyanus) (see page 133), from Asia Minor and the Lebanon is the first of the autumn-flowering crocus to bloom in late August, the flowers appearing before the leaves as do those of C. speciosus.

Each corm produces large soft lilac flowers with a yellow throat and they spread freely.

The winter and spring-flowering species are quite exceptional in habit and are free-flowering, producing four or more flowers at a time. The easiest to force indoors in cool conditions are the chrysanthus varieties. Among the many species in commercial cultivation the following are the easiest to obtain:

C. ancyrensis, the 'Golden Bunch' crocus, is the first yellow crocus of the new year, blooming in January. Each corm yields 18–24 brilliant orange-yellow flowers, maize yellow outside and tangerine orange inside. Ideal for borders, rockeries and between paving stones.

C. biflorus, found from Italy to Asia Minor, is often called the 'Scotch Crocus' because an old horticultural variety of this crocus was found in a Scottish garden as early as 1731. The fragrant flowers are white to lilac and feathered or striped purple on the outside of outer segments with a yellow throat. This species likes the sun and blooms from mid-February to March.

C. chrysanthus from Greece and Asia Minor is the most variable of the genus and has lent itself to cross-breeding with an impressive number of horticultural varieties in a host of shades having been developed in both Holland and Britain. This very hardy early spring crocus spreads rapidly and all varieties are about 3in tall. The best varieties available include:

Advance produces abundant large flowers in March, yellow bronze shaded violet outside and buttercup yellow inside.

Blue Bird, a strong grower, flowering in February, has outer petals of light blue with white margin, inner petals creamy white with a bronze base and light yellow centre.

Blue Pearl (see page 133), with globular flowers light lobelia blue on the outside and lighter coloured inside with a yellow centre, has orange stigmata and flowers freely in February.

Cream Beauty is entirely creamy yellow with a bronze greenish base. Flowering in February it is particularly striking when interplanted with iris reticulata.

E. P. Bowles, another variety for February bloom, has abundant dainty flowers of lemon yellow feathered purplish brown.

Ladykiller, a dainty and aptly named February-flowering variety, possesses blooms of purple violet margined white, the inside pale lilac white.

Page 207 (*above left*) Crocus speciosus; (*above right*) Crocus biflorus; (*below left*) Eranthis hyemalis; (*below right*) Erythronium tuolumnense

Princess Beatrix, an outstanding February–flowering gem, has clear lobelia blue blooms with a golden yellow base.

Snowbunting produces masses of white flowers faintly feathered indigo in February.

Zwanenburg Bronze has large flowers in February, the outside almost entirely garnet brown with yellow margins and inside saffron yellow. Most larger bulb merchants have mixtures of chrysanthus varieties on sale.

C. laevigatus, from Greece, flowering in December–January, is a delightful species with numerous flowers of pale lavender feathered mauve outside and lilac blue with a yellow throat and white anthers inside.

C. sieberi from Greece and Crete is among the most beautiful species of crocus and several distinct varieties have been named, all with an orange yellow throat. The best is undoubtedly **Violet Queen** with blooms of amethyst violet with a purple sheen, marked gold. The dainty medium-sized flowers appear in profusion in February.

C. tomasinianus, from Dalmatia, the 'silvery lilac' crocus, blooms in March and is superb for naturalising. A number of named varieties have been developed, the best of which are:

Ruby Giant, with long slender heads of gleaming purple lit with wine purple towards the pointed petal tips, has a silver throat and brilliant orange stigmata.

Whitewell Purple, produces a mass of slender small flowers of rich violet purple, softer inside with bright marigold stamens.

To distinguish them from the smaller flowering botanical species the bigger crocus are called 'Dutch crocus' and all are horticultural varieties stemming mainly from the species C. vernus, the wild crocus of the Alps and Pyrenees. Both the corms and flowers are outsize. They appear in the garden in March and April in a vast range of colours and can be planted later than other crocus, in October. The Dutch crocus are versatile for they can be used for bedding, in borders, in outdoor containers of all kinds, for naturalising in rough or smooth grass, as well as for growing indoors. Collections (see page 133) are on sale at special bulk prices. Named varieties marked (1) will flower somewhat earlier than those marked (2).

2	**Enchantress**	soft pale blue with silvery gloss
2	**Flower Record**	rich violet blue
2	**Grand Maitre**	dark blue, prolific

2	**Jeanne d'Arc**	pure white, large flowers
2	**King of the Striped**	white striped lilac, large flowers
1	**Large Yellow (Mammoth)**	bright golden yellow, large flowers
2	**Negro Boy**	darkest purple
2	**Peter Pan**	ivory white
2	**Pickwick**	white striped violet, prolific (see page 51)
2	**Purpureus Grandiflorus**	uniform rich purple, free-flowering (see page 52)
2	**Queen of the Blues**	porcelain blue, giant flowers
1	**Remembrance**	violet with silvery gloss (see page 52)
2	**Sky Blue**	heliotrope blue, dwarf flowering
1	**Striped Beauty**	white, striped violet, large flowers
1	**Vanguard**	pale silvery lilac
1	**Victor Hugo**	glowing light purple

ERANTHIS

The golden buds of winter aconites, botanically eranthis and native to both Western Europe and Asia Minor, set in a rosette of frilly, finely-cut leaves, are among the first of the 'little' bulbs to flower, emerging even through snow or hard frost as early as January.

The round golden balls on 3–5in stems, very close to the ground, open up like buttercups and look so charming in their green ruff, which is actually a bract and not true leaves. The real foliage, palmately cut leaves which shoot up beside the flower stalk, appears as the flowers develop forming a delicate carpet for a short while and vanishing as the season advances.

Members of the ranunculus family, eranthis are actually perennials with minute irregularly-shaped brown rhizomes which put them in the bulbous category. They do not like being out of the ground for any length of time, so order early and plant them promptly in the autumn. If the shrivelled rhizomes seem dry cover them with moist peat or sand overnight to help plump them up before planting. Choose sites under deciduous bushes or trees where they will get the maximum amount of available winter sunshine and shade during the summer. Set the rhizomes about an inch or so deep and 2–3in apart in colonies. They are lovely interplanted with snowdrops. Once established, eranthis spread rapidly by self-seeding, forming thickly populated colonies. Once the leaves die away the plants are invisible and sites should be clearly labelled.

E. cilicica from Asia Minor is the most robust of the available species and is distinguished by its pink 4in stem, its thicker foliage and larger deep yellow flower which blooms later than the common European species.

E. hyemalis, the common winter aconite found in Switzerland, has been grown in gardens since 1570. It is the earliest to flower with golden yellow blooms on 3in stems. It is still very popular with gardeners for its very early splashes of colour.

EREMURUS

Eremurus are rated by many as the most spectacular of all garden flowers, looking like king-size hyacinths or giant candles. Though not yet widely grown, they certainly should be. Eremurus do not have bulbs as such but the dormant crowns look like a star-shaped tangle of long, thick and fleshy white roots. The glossy green foliage forms a full rosette rapidly with leaves up to 3ft long. The floral stem ranges from 2–9ft according to species, the upper half bearing the floral raceme, 1–3ft in length with hundreds of star-shaped flowers close to an inch in diameter.

All species are native to Asia and those available to British and American gardeners are hardy, although it is wise to protect the crowns with a mulch of leaves or peat in winter. They are not difficult to grow but soil must be well drained with plenty of organic matter. In September or October dig over sunny sites well mixing in leaf-mould or well rotted manure. Spread out the roots, carefully covering the crown with a few handfuls of sand. Planting must be shallow, the central bud being level with the soil. Space the crowns 2–3ft apart. They should be left for at least three to four years when crowns may be divided and leaf-mould or manure be renewed in planting.

Site eremurus in herbaceous borders, in clumps in the middle of the lawn or against a background of evergreen shrubs or cupressus. The flowers are very long-lasting and make excellent cut flowers.

E. bungei from Turkestan and Afghanistan is a dwarf species only 2–5ft tall, bearing a raceme of bright golden yellow flowers in late June or July. The leaves are rather narrow.

E. robustus from Turkestan is the largest species of all, with stems up to 9ft high and racemes of lovely peachy pink flowers which bloom in June.

The **Ruiter hybrids,** obtained by N. C. Ruiter from crossing Shelford and natural warei hybrids, with all the colours of the former but flowering somewhat earlier are available from suppliers as mixtures.

The **Shelford hybrids,** obtained in 1902 by Sir Michael Foster, are the result of crosses between E. bungei and E. olgae, the latter from Turkestan too and bearing tall dense racemes of pale pink to white flowers. A mixture of forms are retailed in pink shaded orange, bright pink, pale yellow and white. The floral stems, like those of the Ruiter hybrids, range from $4\frac{1}{2}$–6ft tall. Flowering time is June.

ERYTHRONIUM

Erythronium are among the most beautiful and graceful spring-flowering bulbs with flowers rather like martagon lilies in shades of cream, pink, violet and yellow. Enough species and hybrids of this comparatively little cultivated member of the lily family are now available at such reasonable prices that gardeners no longer need regard it as a stranger. Only one species is native to Europe, the remainder are North American forms, but culture of all is the same.

They are not difficult to grow although these woodland plants have small whitish bulbs which tend to dry up easily. They should therefore be planted upon receipt in early autumn, choosing slightly shady positions in rich soil, setting the bulbs 4–6in deep and 2–3in apart, always planting in groups. They should be left undisturbed in rockery sites or beneath shrubs and trees. Transplanting checks growth and if they are lifted for any reason they should be replanted immediately.

E. dens-canis (see page 134), known as the 'Dog's Tooth Violet' because of the shape of the bulb, is the only European species. Bulb retailers offer fine mixtures of varieties in shades of clear pink, red, deep violet and white, all producing in March–April graceful and dainty reflexed-petal blooms on 4–6in stems. They have the added attraction of marbled leaves of green and reddish brown.

E. revolutum, often called the 'Trout Lily' because of the beautifully mottled and blotched leaves, is the most splendid of the native California species with a number of gorgeous hybrids flowering in April and May. These include **Kondo** with 10in stems carrying 3–4 blooms of pale yellow ringed deep yellow round the centre; **Pagoda** with 4–5 golden yellow

Page 212 (*above left*) Fritillaria meleagris; (*above right*) Fritillaria imperialis;
(*below left*) Galanthus nivalis; (*below right*) Galanthus nivalis flore pleno

flowers ringed brown round the centre on somewhat taller stems; and **White Beauty,** its snow white flowers chocolate zoned on sturdy 8in stems.

E. tuolumnense (see page 133), also native to California, produces 2–3 orchid-like flowers of golden yellow with pale greenish yellow base on each 10in slender stem in April. The foliage is uniform green, glossy and unmottled and this species makes a lovely cut flower.

FRITILLARIA

The fritillaries are members of the lily family, species of which are at home in the temperate zones of the northern hemisphere. Of the 100 species known to botanists only a few have been brought into garden cultivation or are available to British and American gardeners, but these are beautiful and most unusual.

Perhaps the most handsome plant that can be grown in any garden border is **F. imperialis** (see page 212). The giants of the clan, known as 'Crown Imperials', they are tall conspicuous plants growing all of 30–36in high. Each stem supports a leafy tufted crown beneath which appears a hanging, umbel-like group of brilliantly coloured large flowers. Named varieties available include **Aurora** in rich orange red, **Lutea Maxima** (see page 134) in deep lemon yellow, and **Rubra Maxima** in rich burnt orange shaded red.

Spectacular when grouped in sunny or partially shaded sites the big white bulbs of all varieties must be planted no later than September in humus-filled soil a good 8in deep and about 12in apart for April bloom.

Fritillaria meleagris are the delightful April-flowering dwarfs only 10–12in tall and known as 'Chequered Lilies' or 'Snakeshead Fritillary'. They have 6-pointed, squared off, drooping bells, 2–3 of which appear on each leafy stem. They are available in mixtures of chartreusy tones, in curious reddish browns and purples with deeper markings, and in white with green veinings, all chequered, or in named varieties. These include **Aphrodite** with large almost pure white flowers; **Artemis,** prettily chequered purple with green; **Poseidon** with large white flowers chequered purple; **Purple King** in dusky wine red; and **Saturnus** with large red violet blooms.

Although found wild in damp meadows **F. meleagris** will flourish in almost any well drained soil but prefer cool situations. Plant the bulbs in August–September about 3–4in deep and 4–8in apart in groups. They are ideal in rockeries, at the edge of borders and can also be naturalised in grass, where they seed themselves freely. They can also be grown in pots like crocus but require earlier planting.

GALANTHUS

Gardeners everywhere call them snowdrops although botanically they are classified as 'galanthus' which means 'milk flower'. These members of the amaryllis family stem from the Eastern Mediterranean but are perfectly hardy in Britain and America and very easy to grow. Although there are species that flower from October to April only those blooming from January into March are easily obtainable.

As early as January the tiny bulbs send up pearl-like buds protected by two green leaves. If it is cold the buds will remain closed waiting for the sun's warmth. When the sun shines the long outer segments of the frosty white flowers open in the shape of an ovoid bell, revealing the inner tube with each of its three segments tipped with a semi-circle of emerald green. The flowers go on giving pleasure for weeks on end.

Like eranthis rhizomes, snowdrop bulbs should be out of the ground as short a time as possible. The bulbs should be planted on arrival in September to mid-October about 3–4in deep in light soils and up to 6in deep in heavy soils, spaced some 2–3in apart. They prefer fairly solid heavy soil, moist but not wet.

Snowdrops spread rapidly by bulb division and self-seeding. If clumps become too thick they should be divided after flowering but before the foliage changes colour. As snowdrops do well in sun or partial shade they can be planted with winter aconites between paving stones, beside terrace steps, in urns or tubs or windowboxes, in fact almost any-where you can find a square foot of space in the garden. They can also be naturalised in grass or on sloping sites. Never cut the foliage, even if you use snowdrops as dainty cut flowers, but allow it to ripen naturally. Galanthus are seldom grown indoors simply because few gardeners seem to be aware that they can be. Indoor culture is as for crocus but snow-drops must be kept out of the midday sun and watered with care.

G. elwesii yields distinct and beautiful single flowers of broad globular shape, the inner segments of white marked heavily with green at the base. Stems are 7in tall, the leaves broad and glaucous, and this species flowers somewhat later than the others mentioned here.

G. nivalis (see page 134) is the common snowdrop of European origin, distinguished by comparatively narrow strap-shaped leaves pressed flat against each other when they emerge and which, as they grow, are of equal width throughout their length. The single flowers are pure white with a touch of green and stems are 6in tall.

G. nivalis flore pleno is the exquisite double form with large globular flowers of peerless white lightly touched emerald green. It flowers at the same time as the single form on slender 6in stems and is equally excellent for naturalising.

Chapter Nine

REWARDS FROM 'LITTLE' BULBS, IRIS—STERNBERGIA

IRIS

Dutch, English and Spanish iris are on most gardeners' shopping lists but the dwarfs of the clan which flower months before their bigger sisters are all too often overlooked. Yet they are as enchanting as butterflies and provide an incredible range of colour early in the year. In fact, the species iris produce the richest colours of all hardy spring flowers.

For maximum impact they should be planted early in the autumn about 3–4in deep and 4in apart in semi-shaded positions where their rich colourings are more pronounced and their flowering period is lengthened. The secret of successful cultivation is simply to keep them moist while growing and dry and warm during their summer resting period.

The easiest to grow indoors are **I. danfordiae** and the **reticulata hybrids.** Plant the bulbs in pots in October some 2–3in deep and about 3–4in apart, using any good compost. Place the pots in a garden plunge or cool cellar for eight weeks or so before bringing them into the living room or greenhouse, where temperatures should not exceed 50–55° F (10–12° C). For a few days after bringing iris in from the plunge cover them with tissue paper to enable them to adjust gradually to the light. Keep well watered, applying liquid fertiliser about once a week. Forced bulbs are of no further value for indoor growing but after the foliage dies they can be dried off and stored for planting in the garden the following autumn.

I. bakeriana from Asia Minor have slender soft blue standards and unusually marked falls of ivory heavily dotted deep purple. They grow just 4in tall, their stiff leaves distinguished by eight ribs, and they flower fragrantly from late January and February.

I. danfordiae (see page 151) from eastern Turkey sparkles with slightly scented lemon yellow standards, the falls spotted brown. The very dainty flowers on 3in stems last well even in bad weather and after flowering in February with the reticulata hybrids, the bulbs sometimes split up into many little offshoots which themselves flower in 3–4 years.

I. histrioides major (see page 134) is a fine naturaliser withstanding frost, rain or hail. It comes from northwest Persia and boasts pure gentian blue flowers with white spots on 3in stems. Flowering in March or somewhat earlier it does well on a sunny terrace or in rockery nooks and can also be grown in pots indoors.

I. reticulata (see page 52) is the best known of the dwarf iris, its fragrant rich velvety blue purple flowers with an orange gold splash on the falls appearing in February or March. About 5in tall, it has long, stiff, erect filiform leaves with four ribs. It is easy to grow and flourishes among rocks.

There are a number of delightful reticulata hybrids available now in named varieties. **Cantab** (see page 151), 4in tall, has dainty flowers of flax blue with lighter tips and a yellow blotch. **Harmony,** about 4–5in tall, has standards of bluebird blue and falls of royal blue with a yellow blotch. **Hercules,** 5in tall, is a bronze introduction with an orange blotch on the falls. **Joyce,** also 5in in height, possesses lavender standards and deep sky blue falls with a yellow blotch tigered greyish brown. **J. S. Dyt,** 5in tall too, has sweetly scented reddish purple standards with a narrow sword of orange on the falls.

I. tuberosa is the odd flower out. Officially reclassified Hermodactylus tuberosus, it has been in cultivation since 1574 as the 'Snakeshead iris' or 'Widow iris' and bulb merchants and gardeners of today pay little attention to its botanical nomenclature. It is grown exactly like other bulbous iris and the narrow, almost tuberous bulbs, can also be forced indoors for February or March bloom. Grown in the garden, however, this gem from Greece and Asia Minor will bloom in April–May, each 8–10in stem producing a curious single flower of light green, the outer segments blotched purple brown.

Today Dutch iris are by far the largest cultivated group of the huge iris genus, popular not only with gardeners who like them best in clumps in the rockery or border or to set off evergreen shrubs, but with housewives who find them invaluable for floral decoration in the home. Dutch iris are, of course, widely grown commercially as cut flowers, available in the shops from well before Christmas into May.

They are called Dutch iris not just because the top quality bulbs come from Holland (which also exports mixtures of English and Spanish iris) but because they are a distinctly different breed obtained in 1909 by a famous Haarlem breeder and are botanically classified as Iris hollandica. Their evolvement took many years and involved multiple crossings between species in the xiphium section of the genus native to Southern Europe and Northwest Africa to broaden the colour range to encompass whites, yellows, blues, mauves and purples. To create such a handsome breed in a clan comprising nearly 200 species in 12 different sections is no mean achievement. In the past few decades in particular new breeding advances have been made in Holland resulting not only in improved varieties and new novelties but in a whole series of modern plants with noticeably larger flowers (marked * in the descriptive list).

Dutch iris are particularly fine plants with larger flowers too than the somewhat similar Spanish iris and are sturdier and stronger in growth. Compared with English iris, the Dutch iris are not only more colourful (there are no yellows among English iris) but boast exotic and delicate blooms with more graceful stems and foliage. Dutch iris have tall stems, ranging 20–24in in height, are long lasting and are the first of the cultivated iris to bloom. When planted in September some 3–4in deep and about 5–8in apart, they will flower as early as mid-May, depending upon the season, or in June. Spanish iris bloom at least a fortnight later and English iris do not flower until late June or July. Dutch iris are hardy and accommodating but for best results plant them in sunny positions in soil with plenty of humus. By covering Dutch iris positions in early spring with an inch or two layer of peat you will prevent the soil from drying out and help your iris to develop perfect flowers. They need little care and attention. They need not be lifted until clumps become overcrowded and the little bulbils that form round the mother bulb will bloom too after 2–3 years. When lifted after the foliage dies down the bulbs should be kept dry until replanting time in September.

Dutch iris will grace your rockery, border, foundation planting, shrubbery or narrow bed along a fence. Plant some too in the cutting garden. Many varieties can be forced in the cool greenhouse, the most suitable marked (f) in the descriptive list. Pot them in October about 4in apart with the compost covering the tops of the bulbs for a good inch. Plunge outdoors or place in a cool cellar until well rooted, then bring

Page 219 *(above left)* Dutch Iris Golden Harvest; *(above right)* Muscari botry-oides album; *(below left)* Ornithogalum nutans; *(below right)* Ornithogalum umbellatum

them into the greenhouse, maintaining a night temperature of 45–50° F (8–10° C). Keep well watered, adding liquid fertiliser to the water twice weekly. Bulbs cannot be used again for forcing but should be relegated to the cutting garden.

More and more varieties of Dutch iris are coming on to the market and among the best currently available are:

Angel's Wings* (f)	pure white, deep yellow falls blotched orange (see page 151)
Golden Emperor (f)	bright golden yellow
Golden Harvest*	golden yellow shaded orange
H. C. van Vliet (f)	dark violet blue, grey blue falls blotched browny orange
Ideal* (f)	lobelia blue sport of Wedgwood, bluebird blue falls blotched yellow
Imperator (f)	indigo blue with orange blotch
Professor Blaauw (f)	gentian blue with narrow yellow stripe
Purple Sensation* (f)	violet purple with yellow markings
Royal Yellow* (f)	buttercup yellow with sunflower yellow falls
Wedgwood (f)	lobelia blue with flax blue falls blotched yellow
White Excelsior (f)	white with yellow blotch
White Perfection* (f)	snowy white with ivory white falls striped yellow
White van Vliet* (f)	greyish white with violet gloss, ivory white falls blotched golden yellow
White Wedgwood* (f)	creamy white with greenish white falls blotched buttercup yellow
Yellow Queen (f)	golden yellow with orange blotch.

IXIA

Ixia (see page 151) or the South African 'Corn Lilies' require late planting, protection from frost and moisture in the spring but the little extra attention you give them produces a fine reward. These members of the iris family are free-flowering, the small corms producing in June and July long graceful racemes of delightful blooms in a wide range of yellows, oranges, pinks, reds and purples on thin but wiry 16–18in stems. Each stem carries six or more handsome wide-mouthed bell-shaped flowers of striking beauty, most having a dark prominent centre. The narrow and grassy foliage is an added bonus. They can be purchased in mixtures from most bulb merchants.

Planting should be delayed as long as possible, certainly not before late October and preferably in November so that the leaves do not emerge too early. Ixia require sunny positions and should be planted 3in deep and 3in apart in sandy soil to which peat and leaf-mould and additional sand can be added. A winter mulch to protect top growth should gradually be uncovered in spring to accustom the young shoots to light and air.

Ixia make marvellous cut flowers and can also be grown as pot plants. Between September and October plant 5–7 corms in a 6in pot containing a mixture of sand, leaf-mould and good garden soil. The pots should be plunged in a sheltered area of the garden and be protected by glass or straw. Once the shoots appear the pots can be brought into the cool greenhouse or the home, where they should be given as much light as possible. They grow best under cool conditions and must be kept moist.

IXIOLIRION

Ixiolirion are often confused with ixia because they are frequently called 'ixia lilies'. But this small genus is a member of the amaryllis and not the iris family to which ixia belong, and is native to the steppes of Central Asia.

Ixiolirion are not widely grown, probably because of this confusion, but they make a distinctive contribution to the rockery or border and are excellent for cutting. The thin stiff stems are 15–18in tall according to type and bear a loose umbel of graceful tubular star-shaped flowers in shades of blue and violet blue. The leaves, which appear in spring, are long, narrow and greyish green.

The small ovoid, long-necked bulbs should be planted in autumn 3–4in deep and 4–6in apart in sunny sheltered positions in well-drained and preferably sandy soil and be left undisturbed. Like ixia, ixiolirion are not entirely hardy in Britain and America and appreciate a winter mulch but otherwise need no special attention. They can be grown in pots in the greenhouse in the same way as ixia.

Two types are available to gardeners.

I. ledebourii (montanum) is the earliest to bloom in June with light violet blue flowers, about 2in in diameter, on 15in stems.

I. pallasii, technically a variety of montanum but always catalogued as pallasii, has somewhat showier and larger flowers blooming about a fortnight later. The long-lasting blooms are violet blue tinged rosy purple and with a darker coloured band down the centre of each segment. The taller 16–18in stems are strong and this variety makes particularly elegant cut flowers.

LEUCOJUM

All gardeners know the snowdrop but the genus leucojum or snowflake, ostensibly named by the Greek philosopher and naturalist, Theophrastes, several hundred years before the birth of Christ, is a stranger to most gardens.

This member of the amaryllis family is native to both Europe and Asia Minor and there are species available for both spring and summer bloom. The cultivation of leucojum presents no problem because they adapt themselves to almost any soil and every kind of location although summer snowflakes welcome rich, moist soil. Spring snowflakes are particularly happy in the rock garden while summer snowflakes are suitable for borders, naturalising and for cut flowers.

Leucojum bulbs should be planted in autumn 3–4in deep and the same distance apart. Both the spring and summer snowflakes are hardy and bulbs should be left undisturbed until clumps become too thick. They should only be lifted and divided after the leaves have withered and be replanted immediately.

Snowflakes are quite similar to snowdrops but a discerning eye will notice that the six segments of the perianth are all of the same length while in the snowdrop the three inner segments are considerably smaller than the outer ones.

L. aestivum, the summer snowflake, is the largest species with stems 18in tall bearing umbels of 4–8 nodding white flowers with green markings near the tips of the segments. They flourish in sun or partial shade but prefer a cool place. Flowering time is May–June.

L. aestivum Gravetye, an improved form with larger flowers up to an inch across, produces elegant drooping white bells tipped green in May–June. Like L. aestivum the leaves are long, strap-shaped and bright green.

L. vernum (see page 151), the spring snowflake, is only 6in tall but the lovely little white bells tipped pale green, one or two per stem, are somewhat larger than the blooms of snowdrops. The leaves are broad, strap-shaped and deep green. They are particularly valuable for massing and naturalising, preferring somewhat shady locations. They increase rapidly if left undisturbed, by self-seeding.

MUSCARI

The muscari genus, a member of the lily family, is one of the most free-flowering to bloom in spring and because many of the species are scented are referred to as 'grape hyacinths', 'musk hyacinths' or 'tassel hyacinths'. They are in fact related to the hyacinth and are as easy to grow, adapting themselves to a variety of soils.

All muscari are of dwarf habit and lend themselves to naturalisation as they spread so incredibly freely, to the rockery, to border clumps, to fringes of the shrubbery, to terrace containers and windowboxes and to cultivation in pots or bowls in the cool greenhouse or in the home.

The flowers of all species are shaped rather like American or Rugby footballs, the small bells being borne in dense racemes. The leaves are mostly grass-like but in some species are broader and strap-shaped.

The fleshy globose bulbs of all species should be planted in September and October *en masse* about 3–4in deep and 2–3in apart, and once planted should be left undisturbed to increase and multiply. Clumps should be divided every 3–4 years. Provided bulbs are pre-cooled for 4–6 weeks before planting muscari will flourish in most warm climates of the United States.

Species recommended here for indoor cultivation should be grown like crocus although bulbs should be planted in October about 1in deep and fairly close together in any good compost. They can also be grown in bowls with bulb fibre. Muscari take 6–8 weeks to root in the garden plunge or cool cellar and are easy to force if not hurried.

M. armeniacum from Northern Asia Minor, sometimes catalogued as **Early Giant,** produces a 6–9in stem bearing a dense cluster of scented flowers of bright cobalt blue with a distinct white rim. Flowering in April it increases very rapidly by division or self-seeding and is excellent for naturalising in borders, rockeries or woodland. Interplanted with trumpet daffodils or fosteriana tulips this species creates a beautiful contrasting background. It is also suitable for indoor forcing.

M. armeniacum Blue Spike (see page 34) boasts large double flowers of flax blue, sometimes tipped greenish yellow, always scented and on stems 6in tall. This variety flowers a bit later.

M. botryoides, native to Europe, bears dense spikes of violet blue flowers rimmed white in April or even earlier on 6in stems. It is not as vigorous as armeniacum and is ideal for the rockery.

M. botryoides album (see page 219), the exquisite white form, produces a compact cone of fragrant white flowers, looking like an elongated bunch of pearls, on 6–8in stems in late March. It is an attractive pot variety too.

M. plumosum (comosum), native to Southern Europe and Asia Minor, is rather distinct from other species and is known as the 'feather' or 'tassel' hyacinth. Its flowers are sterile and their segments are transformed into long bluish violet filaments forming a huge tuft. It is a most attractive and unusual May flower on 12–18in stems. The leaves are broader than in most other species and clearly strap-shaped. The bulbs are larger too with rather pinkish tunics and because of the size of the bloom should be spaced about 6in apart.

M. tubergenianum from Northwest Persia is a spectacular species introduced as recently as 1940. It flowers in late April but is at its best in May. Commonly called the 'Oxford and Cambridge' muscari in Britain, it produces several 8in stems during the flowering season with dense clusters of globular flowers, bright clear blue at the top of the spike and deep Oxford blue lower down. It is a must for every rockery or border.

Muscari foliage often appears in the autumn but gardeners need not be alarmed for it withstands the winter weather without damage.

ORNITHOGALUM

Ornithogalum are those unusual members of the lily family that bloom from spring into summer when naturalised in woodlands, shrubberies, grassy banks or borders. Some are a real asset in the rockery too, for they produce masses of star-like or cup-shaped flowers. The large genus has many species native to southern Europe, Asia Minor and South Africa but only a handful are sufficiently striking for garden application. The European species are quite hardy but the South African are not. The flowers are inevitably white, some tinged with green, and the leaves are linear or strap-shaped, often with a silvery line down the middle.

There are two early-flowering species, readily available from most bulb merchants.

O. nutans, of European origin, will flourish in sun or partial shade and will quickly form colonies that decorate the garden with large flowers of greenish white on drooping one-sided racemes. The 9–12in stems bear as many as 6–12 widespread flowers, which are excellent for indoor decoration too. Shortly after flowering in April–May the plant withers and disappears and planting sites should be labelled.

O. umbellatum (see page 219), native to Europe, Asia Minor and North Africa, is another hardy species popularly known as the 'Star of Bethlehem'. It has attractive pure white flowers in large umbels on short 6in stems, flowering in May. This species, whose flowers only open when the sun is shining, is most effective for massing and edging and likes sunny locations.

Any ordinary well-drained soil suits the bulbs of these two species. Plant them 3–4in deep and about 4in apart but not too early in the autumn, certainly not before late September. Fertilise them each spring by all means but there is no need to lift and replant until sites become crowded.

O. thyrsoides from South Africa is the best known of the ornithogalum clan because this species is now cultivated widely on a commercial scale for cut flowers. Its common name is 'chincherinchee', given it by the natives because of the sound the dry stalks make when rubbing together in the wind.

This species is not hardy in Britain and most of America and properly belongs among the summer-flowering miscellaneous bulbs but is included here for easier reference. The inexpensive bulbs should not be planted until March in rich porous soil and always in warm and sunny positions. The leaves do not develop fully outdoors and consequently the bulbs will not flower a second year. It is worth planting fresh bulbs each year for the flowers, when picked in bud, will last as long as 6 weeks in water. If grown in a cool greenhouse chincherinchee bulbs will bloom annually, however. Pot up bulbs in good rich compost, about 1in of covering over the top of the bulb, in late autumn. After bringing in from the plunge, water early growth moderately and then more freely throughout active growth. When the foliage begins to die naturally after flowering, gradually reduce amount of water, then withhold entirely, keeping the bulb dry through its dormant season. Repot in fresh compost each year.

The 15–30in stems carry dense racemes of lovely white cup-shaped flowers with prominent yellow stamens, very long lasting. Each round white bulb will produce up to 3 floral stems. The first flowers bloom in July and thereafter in succession until autumn.

OXALIS

Only one species of this vast genus is widely cultivated but it deserves a place in every rockery for its bright display.

O. adenophylla (see page 152), hails from Chile and this graceful dwarf that looks like a pink cushion framed by silvery green leaves is quite hardy. It produces small rich pink flowers almost lilac in colour with deeper marked veins in the throat on 4–6in stems in succession from late May into July. The foliage forms a compact rosette close to the ground.

Plant the scaly bulbs about 2–3in deep and 2–4in apart in a good loam, preferably chalky, in September–October. Site them in warm spots in the rockery, in full sun or very light shade, and the clumps will increase from year to year.

PUSCHKINIA

This pretty scilla-like plant of the lily family is native to the Caucasus and Asia Minor and was named puschkinia after the Russian botanist, Count Puschkin. Only one of the two known species of this genus is cultivated but it is a charmer, and is often called the 'striped squill'. Drifts of puschkinia in partially shaded positions create a most pleasing effect in the garden in March and April. They also like sunny spots in the rockery and do well in outdoor containers. Puschkinia can be grown indoors like crocus too.

The fluffy striped bells resemble scilla, each 4–6in stem bearing a cluster of a dozen or more pale silver blue blooms, each segment marked lightly with a slightly darker prussian blue line. The blooms are made up of segments joined at the base in a kind of tube widening into a crown.

P. libanotica (scilloides) is the species you ask for. There is also a pure white form, **P. libanotica alba,** which blooms at the same time. The flowers are beautiful, very solid in texture.

The small tunicated bulbs should be planted in September–October in fertile well-drained soil about 3in deep and 3in apart. Choose sunny locations where the bulbs need not be disturbed.

For indoor cultivation plant the bulbs in rich but light soil in October, about 1–2in deep and ½–1in apart, in 5in pots. Plunge the pots outdoors in the garden or place in a cool cellar for about 8 weeks before bringing them indoors to a living room temperature of 50–55° F (10–12° C). Shade them from direct sun for a few days before exposing them to full light. They can also be forced in a cool greenhouse.

Page 227 (*above*) Puschkinia libanotica; (*below left*) Scilla tubergeniana;
(*below right*) Scilla siberica Spring Beauty

SCILLA

There are basically two groups of scillas available to the gardener—the early-flowering Siberian squills for intense blues at the base of shrubs and trees, in the rockery or in pots indoors; and the later May-flowering and much taller 'wood hyacinths' or 'Spanish Bluebells' so delightful for woodland areas and the front of the border, where their tall clusters of blue, white or pink bells contrast well with other May blooms.

This large genus of bulbous plants in the lily family with both hardy and tender bulbs from Europe, Asia and Africa is closely related to chionodoxa, from which the flowers are distinguished by the complete division of their perianth segments. Only the hardy kinds are in general distribution, and are easily cultivated. The bulbs, which vary in shape and colour according to species, should be planted in well-drained soil with plenty of humus in October or November. Plant 3–5in deep and 3–5in apart according to size of bulb, at least 12–15 bulbs in a group. All the species are prolific, multiplying every year, and clumps should be divided every 4–5 years.

S. bifolia, siberica, siberica Spring Beauty and **tubergeniana** are very easy to grow indoors and the novice need not fear failure with them. Any good compost or bulb fibre will suit scilla. Plant in pots or bowls from early September to the end of October in succession, placing the bulbs ½in apart and about 1in deep. Their roots will develop within 6–8 weeks and then, when brought into the house from the garden plunge, they should be kept as cool as possible. Grown by themselves in a fairly large pot they will compete with the bluest of skies. Send the bulbs into garden locations as soon as possible after flowering.

S. bifolia, from Central Europe and the Mediterranean area, is the earliest to flower, sometimes sending its small nodding bells of star-like gentian blue flowers on 4–6in wiry stems right through the snow in February. There are 3–4 flowers per stem and the leaves, as the name implies, are two in number, green and linear shaped. This species can do with a bit of winter protection in colder climates.

S. campanulata (hispanica) (see page 152), from Spain and Portugal, now officially classified as **Endymion hispanicus** but still catalogued and sold as scilla or Spanish bluebells, bloom in May. Tall straight stems, carrying 12–15 or more distinctly bell-like blossoms, similar to the wild hyacinth, in white, pink or blue, rise 12–18in above lush clumps of linear leaves. These woodland plants do well in open woods, along shady paths, at the edge of wild gardens or in the front of a lightly shaded border. Hardy and robust they will even flourish beneath pines and hemlocks. whose old needles build up a woodsy soil. The bulbs are good-sized and should be planted 4–5in deep. This species will bring a particularly bright note to spring in many warm climates of the United States if pre-cooled bulbs are planted 3in deep in drifts under trees.

S. nutans (non-scripta), is the common bluebell of Britain and Western Europe and technically classified as **Endymion non-scriptus** although generally sold as scilla or English bluebells. Grown in European gardens since 1500, the plant, 10–12in tall, blooms in May, producing pendulous spikes of rich violet blue bell-shaped flowers attached to short pedicels. The anthers are cream compared to the blue anthers of the Spanish bluebell. They do best in open glades or semishade and planted with Spanish bluebells the two species will readily hybridise together.

S. siberica (see page 227), from Siberia, is the best known species, its prussian blue bells intensified by grey blue anthers on 3–4in stems. The flowers, about 1in in diameter, appear in March–April and contrast well with the golden yellow buds of dwarf daffodils. **S. siberica alba** is the pure white form sometimes available. A beautiful variety, **Spring Beauty,** has prussian blue bells, twice as large as the species, on stems 6–8in tall. All are sturdy and strong and can be naturalised in grass.

S. tubergeniana (see page 227), native to Northwest Persia, and another comparatively recent introduction, is very early-flowering, appearing frequently in milder Februaries. The delicate soft blue flowers on a silvery white ground pale as they age. The large flowers have a line of hyacinth blue down the centre of each petal. The leaves are broad and bright green and the stems are but 4in tall, usually 3–4 per bulb. This scilla closely resembles puschkinia libanotica in colouring and is superb for the rockery.

SPARAXIS

The small corms of this small genus of South African plants produce very variable but brightly coloured flowers and in their native land are often called 'Harlequin flowers'. These members of the iris family are related to ixia and freesia and are not very hardy. In all but the warmest climates of Britain and America they are best grown in pots or raised beds in the cool greenhouse like ixia.

When planted in the garden they should be assigned warm and sunny positions. Plant the corms in late November in light, fertile soil, 3–4in deep and 3–4in apart, and protect them with a winter mulch of peat or dried leaves. They have to be lifted after the foliage has died down, dried, cleaned and stored in a cool, dry, shaded place until planting time comes round again.

The 6–9in stems of sparaxis yield a host of large freesia-like flowers in April–May ranging in colour from white and yellow through all shades of red and orange to dark purple. The throats of the flowers are yellow and orange and the narrow foliage is as graceful as the blooms, which have six equal segments forming a widespread perianth with a short, floral tube.

Sparaxis mixtures are available from most bulb merchants, made up of a large number of horticultural varieties of S. tricolor, native to the steppes of Cape Province.

STERNBERGIA

Least known of the autumn-flowering bulbs is sternbergia, often called the 'autumn daffodil'. Named after a Czech botanist, Count von Sternberg, the plants are members of the amaryllis family and the flowers are distinctly crocus-like. They can be distinguished from crocus because they have six stamens instead of three.

S. lutea, native to South Europe and North Africa, with handsome and rich clear yellow flowers, solitary, erect and rather globe-shaped, is easy to grow and one of the genuine beauties of the autumn garden. Growing about 4–6in tall with strap-shaped leaves, they are very effective when planted on grassy banks or in rockeries or borders. They like sunny positions. If left undisturbed over a long period—and do give them a year to establish themselves—they will form large clumps and provide ever-expanding patches of bright colour.

Plant the bulbs, which have black tunics, 6in deep and 3–4in apart in any good soil with leaf-mould in July as the roots start growing in August and late planting will endanger flowering from late August into October. Ensure that positions are well-drained for sternbergia detest wet conditions.

If planted in good-sized pots or bowls S. lutea will flower a few weeks after planting for an unusual indoor display.

Chapter Ten

GLADIOLI

GAY GLADIOLI have risen to the top of the popularity polls among summer-flowering bulbs simply because these handsome and decorative members of the iris family have so many good and rewarding qualities. Although introduced into horticulture only comparatively recently, skilful hybridisation has provided not only a choice of types but a fabulous selection of beautiful varieties in an almost unlimited range of colour.

Gladioli, botanically corms and not true bulbs, are remarkably easy to grow, thriving in any garden location that catches the sun and in virtually any well-drained soil. They are the most cheerful and long-lasting of cut flowers too, the florets continuing to open in succession from the bottom to the very tip of the long, tapering flower spike which makes so apt the common name of 'sword lily'.

There are some 150 species in the genus, native to South and Central Africa, Asia Minor and Southern Europe. Very few of these species are cultivated today. The earliest gladioli species introduced into Europe came from South Africa and the new plants were first grown by English horticulturalists. In the early days each selector created his own strain, eventually elevated to species status. The oldest known strain, G. colvillei, was named after its nurseryman creator, Colville of Chelsea, who developed it from a cross between the yellowish white G. tristis and the red G. cardinalis. Some varieties derived from this strain are still available but are now generally included in the early-flowering dwarf nanus group, which require different cultivation than the modern hybrids. In the early days gladioli plants were short and slender in stem and produced smaller, more closed florets than modern varieties.

Gradually other selectors, in Belgium, France, Germany, Holland and the United States, produced new strains. The first large-flowered gladioli did not come on to the market until 1841. Nowadays, the various strains have joined forces and over the past 100 years thousands of new varieties have been introduced largely replacing the gladioli in cultivation before the mid-nineteenth century.

There are many systems of classifying gladioli, by form, floret size and colour, and various gladiolus societies have their own standards for show purposes. The average gardener, as opposed to the gladioli fancier, will only be confused by detailed explanations of these systems and consequently this book will divide available gladioli into the four main types as catalogued and offered for sale by bulb retailers. All British and many American retailers follow this system, although some American retailers still divide the corms into large-flowered and small-flowered and sell by colour rather than named variety.

Because the early-flowering **nanus** type require different treatment than the other three types available I propose to deal with them separately. They are smaller and more delicate in flower than later flowering hybrids and shorter in stem, growing only 18–24in tall. They are invaluable in the border, extremely useful for pot culture and their brilliantly coloured blooms are excellent for cutting, giving a prolonged period of display.

Unlike any of the other types the corms of nanus varieties should be planted in late autumn outdoors, in rich soil about 3in deep and 6in apart, mixing bonemeal into the soil before planting. Outdoor planting is not recommended in areas subject to severe frosts and even in warmer regions a protective winter mulch should be applied. They flower from early June if planted in sunny sheltered spots, and generally last a very long time, throwing up secondary floral spikes when the first are nearly over.

For indoor culture pot up the corms in autumn, about 5 to each 6in pot, using any good potting compost. Plunge the pots outside until there is good root development—about 8–10 weeks—and then bring into a cool greenhouse. Very little if any heat is required until the plants begin to show colour and even then only a little heat is warranted.

Nanus mixtures, representing a wide range of colours, are available in the autumn from many suppliers and larger bulb merchants will offer a limited range of named varieties, including:

Blushing Bride	waxy white, flaked bright crimson
Charm	magenta rose, blotched greenish yellow
Peach Blossom	rose pink with white centre
Spitfire	scarlet, blotched pale blue, edged lilac
Suzanne	dawn pink, splashed cream, outlined red
The Bride	pure white (sometimes catalogued as Colvillei The Bride)

Most catalogues and suppliers ranging from garden centres to nursery-men and local garden shops will have on offer as winter creeps up on spring, a good choice of 'large-flowered', 'primulinus' and 'butterfly' hybrids.

The large-flowered gladioli (see page 153) with brilliantly coloured florets all of 4in in diameter and often 5–6in or more on stems growing 30–60in tall produce the longest and most dramatic garden display from July through September. This type has the biggest choice of named varieties for early, mid-season and late flowering. In colour they range from white to almost black and come in so handy for all those places in the garden where height is wanted—such as against fences or walls, at the back of borders, amongst evergreens or small shrubs. They are valuable for cutting too, for just a few stems will make a colourful and effective display indoors.

Primulinus hybrids (see page 234) boast elegant hooded flowers, mostly of soft delicate colours on slender and graceful stems between 30 and 36in tall. Each floret has a delicately hooded top petal about 2–3in across formed as if to protect the stigma and stamens from the elements. The arrangement of florets on the spike is not as straight and regular as with the large-flowered gladioli, for though evenly spaced, primulinus florets are wider apart and staggered up the stem. Although they have a slightly shorter flowering season—July and August—than large-flowered hybrids, they are sturdy plants and splendid for table decoration, lasting for a long time in water and under artificial light.

A new race of small-flowered gladioli recently introduced by the Dutch under the name 'butterfly gladioli' (see page 153), has caught the imagination of so many gardeners. The florets are just a little larger than those of primulinus varieties but still under 4in in diameter, and they are distinctly different. Butterfly florets are not hooded and come in most attractive colour combinations with petals beautifully ruffled. Each stem grows about 36in in height and spikes have 6–8 florets open at a time.

Page 234 Primulinus gladioli

Many butterfly varieties have vivid throat markings. Flowering in the garden in July and August, they are ideal grouped in borders where brilliance and dash is wanted. And butterfly gladioli lend themselves to charming and dainty floral arrangements too.

Gardeners could not do better than to try varieties of each type but should remember that both the primulinus and butterfly varieties are almost exclusively restricted to early and mid-season flowering and that for a longer season, more varieties from the large-flowering group is a wise investment. As a rough guide early-flowering gladioli take 90 days from planting to produce flowering spikes, mid-season varieties take 100 days and late-flowering varieties 120 days.

The corms of large-flowered, primulinus and butterfly gladioli can begin to be planted any time after the frost is out of the ground and it is dry enough to work easily. This is usually from mid-March or when the trees begin to make leaf. To get three full months of gladioli bloom, plant the corms at fortnightly intervals from mid-March to the end of May or early June. Extra-early blooms may be had by planting in a cold frame about a month before it is safe to plant in the garden, or by potting corms singly in 4in pots a month ahead of planting time and transplanting them into the garden when the danger of frost is past. A regional gladioli planting guide for North American gardeners is on page 23.

Corms should be planted in the garden 4in deep and 6–10in apart although in cutting gardens rows should be a good 24in apart. Almost any well-drained soil will do, though a light sandy soil is ideal. For best results, work in some fertiliser while digging over and raking the planting sites. An all-purpose balanced commercial fertiliser at the rate of 2–4oz per sq yd is most suitable and if soil tends to be heavy do work in some peat, compost or sand. The taller varieties will require staking, particularly if they are sited in exposed positions. The time for staking is at planting time, to avoid damage to corms. Stakes can be of wood, bamboo or metal but should be as tall as the flowering stems and driven into the ground for at least 18in or more.

All gladioli like sunny positions but will take some shade, especially at midday or during late afternoon. Wind-swept locations should be avoided. Plant in groups or clusters of a dozen corms or more for spectacular display. Colours of gladioli won't clash with other blooms and sites among rhododendrons, lilies and even iris can be very effective.

Gladioli do have one pest—thrips—an insect so tiny it cannot be seen. They cause mottled flowers and streaked foliage but are easy to check.

Simply put the flattened corms in Captan—1oz to 5 pints of water—for an hour before planting them, or roll the corms in DDT powder or Sevin dust as a preventive measure. Some gardeners also use DDT-based sprays once the shoots stand 6in high.

Plants should be watered freely during their growing period. Mulching with moist peat is also helpful and keeps weeds down as well. Clean cultivation is essential and it is worthwhile to cultivate the soil round the plants frequently but shallowly. The most critical period of growth is when the flower stalks are forming, as new corms are developing under ground at the same time. Applications of liquid fertiliser when watering at this stage will be beneficial.

Be sure to leave at least three leaves when cutting gladioli for indoor decoration so that the young corms for the following season obtain proper nutriment. To produce healthy cormlets gladioli like a spell of dry weather for about 6 weeks after they have finished flowering, by which time the foliage will have turned brown and they will be ready for lifting.

Lift the plants out carefully with a fork to save all small corms and cormlets from damage. Label each variety and then cut off the dried tops, an inch or so above the corms. Dry off the corms for a few weeks on a bench or in boxes, then separate the corms, discarding husks and remains of old corms, and place in paper bags or shallow boxes for the winter. Store in a cool but frost-free and well-ventilated place until planting time comes round again. The very small cormlets cannot be expected to produce full size flowers the following year but if planted in rows about 2–3in deep they will produce larger corms for the subsequent season, particularly if planting sites are enriched. Many gardeners short of space discard the smallest corms and most gardeners, in any case, tend to want to purchase new varieties each year.

As so many flower lovers use gladioli as cut flowers, here are a few tips about making the most of them. Cut them in the early morning or late evening, taking the minimum of sword-like and plaited foliage with the floral spike when the bottom florets are just opening. Plunge them in deep water in a cool place for at least a few hours or overnight before arranging. The florets will gradually open all the way up the spike. As the florets fade they should be removed and the stem shortened. The last few florets can be used effectively in shallow bowls or dishes.

New varieties of gladioli are constantly being introduced and lists in bulb catalogues are subject to change frequently. The varieties I am recommending are all economically priced, are known to do well both in

Britain and America, and include very recently introduced plants. In addition to colour descriptions each variety is keyed to indicate (1) early flowering, (2) mid-season flowering, and (3) late flowering. For convenience I have separated the three types and because there are so many large-flowered varieties have grouped them according to colour.

Large-flowered gladioli

RED

1	**Agnita**	deep scarlet
3	**Albert Schweitzer**	mandarin red, darker blotch
1	**Auber**	mandarin red
1	**Carmen**	scarlet red, marked white
1	**Cordula**	signal red
2	**Dr. Salk**	poppy red, striped purple
2	**Eurovision**	light vermilion red
2	**Herman van der Mark**	pepper red
1	**Joli Coeur**	orange red
2	**Jo Wagenaar**	dark carmine red, striped white
1	**Life Flame**	cochineal red, striped yellow
3	**New Europe**	geranium red
2	**Oscar**	blood red
2	**Rotterdam**	signal red, blotched purple
3	**Sans Souci**	scarlet, striped yellow

PINK AND SALMON

2	**Alfred Nobel**	salmon rose
1	**Allard Peirson**	salmon pink
2	**Ben Trovata**	light rosy red, purple throat, yellow blotch
3	**Bloemfontein**	salmon, blotched yellow
1	**Bon Voyage**	pink, tinged salmon
3	**Elan**	light pink, creamy white throat
1	**Emilia**	azalea pink
1	**Friendship**	bright rose, striped white, marked yellow
1	**Happy End**	salmon carmine pink, marked creamy white
2	**Leeuwenhorst**	pale lilac rose
1	**Lovely Melody**	begonia rose
1	**Ma Jolie**	deep salmon
2	**My Love**	old rose
1	**Perosi**	salmon pink, striped yellow

1 **Peter Pears**   shrimp red with paler stripe
2 **Spic and Span**   salmon shading to pink
1 **Wild Rose**   pink, blotched creamy white

ORANGE
2 **Hochsommer**   orange red
3 **Princess Beatrix**   scarlet orange, marked purple

WHITE AND CREAMY WHITE
2 **Mary Housley**   creamy white, blotched vermilion red
2 **Snow Princess**   creamy white
2 **Tequendama**   pure white
2 **White Excelsior**   pure white
2 **White Friendship**   creamy white, pale primrose blotch

YELLOW
1 **Aldebaran**   yellow, blotched blood red
1 **Flowersong**   yellow, carmine throat
2 **Polygoon**   butter yellow
2 **Spotlight**   creamy yellow, blotched carmine red
2 **Vink's Glory**   canary yellow

BLUE, LAVENDER AND VIOLET
2 **Blue Conquerer**   deep violet blue, lighter in throat
2 **Lilac Wonder**   lilac, striped white
2 **Modern Art**   purple rose, lighter in throat
1 **Pandion**   cattelya violet, marked red

PURPLE
3 **Aristocrat**   reddish purple, lighter edge
1 **Grock**   purple
2 **Hawaii**   mahogany purple
1 **Memorial Day**   reddish magenta

SMOKY
2 **Silhouet**   lilac, shaded bright red

Primulinus gladioli
2 **Bristol**   lemon yellow, blotched red
2 **Carioca**   warm orange, feathered yellow

2 **Columbine**	soft carmine rose, marked creamy white
2 **Comic**	peach, flushed orange, flecked crimson
2 **Daisy**	soft primrose yellow
2 **Harmony**	cyclamen purple, marked white
2 **Lady Godiva**	pure white
1 **Little Trophy**	ivory white
2 **Mephisto**	mandarin red
2 **Page Boy**	mandarin red, edged yellow
1 **Pretoria**	coral red, flecked apricot and gold
2 **Robin**	pinkish purple
2 **Rosy Morn**	shell rose, creamy white centre
1 **White City**	pure white
1 **Yellow Special**	amber yellow

Butterfly gladioli

1 **Ares**	creamy white, blotched red
1 **Areta**	rose, overlaid cardinal red
2 **Cormbra**	apricot orange, blotched orange red
2 **Delphi**	carmine pink and soft yellow
2 **Golden Horn**	soft greenish yellow
2 **Green Bird**	greenish yellow, flushed rose pink
2 **Green Woodpecker**	greenish lemon, blotched red in throat
2 **Hoax**	greenish yellow, edged old rose
2 **Ice Follies**	pure white
1 **Mavoureen**	lilac
2 **Mykonos**	soft butter yellow, splashed red
2 **Pink Pearl**	shell pink
2 **Prairie Fire**	bright orange red
1 **Repartee**	pure white, marked red
2 **Salina**	burgundy red, splashed yellow
2 **Storiette**	azalea pink, blotched yellow

Most bulb retailers will offer mixtures of large-flowered, of primulinus and of butterfly varieties.

Chapter Eleven

LILIES

MOST GARDENERS in Britain and the United States either do not grow lilies at all in their gardens or only one or two kinds of them. There are three basic reasons for this, the assumption that lilies are fragile and delicate, that they are difficult to grow and that they are expensive. And all three assumptions are excessive.

Lilies are the hardiest of all summer-flowering bulbs, vigorous and resistant to disease, and once planted need not be lifted for annual winter storage. Lilies are no more difficult to grow than other bulbs, although a few will not tolerate lime and all like to have their roots protected from the sun. Lilies may not be the cheapest of bulbs but they are not as dear as many suppose, particularly in that they provide tremendous value for money by providing a great mass of flowers and by increasing rapidly.

The lily is, of course, a member of the enormous lily or 'liliaceae' family consisting of over 200 genera, among them hyacinths and tulips, with over 2,500 different species. The lily genus itself has some 80 species found growing in America, Europe and Asia. These have been cultivated and hybridised to produce a fascinating collection of lily strains and varieties for garden use.

Lilies, once one gets to know a bit about them, are the most fascinating of bulbous plants. These symbols of religion, royalty, heraldry and purity range in height from $1\frac{1}{2}$–10ft, come in a host of flower forms, produce a galaxy of colours that exclude only blue, and flower from May to October, many with delightful fragrance. They are most adaptable too, for they can be planted in beds, borders, rockeries, wild gardens, woodlands, among grass, between evergreens and flowering shrubs, in outdoor pots and tubs, in the cutting garden, in fact, in almost any sunny or partially shady site. Many can be grown in cool greenhouses and the majority make long-lasting cut flowers.

Everything about the lily is distinctive. The bulbs are different from those of all other genera in that they are made up of a number of overlapping fleshy scales without an outer skin or tunic, and are highly variable in character, shape, size and colour. The lack of tunics is a warning to all gardeners not to permit lily bulbs to become really dry. Clumps may in time have to be divided but when lifted they should be replanted immediately or covered with slightly moist peat until they can be replanted.

Bulb shapes may be round, almost round or egg-shaped and vary from 2–6in in diameter. Bulb sizes vary by species, smaller species generally having smaller bulbs. But bulb size is not a guide to flower size as it is with hyacinths and tulips, only an indication of different species. Bulb colour also varies by species, most bulbs having whitish, yellowish, browny yellow or pinkish scales.

The form of bulb varies according to different types of bulb reproduction. Concentric lily bulbs are single bulbs that reproduce by forming offsets, like tulip bulbs. Rhizomatous bulbs develop new bulbs in scaly clusters on a thick rhizome-like root underground. Stoloniferous bulbs produce stolons or creeping underground shoots or branches. The original bulb dies, new bulbs produce new stolons and die in turn, but the stolon keeps on growing and producing new bulbs.

Just as lily bulbs reproduce themselves in a number of ways so too do lily growers raise bulbs commercially in different ways. Lily bulbs raised from bulbs are called clones and clones are produced by dividing rhizomatous and stoloniferous bulb clusters, by taking scales from lily bulbs and planting them, and by cultivating bulblets. The small fragments and offsets are then grown until they become flowering-sized bulbs and as this takes several years lily clones are more expensive than lilies raised from seed. There is an advantage, however, in that clones identically repeat the characteristics of a given lily variety in each generation and each individual lily plant.

Lilies grown from seed vary, and often considerably, from one another. These lilies, grouped as strains, include all lilies obtained from a single source or particular crosses, and include a varied group of flowers. This provides a broader range of bloom. Lily growers, of course, discard any inferior plants each season, retaining only those of better quality and greater vigour. Seed-raised lilies can consequently be improved more quickly than lilies raised from bulbs.

Some lilies, primarily American species, put out basal roots coming from the lower part of the bulb, like tulips. Most Asiatic species, on the other hand, form roots on the stem of the bulb. Whether lilies are base-rooting or stem-rooting is important for the amateur to know, for they must be planted differently to survive. This is fully dealt with in the section on lily cultivation in this chapter.

Lily leaves, although generally short and narrow, may be arranged either in whorls at intervals up the stem or they may be arranged irregularly up the stem. In a few species combinations of whorled leaves and single irregular leaves are noticeable.

Lily flowers are invariably arranged in six parts. There are six petals or segments forming the perianth; there are six stamens constituting the male reproductive organs, and six rows of seeds in a tri-lobal capsule forming the female ovary.

Not surprisingly, there are a number of methods of classifying lilies, some extremely complicated and not really all that useful to the average gardener. They are often divided into trumpet lilies with narrow funnel-shaped flowers, trumpet lilies with broad, open flowers, upright or vase-shaped lilies and martagon-type or Turk's cap lilies in which petals are reflexed, turning upwards and backwards. The name martagon is quite an old one derived from the Turkish word 'martagan' describing a special form of turban adopted by Sultan Muhammed I, hence the 'Turk's cap'. The problem is, that over the entire genus with its broad range both of species and hybrids, there is a host of intermediate shapes.

The most practical and beneficial system of classification is the new one adopted by the Royal Horticultural Society in Britain and the North American Lily Society, which divides lilies into nine divisions.

Division One—Asiatic Hybrids
    (a) Early-flowering upright lilies, mostly stem-rooting
    (b) Lilies with outward facing flowers, mostly stem-rooting
    (c) Lilies with pendant flowers, usually on longish pedicels

Division Two—Martagon Hybrids revealing the characteristics of L. martagon and L. hansonii, with small pendant flowers, recurved at petal tips; stem-rooting.

Division Three—Candidum Hybrids revealing the characteristics of the classic Madonna lily with wide open, trumpet-shaped flowers; base-rooting.

Division Four—American Hybrids mainly tall-stemmed with Turk's cap flowers borne on long pedicels; semi-rhizomatous and sparsely stem-rooting.

Division Five—Longiflorum Hybrids revealing the characteristics of the trumpet-shaped Easter lily. (Few grown in commercial quantities but the species and varieties derived from it are easily obtainable.)

Division Six—Trumpet Hybrids. A big group derived from Asiatic species but excluding L. auratum and L. speciosum hybrids.
   (a) Chinese trumpets with true funnel-shaped flowers
   (b) Bowl-shaped flowers
   (c) Pendant-type flowers
   (d) Sunburst-type flowers, star-shaped and opening flat.

Division Seven—Oriental Hybrids. A group derived from L. auratum pictum and L. speciosum crosses; stem-rooting.
   (a) Hybrids with trumpet-shaped flowers
   (b) Hybrids with bowl-shaped flowers
   (c) Hybrids with flat-faced flowers
   (d) Hybrids with recurved flowers

Division Eight. Contains all hybrids not provided for in any previous division.

Division Nine. Contains all true species and their botanical forms.
   Species lilies have, of course, been cultivated directly from the wild species gathered from all over the world. Hybrid lilies, usually named both by strain and individual variety, are new lilies developed by crossing various species lilies, and then frequently by further crossing of the hybrids with species lilies and other hybrids. Such a large number of crosses has been made to raise the strain of Olympic Hybrids, for example, that it is now impossible to trace their descent.
   The classification above clearly discloses the variations in flower shape or form among lilies but they also vary in habit. I have already mentioned

that the leaves vary both in shape and relationship to the stem. The flowers bloom either in pedicels which are stalks bearing flowers in a branched inflorescence, the pedicels arranged in racemes rather widely spaced one above the other; or in umbels, from the Latin word for 'umbrella', which are clusters of flowers growing from a central point at the top of the stem. Whether in pedicels or umbels, lilies generally bloom in clusters of flowers rather than singly. The number of blooms varies tremendously, some lilies having only 2–3 flowers while others have up to as many as 75 flowers in each cluster.

With all this variation in form, habit, colour and flowering time gardeners can have a fascinating time choosing lilies from among both the species and their botanical forms and the great range of hybrids. And many gardeners go for fragrant lilies in the same way as they seek out scented roses.

LILIES IN THE GARDEN

When planting lilies in your garden the most important factor to bear in mind is that they must have good drainage. All bulbs require adequate drainage so this is not a special requirement for lilies but soil that remains waterlogged after rain is literally death on lilies. Humus, and plenty of it, is also of great importance. Although some lilies grow wild in very poor soil, all profit from soil that is enriched with compost, peat and leaf-mould and will respond by producing more brilliantly coloured blooms more prolifically as well as glossier and greener leaves.

Lilies prefer neutral or slightly acid soil and dislike chalk and lime on the whole, but many are lime tolerant as indicated in the recommended list at the end of this chapter and a few, like L. amabile, L. candidum, L. henryi and L. martagon, not only tolerate lime but need an alkaline soil to produce their best flower.

Base-rooting lilies can be planted in November–December but it is best to wait for early spring—late February to April—before planting stem-rooting types. Lilies like open, porous soil, so if your garden is heavy clay, deep-soil preparation is the traditional way to provide good drainage. If you have heavy soil dig it over in advance of planting to a depth of 12–18in, being careful to avoid leaving a hard base, and liberally add compost with peat or leaf-mould. If you haven't the time or cannot face the job of deep-soil preparation an alternative method of providing good drainage is to make raised beds. This is simply done by digging out

Page 245 (*above left*) Lilium auratum; (*above right*) Lilium Harmony; (*below left*) Lilium regale; (*below right*) Lilium henryi

sunken paths from an area in the garden and placing the top soil removed on top of the bed or beds in between, using stone, tile or brick edges to retain the beds. Or you can just provide hills of raised soil for your lilies if it is impractical to raise a whole area. But don't just dig out a hole, fill in with compost and humus, and then put the soil back on top to make a hill. All your hole will do is act as a sump to collect water and drown your lily bulb. You should also dig some distance round each hill and add humus. If you have a slope in your garden or light porous soil no deep-soil preparation or formation of hills or raised beds will be necessary, as surface water will drain off.

Whether you are planting base-rooting or stem-rooting bulbs a hole deep enough and of sufficient size to accommodate the bulb and allow for root spread should be dug out, and surrounding the bulb with sand helps drainage and discourages slugs. Small bulbs should be about 12in apart and larger ones about 18in apart or more. It is advisable to plant at least three bulbs in each site. Work the soil well round the bulbs and then water them well.

Base-rooting lilies, which include L. candidum, L. martagon and L. pardalinum, should be planted 4–6in deep, the depth measured from the top of the bulb, with the sole exception of L. candidum which only needs a covering of 1in of soil. Stem-rooting lilies, which include L. amabile, L. auratum, L. hansonii, L. henryi, L. pumilum, L. regale, L. speciosum and L. tigrinum, should be planted about 8in deep in light soil but in most gardens 6in deep is usually enough. It is better to make little mounds of earth above the bulbs than to plant them too deeply. After planting add a surface mulch of 2in of peat or leaf-mould to all stem-rooting lilies.

Lilies may be planted in sun or part shade but never in windswept positions. The ideal conditions for most lilies is to have the roots and lower stem shaded by other plants and the flower heads in the sun. Some of the larger lilies will need staking. Use a small stake when planting to act as a marker for a taller one when support is needed.

Lilies should never be allowed to dry out and need good and regular waterings rather than sprinklings from the time the shoots first emerge in spring until the stems and leaves lose their green colour in the autumn. All lilies, and especially stem-rooting types, should have a 2in mulch of peat or leaf-mould throughout the summer to help retain moisture. By planting lilies among azaleas or rhododendrons or other shrubs or with a ground cover of low growing plants you will help conserve moisture and provide shade to the roots and lower stems.

Faded flowers should be removed as necessary but don't cut back the whole stem until the autumn. Stems should be completely cut back in autumn, as a disease-control measure. Lilies are hardy but a winter mulch is recommended for most parts of the country to keep soil temperatures evenly low.

The only reason to lift lily bulbs is to space them farther apart as a site becomes overcrowded due to the natural increase of the bulbs. Lifting should be done with great care to avoid damaging bulbs and roots and is most safely done when the leaves begin to turn yellow. Once bulbs are lifted they should be replanted at once.

Do not be concerned if some of your lily bulbs do not flower in the first season after planting. Some lilies take a season to become established and if left alone will produce glorious blooms in the second season.

The plants can be fertilised twice a year, once in the spring when the shoots are about 2–3in tall and once in the summer after flowering. Bone-meal is the safest fertiliser for lilies and may be worked into the soil round the plants. Wood ash can be safely added to the soil for lime tolerant lilies but fresh manure is taboo for all lilies. Well-decomposed manure may be dug in when planting but even then should not be allowed to touch the bulbs. Leaf-mould should always be used in mulches to keep lily bulbs nourished.

Precise sites in the garden for lilies is a matter of individual taste and locations are suggested by the individual characteristics, such as height, form of flower, colour, time of bloom and habit. Generally speaking taller lilies are best planted in a border with other summer-flowering subjects or as vertical accents among evergreens or shrubs. Dwarf lilies look delightful planted in random clusters like tulips or daffodils, and many are charming in terrace tubs. Some, like L. amabile, are excellent rockery plants. There are a number which are suitable for naturalising in a semi-cultivated, a wild or a grassy garden. These include the Aurelian and Bellingham hybrids, L. hansonii, L. henryi, L. marhan, L. martagon, L. pardalinum, L. regale and all the speciosum and tigrinum varieties.

Lilies make delightful cut flowers and among the most effective and long-lasting for floral arrangements are L. auratum, Aurelian hybrids, L. Bright Star, L. candidum, Fiesta hybrids, L. henryi, L. Limelight, L. longiflorum, Mid-century hybrids, Olympic hybrids, L. pardalinum, L. regale and the speciosum and tigrinum varieties. When cutting lilies for flower arrangements, however, the entire flowering section of the plant can be taken provided the cut is made on the stem above the leaves. If you

cut long stems and take most of the leaves the plant will be unable to
build up nourishment in the normal way and will probably die. L. auratum, L. martagon and the speciosum varieties in particular suffer when
leaves are removed.

One last word about lilies in the garden. The thoughtful gardener will
plant some bulbs in pots which can be sunk into the earth outdoors or
placed in a cold frame. These extra lilies in pots can be used later to fill
gaps in the summer garden and also function as mobile lilies for display
in the house or outdoors on patios or porches.

LILIES INDOORS

For gardeners with unheated greenhouses it is eminently feasible to have
a gorgeous show of lilies in pots from early summer to autumn. Lilies
recommended for pot culture include L. auratum, L. henryi, L. Limelight,
L. longiflorum, the Mid-century hybrids, L. regale and the speciosum
varieties. Others which can be grown in pots with care are included in the
list at the end of this chapter.

The time to pot is when the bulbs become available in the retail shops
and potting up should be done immediately to prevent bulbs from drying
out. When potting use a compost of $\frac{2}{3}$ fibrous loam and $\frac{1}{3}$ well-decayed
leaf-mould, adding plenty of coarse sand and a few pieces of charcoal.
Bonemeal can, of course, be well mixed into the compost. Do ensure good
drainage by adding crocks to the bottom of each pot. Normally 6in pots
are adequate but some of the larger bulbs like L. auratum, L. regale and
L. speciosum may require an 8 or 9in pot.

Pot firmly just covering the top of the bulb and leave room to add more
soil when the stem roots appear. Choose a position out in the garden
preferably facing north, and stand pots on a raised bed of weathered
ashes. Then cover with a good 6in of peat or leaf-mould to keep off excessive rainfall. When top growth is about 1in tall, the pots can be removed
to the greenhouse or cold frame and be watered sparingly.

If you want the blooms very early the lilies can be forced in gentle heat
but must be kept near the glass to prevent the growth getting drawn.
Shade should be given the lower part of the stems to help stem-root
development and these should be top-dressed with peat as they appear.
Always ensure that your greenhouse or cold frame has adequate
ventilation, and give air freely to the lilies. Although watering should be
moderate at first it should be given liberally when the plants are in full

growth and pots are well filled with roots. When plants are in full growth dilute liquid fertiliser applications are advantageous. Feeding with bone-meal or dried blood is also fine.

Lilies planted in smaller or medium-sized pots should be re-potted each year but those grown in very large pots or tubs, where a number of bulbs are planted together, repotting every second or third year will be sufficient provided top soil is removed and fresh compost substituted. Lilies in pots should be kept dry during the winter either plunged in a cold frame or in a cool greenhouse. Its a good idea to cover the tops of the pots with peat, which will help keep out mice.

YOUR CHOICE OF LILIES

There are so many different kinds of lilies obtainable in Britain and America that any selection is necessarily arbitrary. Gardeners should really please themselves and while continuing to grow old favourites should also introduce some new species and new hybrids each year. For the amateur who has never grown lilies before I can say that the easiest to grow are L. amabile, L. candidum, L. hansonii, L. henryi, L. martagon, L. pardalinum, L. regale and L. tigrinum as well as the vast majority of horticultural hybrids.

Lilies I can most strongly recommend are listed in alphabetical order with the fullest possible pertinent information, including horticultural classification and any special requirements.

L. amabile (Div 9), a martagon-type stem-rooting lily from Korea, bears up to six vivid reflexed red Turk's cap flowers spotted black on sturdy 2–3ft stems in July–August. It is free-flowering, lime tolerant, and prefers partial shade. Plant 5–6in deep in borders or the rockery.

L. auratum (Div 9), the golden-rayed lily of Japan, is stem-rooting and produces many highly scented pure white large open flowers with brown and crimson spots, each petal marked with a golden ray. The blooms on stems 4–7ft high often measure 10–12in across and flower in August–September. Plant the bulbs 3–4in deep among paeonies or in sheltered positions near evergreens in partial shade. They like plenty of peat or leaf-mould. Excellent for cutting, this species is also ideal for pot culture.

L. Brandywine (Div 1b) has wide-petalled large, outward-facing orange flowers spotted with minute dots of oxblood red. This stem-rooting variety is free-flowering, blooming in June on 3–4ft stems. Plant 4–6in deep in full sun or partial shade.

L. Bright Star (Div 6d) is an Aurelian hybrid producing from 7–14 large 5in diameter, flaring star-shaped but broad-petalled flowers which open flat with slightly recurved tips on each 3–4ft stem. The finely textured petals of ivory white contrast beautifully with the apricot orange star pencilled in the centre of each flower. They bloom in July and may be planted in either full sun or partial shade. This lime tolerant variety is an excellent cut flower and can be naturalised in wild gardens or grass. It is stem-rooting.

L. candidum (Div 9) is base-rooting and the oldest lily cultivated in Europe. Known the world over as the 'Madonna Lily' it produces pure satin white chalice-like flowers of outstanding fragrance on 3–4ft stems in June–July. It is only available in the autumn and can be planted any-time between August and December in full sun. This lime tolerant species can also be grown in pots and is superb for floral arrangements.

L. Cinnabar (Div 1a) is a fine vivid maroon red mid-century hybrid whose flowers are borne on long pedicels in well-spaced array. The blooms on 2–3ft stems literally glow in the sun. All mid-century hybrids are valuable as border plants and also thrive in grass and in the wild garden, rarely requiring staking unless in exposed positions. They are lime tolerant and do well either in full sun or partial shade. They are also excellent for forcing in pots in the cool greenhouse. They flower outdoors in June.

L. Citronella (Div 1c) is a robust and hardy strain bearing huge quanti-ties of large, bright pure lemon yellow recurved flowers spotted with small black dots on each 3–4ft stem in July. The pendant flowers are borne on short pedicels and are magnificent in sunny or partly shaded borders.

L. Destiny (Div 1a) is a superb upright flowered mid-century hybrid of purest lemon yellow with just enough brown spots to produce a fine colour contrast. The flowers appear in June on 3–4ft stems. This is a most vigorous free-flowering variety, excellent for early forcing.

L. Enchantment (Div 1a) (see page 154), another prolific mid-century hybrid blooming in June, has large cup-shaped upright flowers of brilliant orange red, 16 or more on each 2–3ft stem. It is outstanding as both a garden flower and pot plant.

Fiesta hybrids (Div 1c) have tall 3–5ft stems bearing as many as 30 nicely spaced pendant reflexed flowers ranging from pale straw yellow through orange to vivid dark red, sprinkled with small maroon black spots, in July. Plant 4–6in deep in sunny or partially shady sites. These hybrids can also be grown in pots and make lovely cut flowers.

L. Fire King (Div 1b) (see page 154) has sturdy 2–3ft stems carrying as many as 20 large, open campanulate flowers of vivid nasturtium flame, heavily dotted with brown purple spots towards the throat and with rich brown anthers. This stem-rooting gem flowers in July and prefers sunny positions.

L. Golden Splendour (Div 6a) is a strain comprising only those lilies which are of deepest gold with a definite maroon stripe on the reverse of the petals. As the flower opens it lifts its head to reveal the really deep yellow flowers. This darkest strain of true yellow trumpets has 4–6ft stems and blooms in July. This stem-rooting strain likes a bit of shade.

L. Golden Sunburst (Div 6d) is a recently introduced very vigorous strain derived from a cross between L. henryi and L. aurelianense which will bring a golden glow to any garden. Each 4–5ft stem carries about 8 or more large flowers, up to 8in in diameter, of golden yellow. The finely textured petals, with green-veined reverse form the widely expanded typical sunburst-type flower. The petals, recurving slightly, are long and wide. Flowering time is July–August.

L. hansonii (Div 9), often called the 'yellow martagon lily', is easy to grow, thriving in any position in well-drained soil but does like a little shade. Native to Korea, it was introduced to Europe about 1870. Each 4ft stem bears 6–12 fragrant, nodding Turk's cap flowers of great substance, coloured bright golden yellow with crimson brown spots, in June. I like them naturalised as well as in pots.

L. Harmony (Div 1a) (see page 154) is another of the fabulous mid-century hybrids descended from L. tigrinum. This variety has large, upright flowers of bright orange on 2–3ft stems in June–July. It is splendid in borders, for cutting or for forcing.

L. henryi (Div 9) a graceful and tall stem-rooting species discovered in 1888 in North China grows all of 5–7ft in height, flowering profusely in August–September with up to 30 large, nodding and fragrant flowers of rich deep orange yellow with back curving petals and prominent stamens on each purple black stem. The foliage is glossy deep green. The bulbs like lime and appreciate being planted 8in deep in partial shade. Hardy, vigorous and free-flowering, this species is one of the finest late-flowering lilies available for the garden and is valuable for cutting too.

L. Joan Evans (Div 1a) a mid-century hybrid, is brilliant golden yellow beautifully spotted maroon. The flowers are broad petalled and upright and there are as many as 6–9 on each wiry 3–4ft stem in July. It is very attractive in borders, a good cut flower, and can be grown in pots.

L. Limelight (Div 6a) is one of the most sensational hybrids of recent years, strong, tall, fragrant and an unusual chartreuse yellow. The handsome flowers are magnificent tight funnel-shaped trumpets borne on 4–6ft stems in July. This prolific hybrid should be planted in groups of half a dozen. The blooms last long in floral arrangements.

L. longiflorum (Div 9) is a stem-rooting favourite producing several huge, trumpet-shaped, elongated flowers, pure white and highly scented, on each 2–3ft stem. It is native to the Ryukyu Islands, Okinawa and Formosa and does beautifully in pots in the cool greenhouse or in sheltered positions in the garden, where it flowers in June–July.

L. longiflorum Holland's Glory bears up to 12 large pure white flowers on 3–4ft stems in June–July and is the hardiest of the type in the garden.

L. longiflorum Mount Everest stands 6ft with huge waxy white blooms with a faint golden glow at the throat. It is ideal in semi-shade or woodland positions and flowers in July–August.

L. longiflorum White Queen has a host of long trumpets in white with a greenish throat on 3–4ft stems in July–August. All these longiflorum varieties are first class for forcing in pots and as cut flowers.

L. Marhan (Div 2) is a rather fine martagon hybrid resulting from a cross between L. martagon album and L. hansonii. It has small pendant flowers, recurved at petal tips, of rich orange with reddish spots. It is lime tolerant, likes light shade and can be naturalised. Stems are 4–5ft tall and flowering time is June–July.

L. martagon (Div 9) native to both Europe and Asia and known as the 'Turk's cap lily', will grow in literally almost any soil and in any position although it prefers lime. Each 3–4ft stem carries up to 20 or more flowers varying in shade from light purple to pale purplish pink all spotted in varying degrees with purple. They bloom in June–July. Plant the bulbs of this species and its pure white sport, **L. martagon album** in groups informally under trees or at the edge of herbaceous borders for best effect. Both can be naturalised and the latter can be grown in pots.

L. Maxwill (Div 1c) is an exceedingly lovely lily stemming from a cross between L. Maximowiczii and L. Willmottiae. The slender, graceful stems, 5–6ft tall, bear a pyramidal cluster of 30 or more bright orange red flowers with brown spots in July–August. Plant the bulbs 8in deep in partially shaded positions.

Olympic hybrids (Div 6a) are a top quality fragrant strain of lilies with a colour range from cream through soft pink to cool green. The exterior of the petals of the funnel-shaped trumpets are delicately shaded greenish brown or soft rose. The sturdy stems are 4–5ft tall and flowering time is July. The lime tolerant bulbs do well in sun or partial shade and the scented flowers are ideal for cutting.

L. Orange Triumph (Div 1b) is an outstanding early-flowering garden lily with 2ft stems bearing large clusters of 10–12 upright bell-shaped and outward facing flowers of a vivid orange yellow with violet spots. This stem-rooting beauty blooms in the garden in June and makes an excellent pot plant. It is lime tolerant.

L. pardalinum (Div 9) native to California and Oregon and known either as the 'panther lily' or 'leopard lily', is one of the hardiest and easiest lilies to grow. Each 4–5ft stems bears 12–20 recurving Turk's cap type flowers of brilliant orange shading to crimson with maroon spots in July. It is lime tolerant and will grow in sun or partial shade but prefers rather damp, though well-drained and partially shaded sites. This species can be naturalised and is suited both to pot culture and to cutting for indoor decoration.

L. pardalinum giganteum (Div 9) is a bright orange yellow improved form of stately habit on sturdy stems often reaching 8ft in height. The petals are spotted purple and the flowers appear in July but a little later than the typical form, often as many as 30 per stem. It is a superb variety under trees or in thin woodlands but does equally well in full sunshine.

Also of the pardalinum type are the **Bellingham hybrids** (Div 4), a breed of hybrids raised by the U.S. Department of Agriculture at its Bellingham, Washington research centre over 50 years ago. Unusually vigorous the 5–7ft stems carry up to 25 large flowers in a pyramidal flower head. The July blooms range in colour from clear yellow through orange yellow to bright orange red with pronounced spotting varying from maroon to black. Excellent for the wild garden or naturalising the flowers are particularly long-lasting. If cut when the first blooms open they will remain fresh in water until the entire head is in flower.

L. Pink Perfection (Div 6a) represents a truly fascinating strain of large trumpet lilies ranging in colour from orchid purple to pansy violet which do well in cool greenhouse or garden. The buds are pale green and as the flowers open the colour becomes purplish and finally deep pink. Plant the bulbs in semi-shade for best results in the garden. Stems range from 5–7ft in height and flowering time is July.

L. pumilum (tenuifolium) (Div. 9), or the 'Coral lily', is native to China, Korea, Mongolia and Siberia and is a little charmer with slender 1–2ft stems bearing up to 12 or more scarlet Turk's cap flowers in May–

June. It is one of the finest species for the rockery, preferring sandy soil and a sunny position, and is lime tolerant. It makes a delightful cut flower too.

L. pumilum Golden Gleam (Div 9) is similar in habit but somewhat more robust with fragrant light golden orange flowers. It is considered an 'albino' form of this species.

L. regale (Div 9) (see page 171) is without doubt one of the most popular and accommodating of all lilies, flourishing in light or heavy soils, with or without lime, and doing superbly even in large outdoor containers. The strong, flexible 3–4ft stems are crowned with large funnel-shaped lustrous flowers, pure white inside with golden yellow shading in the throat and golden tipped anthers, and streaked purplish pink outside. The flowers have a pervading scent in July. This species will thrive in sun or partial shade, is fine for pot culture and valuable for cutting, and can be naturalised.

L. regale album (Div 9), also native to Western China and Tibet, is the June-flowering pure white form. Although the yellow throat typical of the species is present the exterior of the petals is white with no markings. It is recommended for herbaceous borders.

L. Royal Gold (Div 6a) (see page 171) is an improved form of L. regale with shining golden yellow trumpet flowers on 3–5ft stems in July. This variety cannot be beaten for providing a really bright splash of colour in the garden.

L. speciosum (Div 9) is one of the most popular lily species boasting many forms and variations, very hardy and suitable for garden or cool greenhouse culture. Of Japanese origin they thrive in sun or partial shade, flowering in August–September on 3–5ft stems. These stem-rooting gems have exotic and unusual large flowers of the martagon type, very fragrant and ranging in colour from pure white through pink to crimson, 5–10 per stem. Always give them rich soil for best results.

L. speciosum album (Div 9) is the beautiful glistening pure white form with golden anthers. The petals are waved at the margins with a cool green band.

L. speciosum Grand Commander (Div 9) is the 4–6ft variety with glowing crimson flowers edged white and spotted all over in blood red. In my own garden in full sun I have had plants of this variety with nearly 40 handsome large perfumed flowers.

L. speciosum Lucie Wilson (Div 9) produces the largest flowers of this section on 5–6ft stems. The abundant and particularly long-lasting blooms are rose pink, edged white and spotted deep red with recurved petals.

L. speciosum roseum (Div 9) has lovely pinky white flowers with rose spots on green 4–5ft stems in August. It is a hardy, robust and rather showy variety.

L. speciosum rubrum (Div 9) (see page 171) is one of the most superb speciosum varieties in terms of size and colour. The giant flowers, measuring all of 8in across, are rich carmine shading to a broad white margin on reddish-brown 5ft stems in August–September.

L. speciosum Uchida (Div 9) also has exceptionally large flowers of really deep red with a white edge and dotted with tiny spots. They are very showy on 4ft stems in August–September.

L. sutchuenense (Div 9) from Mongolia, sometimes referred to as 'Willmottiae unicolor', belongs to the same group as L. davidii but botanists are still arguing about its specific classification. Despite this it is a delightful and graceful lily with flowers of glowing orange red, spotted darker red towards the centre. They bloom in July on 4–5ft stems. As many as 30 recurving martagon-type blooms open on a graceful pyramidal head. This species grows happily in semi-shade.

L. Tabasco (Div 1b) is a 3–4ft tall sun-proof mid-century hybrid with heads of up to 20 broad petalled and wide open flowers of chestnut red, rather reminiscent of the sauce after which it was named, with black spots. It blooms in June–July and the flowers are very long-lasting.

L. Tangelo (Div 1a) is a mid-century hybrid whose name was derived from a fruit resulting from a cross between an orange and a grapefruit and which explains its distinctive orange colouring. It has 7–10 star-shaped flowers in a gorgeous head on each 2½ft stem in June–July. It makes an appealing cut flower.

L. tigrinum (Div 9) (see page 171), the famous 'tiger lily' from China, Korea and Japan, shares with L. candidum the honour of being one of the oldest lilies in cultivation, for it has been grown for food by the Chinese, Koreans and Japanese for over a thousand years. There are a number of varieties flowering in August–September on 4–5ft stems and producing 12–20 unscented martagon-type flowers. These lilies are propagated by bulbils as the flowers are usually sterile. They are easy to grow provided they are planted about 4in deep in any good garden soil that does not have too much lime in it, in full sun or partial shade. They can be naturalised in grass, are excellent as cut flowers, and can be grown in pots in the cool greenhouse.

L. tigrinum flaviflorum (Div 9) is the variety known as the 'yellow tiger lily', flowering in August on 4ft tall sturdy stems. Each stem carries about 20 or more clear lemon yellow flowers with slender pointed and recurved petals spotted lightly with purple. The pollen is noticeably brick red.

L. tigrinum flore pleno (Div 9) is often said to be the most beautiful double-flowered lily. In effect the stamens have been transformed into petals and the perianth has as many as 36 segments. The flowers are bright salmon and profusely spotted, the stems are 4–5ft in height, and flowering time is August–September.

L. tigrinum Fortunei giganteum (Div 9) is the most floriferous of the tiger lilies, bearing as many as 50 large flowers per 5ft stem. They are rich orange scarlet spotted crimson brown. This type was introduced into England by a plant collector called Robert Fortune, and thus the name. It is a superb variety but does require rich soil to produce its abundance of flowers properly.

L. tigrinum splendens (Div 9) is perhaps the most splendid form of tiger lily. Brought to England from Japan in the late 1860s the exceptionally large flowers are rich flame orange spotted glossy black. This robust variety blooms on 4–5ft stems in August–September and is very much a sun-lover.

L. Vermilion Brilliant (Div 1a) is an early-flowering Asiatic hybrid with very showy crimson blood red flowers of fine form and substance on 1½ft stems. It blooms in late June and this stem-rooting gem is as easily cultivated in the cool greenhouse as in warm sunny spots in the garden.

Chapter Twelve

DAHLIAS

DAHLIAS ARE a delight to gardeners who want a continuing bright summer-into-autumn display from July through October as well as a boon to housewives who like cheerful floral decorations in the home. There are dahlias to suit every taste—from the tiny pompons to the shaggy flowers as big as a dinner plate. Whether single or double, giant, large, medium or small, dahlias have velvety petals in myriad brilliant colours and countless shades and hues. Ranging in height from 10–72in or more these tuberous-rooted half-hardy perennial plants are most adaptable and can be sited almost anywhere in the garden that gets the sun. And the dwarf bedding single-flowered dahlias are just the thing to give spectacle to large outdoor containers at the front of the house or on the terrace, balcony or roof garden.

Named after the Swedish botanist, Andrew Dahl, dahlias are members of the Compositae or 'daisy' family. They are native to the Mexican highlands and were cultivated by the Aztecs in numerous forms. A colour illustration of the dahlia appears in the *Badianus Manuscript* of 1552. Although spotted and reported on by Cortes early in the sixteenth century for some strange reason they were not grown in European gardens until about 1789. Interest in the dahlia was quickly awakened early in the nineteenth century as different horticultural types and varieties were developed from the species, now almost unobtainable for cultivation, and this plant with the long flowering season has steadily risen in popularity as a garden subject, as a cut flower and for exhibition. Indeed, there are dahlia cults in many countries today and literally thousands of dahlia shows every year. Today too new dahlia hybrids are developed in Australia, Belgium, Czechoslovakia, France, Germany, Great Britain, Italy, Japan, New Zealand, South Africa and the United States as well as in Holland. Propagation is easy from seed which is evident from the vast number of varieties. Many dahlia fanciers raise their own dwarf bedding hybrids from seed but the larger types are increased by cuttings or by careful division of the tubers in spring. The amateur can cope with the latter by dividing the tubers so that each piece has several young shoots or eyes. These pieces may be grown in boxes until planted out in the garden after the last frosts, towards the end of May or in June.

So many different dahlias are now offered to the gardener that it has become very important to purchase tubers from reliable suppliers. The Dutch bulb industry commercially cultivates not only its own new hybrids but the best garden varieties from round the world and you can be assured of healthy perfection in dahlias by buying Dutch-grown tubers.

CULTIVATION

Many types of soil suit dahlias but they do better in heavy moist soil than in extremely light sandy soil. The most important aspect of growing dahlias successfully from tubers is the preparation of the soil for they are greedy and revel in rich ground. Ideally, a thick layer of well-decayed manure should be spread over dahlia sites in the autumn, the ground dug over and left rough until spring. If this procedure has been overlooked, there is still time to catch up. As long as soil is manured and dug over deeply 2–3 weeks ahead of dahlia planting time the tubers will respond magnificently to the treatment. Planting time is always after the last spring frost, sometimes as early as late May and at other times not until June. Most suppliers will accept orders for dahlia tubers up to the end of May and some despatch them in polythene bags in which they may be safely kept until planting time if stored in a cool frost-free place.

Some gardeners wait until planting time and dig a hole for each tuber about a foot wide and deep and then work about a half a cup of bonemeal plus some well-rotted manure or compost into the soil. I find preparing sites in advance easier and more rewarding. Planting in prepared sites is simple. Dig a hole a good 6in deep for each root and place it at the bottom with growing tip upward. The tubers should be covered with about 3–4in of soil, except for the dwarf bedding varieties which need only 2in of soil over the tubers. Allow 3ft between the larger varieties and 2–2½ft between the smaller varieties. Drive a tall, stout stake into place before you cover the roots so they won't be damaged. Stakes should be 6–8ft high. Bedding varieties, of course, will not require staking.

Keep dahlias well watered at all times—the Mexican name for them means 'waterpipe'. The roots should be watered freely and not with a spray as this does not moisten the roots sufficiently. Except with dwarfs allow only one or two of the strongest shoots to develop. Tips of subsidiary shoots can be pinched off when growth is about 6in high. For really huge and handsome flowers disbudding is necessary. When larger varieties produce terminal buds remove the smaller lateral buds beside them and also all side growths from the axils of 2–4 pairs of leaves immediately below the terminal bud. Some gardeners only allow one stem to develop but this is a matter of individual taste.

Cultivate shallowly round the plants after they are well up. You can start tying stems to stakes when the stems are about 2ft tall and tying should be secure but not tight. Your dahlia plants should have at least one good feed of well-balanced fertiliser low in nitrogen (2-10-6) in late July or early August. Use a handful to each plant, making sure not to touch the leaves, and hoe it into the soil carefully. Some gardeners fertilise their plants with liquid manure every two weeks from the time the buds appear until flowering has ended. Do keep dahlias free of weeds and a mulch of compost, peat or leaf-mould will help here as well as retain moisture for the plant.

All types of dahlias are superb in borders and the dwarf bedding varieties can also be most effective in windowboxes or other outdoor containers. Wherever you plant them they should get as much sun as possible. If the flowers are not intended for indoor decoration it is advisable to remove those that fade, to prevent seeds forming and exhausting the plant to the detriment of future bloom.

Most gardeners grow extra dahlias just for cutting and there is a proper way to cut these flowers. They should always be cut with a really sharp knife in the morning or late evening and never in the heat of the day. Make a slantwise cut at the base of the stem and slit the stem for about 2in from the base to allow for an adequate intake of water. Strip leaves from the parts of the stem which will be immersed in water so that they won't decay.

Immediately after frost blackens and kills the foliage, cut off dahlia stems to 6in or so above the ground, lift the roots carefully out of the ground with a fork, shake off earth that remains and leave the tubers on the ground for a few hours to dry. Put them in a well ventilated, frost-free place indoors to finish drying off for a few days. Then they can be stored in a cellar or other frost-free place over the winter. Tubers should never be heaped on top of each other but stored carefully in slightly moist peat or sand. Examine the stored tubers occasionally to make sure they are not drying out and shrivelling. When storing or during storage if any damage is noted the damaged portion should be cut away and cut surfaces dusted with sulphur. Dormant tubers may be started in growth earlier than usual by potting them in February or March. The tubers should not be buried but pressed into a light fibrous soil mixed with peat. They should not be soaked but only kept slightly moist.

CHOOSING DAHLIAS

Some exhibition varieties of dahlias can be fairly expensive but the average gardener who wants a splendid garden show as well as dahlias for indoor decoration will find that there are scores upon scores of reasonably priced varieties available, every bit as effective as the pricier show blooms.

There have been various systems of classifying dahlias according to habit of growth and size of flower and until quite recently these systems varied from country to country. Classification has now been completely revised and a new system internationally adopted which divides horticultural varieties into ten classes or types. These are:

I. Single. II. Anemone-flowered. III. Collerette. IV. Paeony-flowered. V. Decorative. VI. Ball. VII. Pompon. VIII. Cactus. IX. Semi-cactus. X. Miscellaneous.

The National Dahlia Society in Britain also subdivides four of the classes according to size of flower, which I have used in this text. As the size of flowers will vary in different climates the American Dahlia Society does not follow this specific sizing arrangement.

Amateur gardeners need not concern themselves too closely with the intricacies of the classification system nor with the rigid rules for judging and exhibiting of dahlias in competitive classes set out by the dahlia societies. Varieties from all ten classes are not generally available and the rarer and more expensive hybrids must be searched for in the catalogues of specialist suppliers. But most suppliers will have a good selection of the most popular and easy-to-grow types and varieties at very reasonable prices (see page 261).

Page 261 A selection of dahlias—(A) semi-cactus, (B) decorative, (C) cactus, (D) collerette, (E) ball, (F) pompon, (G) anemone-flowered and (H) Topmix

In recommending varieties I am following the nomenclature used in most catalogues and by the majority of suppliers. The normal heights of plants are given in feet in parenthesis after the name of the variety and those specially commended as long-lasting cut flowers are marked with an asterisk.

Cactus and Semi-cactus Dahlias have distinctive cactus-like or chrysanthemum-type double flowers, the ray florets usually pointed. The flower form varies slightly and you can purchase varieties according to size of bloom. All range in height from 3–5ft, all have cane-hard stems, all come in a wide range of bright colours, and all thrive in sunny border positions.

Large-flowered Cactus and Semi-Cactus Dahlias (flowers 8–10in across)

Belle Dame (4)*   salmon pink (semi-cactus)
Colour Spectacle (4)   orange tipped white (semi-cactus)
Gold Crown (4)*   maize yellow (semi-cactus)
Cina Lombaert (4)*   salmon with yellow centre (semi-cactus)
Moonglow (4)   pure yellow (semi-cactus)
Pride of Holland ($4\frac{1}{2}$)*   deep pink (cactus)

Medium-flowered Cactus and Semi-Cactus Dahlias (flowers 6–8in across)

Apache ($3\frac{1}{2}$)*   bright red, fimbriated (semi-cactus)
Apple Blossom ($3\frac{1}{2}$)*   rose with lighter centre (cactus)
Arsenal (4)   light sulphur yellow (cactus)
Beauty of Aalsmeer ($3\frac{1}{2}$)   dark pink (semi-cactus)
Clarion ($3\frac{1}{2}$)*   brick red (semi-cactus)
Firebird (syn. **Vuurvogel**) ($3\frac{1}{2}$–4)*   primrose yellow shading to orange red (semi-cactus)
Good Earth (4)   pure lilac pink (cactus)
Hazard (4)   mandarin red and apricot (semi-cactus)
Helga ($3\frac{1}{2}$)*   dark cherry red (semi-cactus)
Highness (4)   pure white (semi-cactus)
Hit Parade (4)*   signal red (semi-cactus)
Hoek's Glorie (4)*   lavender (cactus)
Hurricane ($3\frac{1}{2}$)*   cherry red (cactus)
Morning Kiss (4)*   clear pink (semi-cactus)

New York (3)   blood red (semi-cactus)
Orfeo (3½)*   bright purple (cactus)
Piquant (4)*   scarlet red with white tips (semi-cactus)
Pioneer (4–5)   lemon yellow (semi-cactus)
Popular Guest (4)*   purple rose with lighter centre, fimbriated (semi-cactus)
Rotterdam (4)*   dark velvet red (semi-cactus)
Top Choice (4½)*   flame red and yellow (semi-cactus)

Small-flowered Cactus and Semi-Cactus Dahlias (flowers 4–6in across)

Border Princess (2)*   salmon orange (cactus) (dwarf bedding)
Doris Day (3½)*   cardinal red (cactus)
Hoek's Yellow (4)*   creamy primrose (semi-cactus)
My Love (3)*   creamy white (semi-cactus)
Park Jewel (1½)   phlox pink (semi-cactus) (dwarf bedding)
Park Princess (2)*   pink and rose (cactus) (dwarf bedding)
Preference (3)*   coral pink (semi-cactus)
Purity (2½)*   pure white (semi-cactus)
Purple Gem (3)*   cyclamen purple (semi-cactus)

Miniature-flowered Cactus and Semi-Cactus Dahlias (flowers under 4in across)

Dentelle de Venise (2)   pure white, fimbriated (cactus)

Decorative Dahlias are of more or less compact or solid form, producing flat flower heads on strong stems. The fully double blooms show no disc. The ray florets are broad, generally flat or slightly twisted and usually bluntly pointed. They are of vigorous habit, make long-lasting cut flowers, and range in height from 2–6ft. Varieties are available according to size of flower.

Giant-flowered Decorative Dahlias (flowers over 10in across)

Holland Festival (4)*   chinese coral
Jocondo (4)*   reddish purple
Lavender Perfection (4)   lavender pink
Lavengro (4½)*   lilac mauve

Large-flowered Decorative Dahlias (flowers 8–10in across)
Dutch Triumph ($4\frac{1}{2}$)*   primrose yellow tipped peach
Ludwig's Score ($4\frac{1}{2}$)*   purple
Showman's Delight (4)   blend of orange and yellow

Medium-flowered Decorative Dahlias (flowers 6–8in across)
Deuil du Roi Albert (4)*   violet purple tipped white
Deutschland ($4\frac{1}{2}$)*   signal red
Duet (3–4)   dark red and white
Majuba (4)*   blood red
Peter (4)*   purple pink
Peter's Glory (4)*   lilac rose with white centre
Red and White (3)   clear red and white
Rosella ($3\frac{1}{2}$–4)*   lilac pink
Snow Country (3)   pure white
Snowstorm (5)*   pure white
Tartan (4)   deep maroon tipped white
Terpo (6)*   blood red

Small-flowered Decorative Dahlias (flowers 4–6in across)
Arabian Night ($3\frac{1}{2}$)*   deep maroon almost black
Chinese Lantern (4)   orange red on yellow background
Gerrie Hoek ($3\frac{1}{2}$)*   deep pink
Glory of Heemstede (4)*   primrose yellow
House of Orange (4)   soft amber orange
Miramar (3–4)*   light vermilion
Rocquencourt (2)   garnet red (dwarf bedding)

Miniature-flowered Decorative Dahlias (flowers under 4in across)
David Howard (2)   deep orange yellow (dwarf bedding)
Kochelsee ($3\frac{1}{2}$)*   fiery red
Lilianne Ballego (3–$3\frac{1}{2}$)*   bronze
Magnificat (3)*   orange red
Musetts ($3\frac{1}{2}$)*   red and white

Pompon Dahlias, the smaller form of the Decorative type, free-flowering
and producing little compact globular flower heads, used to be classed in
four sizes. Under the lastest classification, however, only those with
flowers under 2in across remain pompon dahlias. All varieties range from

3–3½ft in height and are excellent for cutting as well as graceful and dainty garden plants.

Pompon Dahlias (flowers under 2in across)

Albino* pure white
Doxy* white
Lydia* showy red
Moor Place* deep purple
Potgieter* primrose yellow
Regulus* purple violet

Ball Dahlias are what used to be the larger-flowered pompon dahlias, with flowers 2–6in across. They have fully double flowers, ball-shaped or slightly flattened. Stem heights range from 3–4ft and the neat, compact flowers make them equally useful in the garden and as cut flowers. The ray florets are blunt or rounded at the tips, with margins spirally arranged. They are classed in two sizes, but no varieties with flowers 4–6in across are currently available from Holland.

Miniature-flowered Ball Dahlias (flowers 2–4in across)

Amusing* yellow and red
Ben Hur purple
Deepest Yellow* deep yellow
Frits garnet red with white tips
Little Dirk* soft lilac pink
Nero dark red with purple sheen
Stolze von Berlin (syn. **Pride of Berlin**) pink
Zonnegoud* canary yellow

Single Dahlias. Mignon dahlias have lost their name in the recent reclassification and are now known as single dahlias. These are often catalogued or displayed as dwarf bedding varieties for most of them are 14–20in tall. They produce an abundance of flowers, with a single outer ring of florets, which may overlap, the centre forming a disc, throughout the summer and into the autumn.

Single (dwarf-bedding) Dahlias

G. F. Hemerik soft orange
Irene van der Zwet soft yellow

Murillo   lilac pink with darker centre
Nelly Geerlings   scarlet red
Sneezy   pure white

And don't miss the **Topmix** dahlias, a beautiful recently introduced strain of baby plants with lilliputian single flowers blooming from June into the autumn in a range of bright colours. They are incorporated in the Single Dahlia class; are superb for edging or massing in borders because of their free-flowering habit and dwarf stature with stems only 10in in height. Topmix dahlias are marvellous for table decorations too. They are generally sold in mixtures of pink, red, yellow and white but some suppliers provide the following named varieties:

Bambino   white
Bonne Esperance   pink
Chessy   bronze yellow
Facet   bronze
Reddy   red

Collerette Dahlias (sometimes spelt collarette) are a lovely artistic strain of single-flowered dahlias in a class of their own. They have blooms with a single outer ring of generally flat ray florets, which may overlay, with a ring of small florets (the collar), the centre forming a disc. Free-flowering and long-lasting when cut, they range in height from 30–40in.

Collerette Dahlias

Brides Bouquet   white with white collar
Clair de Lune   pale sulphur yellow with cream collar
Kaiserwalzer   fiery red with yellow collar
La Cierva   purple with white collar
La Giaconda   scarlet red with golden yellow collar
Libretto   velvet red with white collar

Anemone-flowered Dahlias have flowers with one or more outer rings of generally flattened ray florets surrounding a dense group of tubular florets, which are longer than the disc florets in Single dahlias, and showing no disc. The varieties are all 10–18in tall.

Anemone-flowered Dahlias

Bridesmaid ivory white
Fabel cardinal red
Guinea yellow
Honey apricot pink
Roulette pure pink
Siemen Doorenbosch light magenta
Thalia light pink

Chapter Thirteen

MORE BULBS FOR THE SUMMER GARDENS

SUMMER COLOUR and exotic spectacle in the garden is really quite simple with spring-planted bulbs. In addition to the 'big three'—gladioli, lilies and dahlias—there are number of unusual and lesser known bulbs that will provide a succession of display from the late tulips until the autumn frosts.

Summer-flowering bulbs, with the exception of lilies, are not as hardy as the spring-flowering bulbs but given sunny sites and well-drained soil these more tender beauties are easy to grow. Like lilies some of them, including anemones, galtonias, montbretias and ranunculus, can be left in the ground during the winter months, provided they are protected from frosts by suitable mulching. The others must be lifted after the first frosts and stored indoors during winter in a frost-free, well-ventilated place until planting time the following spring.

With spring-planted summer-flowering bulbs any amateur can produce a blazing and exciting panorama in the garden from June into October. With stem heights ranging from a few inches to over 3ft, with a colour range to put the rainbow to shame, with the strangest and most exotic of forms, there are summer-flowering bulbs to bring new life and a new look to every corner of the garden, from beds and borders to the rockery and terrace. Many will help bring summer into the home too, as long-lasting cut flowers.

ACIDANTHERA

Sweetly scented acidanthera with their distinctive star-like flowers and narrow gladiolus-like foliage keep a fragrant breath of spring hovering in the garden from August into October. These tender members of the iris family are native to the Ethiopian highlands but adapt themselves to most climates. There are only a few species in the genus and the most vigorous and easy to grow is **A. murielae** (see page 173), with stems $2\frac{1}{2}$–$3\frac{1}{2}$ft in height. This species from the Goa district of Western Ethiopia was named after an Englishwoman, Mrs. Muriel Arkskine, and when it received a Royal Horticultural Society Award of Merit in 1936 it was actually classified as Gladiolus murielae. It was subsequently identified as an acidanthera species and the Dutch introduced them to the amateur gardener just before World War II.

The flowers are from 2–4in across with a large perianth tube and segments forming a kind of a star, the upper portion lying horizontally. They are clear white with a large dark purple blotch at the throat and really strongly scented. There are 5–6 blooms per stem which open in succession over a period of weeks from about mid-August into October although they have been known to flower as early as late July in specially favourable warm positions. Acidanthera are resistant to wet weather and even heavy rain does not spot them. Consequently they are superb for cutting and will last for a long time in water if picked in bud.

Spring planting should not be undertaken until the soil is reasonably warm, about mid-May. Plant the corms, which are smaller than those of gladioli and fibrous-coated, 3in deep and about 6–9in apart in full sun and in sites sheltered from the wind. Any well-drained soil will do although acidanthera prefer light soil and appreciate the addition of leafmould or thoroughly decomposed manure. They look outstanding in clusters on their own and can be most effectively interplanted with other summer-flowering bulbs like galtonia or chincherinchees in an all-white border display. Although somewhat slow to start, particularly if planted too early, they are strong and rapid growers.

These graceful plants dislike frost and corms should be lifted as soon as the foliage becomes discoloured. After lifting allow the foliage to die off completely before laying out the corms in trays or boxes to ripen. They should be stored in a warm, dry place where the temperature throughout the winter does not fall below 60° F (15·5° C). Gardeners can also grow acidanthera in the cool greenhouse, treating them just like ixia.

ANEMONE

Anemones are discussed in detail in Chapter 8 as they can be planted in the late autumn for bloom in April–May, but I am mentioning them here

Page 270 Anemone de Caen

once more because they can also be planted in March–April for a superb summer show. I usually plant a selection of all kinds in the autumn and extra tubers of the de Caen and St. Brigid strains in the spring.

BEGONIAS

Begonias, named after Michel Bégon, patron of botany and one-time governor of French Canada, are a fantastic and large genus of plants composed of hundreds of species native to warm regions all over the world and incredibly varied in size, form and habit. Only one type comes within the scope of this book—tuberous begonias—(see page 173) which are no longer species but the creation of horticulturalists. The fibrous-rooted begonias are not bulbous plants and are consequently excluded. Even so, tuberous begonias in themselves are extremely diverse with flowers resembling hollyhocks, roses, carnations, camellias and daffodils, both single and double. They are the largest and showiest of shade loving, mid-summer flowers and have more applications than any other summer flowering bulb.

No flower has quite so many ancestors and few have undergone so many complicated modifications. It is virtually impossible to trace accurately the genetic descent of the modern tuberous begonia. The creation of large-flowered begonias dates back to the 1860s and they are primarily the results of work by English and French horticulturalists.

A number of kinds of tuberous begonias are available to the amateur gardener today, each with different applications. The larger kinds of varied shape and innumerable colours with thick stems about 15in high and large leaves are superb plants for a shaded border. Smaller and more compact begonias may be used dramatically for edging borders or paths or as foundation plantings. Or they may be grouped in beds or grown in boxes, urns or other outdoor containers on porches or terraces or in windowboxes. Still another sort of tuberous begonia is a drooper or trailer with showers of smaller blooms in clusters on pendant stems, ideal for planting in hanging baskets suspended from porch roof or terrace post or in boxes or other containers on balconies, terraces or even rooftops.

The colours of tuberous begonias are truly magnificent, ranging from white through all the clearest pinks to rose, vermilion, scarlet and crimson. Every shade of yellow, gold, salmon and orange is also present. Although these members of the begonia family, botanically described as begonia tuber-hybrida, prefer moist semi-shady positions they will also bloom with gay abandon in full sun.

Tuberous begonias, however, need an advance start, for they are so susceptible to cold that they cannot be moved outdoors until the weather is continuously warm. But an advance start indoors will mean prompt bloom after the June move outdoors.

The tubers will sprout indoors as reliably as tomato seeds. When you obtain the tubers in February or March place them close together, level with the surface, in flats or boxes of damp peat. Keep moist and shaded at 50–60° F (10–16° C) until 4–6 leaves have developed (when sprouts are about 2–3in tall), and pot up in 5–7in pots. Begonias need rich soil to produce their marvellous flowers. So fill the pots with a half and half mixture of rich soil, into which well-rotted manure has been mixed, and peat, working a little bone meal into the bottom half of the pot. Grow in shade at 60° F (16° C), watering regularly without wetting foliage. Except in the warm south and southwest of the United States it will be late May or June before the started tuberous begonias can be moved outdoors safely, to garden beds or outdoor containers. Plunge the plant and pot into the ground or, if preferred, take the plants out of the pots and set them into the ground. Tubers can be planted directly outdoors at the same time, of course, but will take a good six weeks longer to start flowering.

There's little to do once the plants have been moved into the garden except wait for the flowers. At the first sign of a bud, tie each stem to a bamboo stake. This is a safeguard since flowers are heavy and stems brittle. Never let the rich soil dry out and water if rainfall is scarce or does not penetrate the heavy foliage. Do avoid overhead drip as well. For gardeners who want the largest flowers allow the central bud only on each stem to develop, removing side buds when tiny.

At the first indication of frost stop watering and prepare the tubers for winter hibernation. After the foliage matures in early autumn, lift and set in boxes of leafy soil, avoiding damage to both tubers and foliage. In a short time the plants will have withered and the stems can then be cut off an inch above the tuber and the roots shaken free of earth. The tubers should then be stored in boxes or flats of dried peat in a warm, frost-free place where temperatures will not fall below 42° F (6° C). To keep track of colours and kinds the tubers should be labelled carefully when lifted and stored separately.

Potted begonias can be placed indoors instead of in the garden. Potting up is done at the same time but a good potting compost enriched with bone meal can be used. The tubers can be potted first in 3in pots and later, when a few inches of growth has been made, be repotted into 5–7in pots. Alternatively tubers can be potted directly into larger pots. Shade and moisture are essential for success, for if they are lacking there will be trouble from bud dropping. When the flowers appear it will be apparent that single female flowers develop on both sides of each male double flower. These feminine intruders should be removed. Flower stems will need support in pots as well as in the garden. Watering should be continued after flowering has ceased until the foliage starts to turn yellow. Dry off the plants then by gradually reducing the amount of water given. When the compost is quite dry the pot-grown begonias can spend the winter dry, as they are, in a warmish frost-free place. In February, before growth begins again, they must be repotted in fresh compost.

The Dutch export to Britain and North America a splendid choice of tuberous begonias. Both the large-flowered single and double begonias are upright plants. The **single-flowered,** single-petalled begonias are sold by colour and come in copper, dark red, orange, pink, salmon, scarlet, white and yellow. Mixtures are also available. There is a single-flowered strain known as **crispa** with deckle-edged flowers, available in the same colours. Leaves are large and broad, differing somewhat in texture and intensity of colour. Some are smooth with a high sheen; others with a rougher surface and even a slight fuzz, and still others with a reddish tinge and red edging.

There are a number of kinds of **double-flowered** begonias available. There is a range of **camellia-flowered** varieties sold by colour and coming in rich scarlet, orange, salmon, dark red, pink, white and yellow as well as in mixtures.

A **rose-flowered** begonia, a lovely two-toned double with neat well-formed flowers in pink toned to white to the edge, is on sale and usually catalogued as **Bouton Rose.**

Fimbriated begonias, sometimes called **double frilled** with full double flowers and finely deckle-edged petals, are obtainable in the same range of colours as the camellia-flowered begonias.

Marmorata begonias are also doubles with bicoloured marbled petals. Excellent for bedding or pots this kind is available beautifully marbled on violet rose or carmine ground, the petals attractively ruffled and waved.

All the other begonias are **small-flowered.** There is **B. bertinii** with orange red single flowers combined with beautiful foliage, very prolific, compact and sun-proof. It is superb for bedding and for cool greenhouse cultivation.

B. multiflora, available in named varieties, is very floriferous, with slender stems of equal height, single- or double-flowered and carrying several flowers per stem, with a neat and compact habit. Varieties include:

Ami Jean Bart   bronze
Flamboyante (double)   brilliant cherry red
Galle Superba   salmon orange
Helene Harms (semi-double)   rich copper yellow
Madame Richard Galle (double)   copper

B. multiflora maxima are a new development in tuberous begonias. They are a double-flowered type with free-flowering blooms larger than B. multiflora varieties, as they are derived from crosses between B. multiflora and large-flowered begonias. They form bushy compact plants ideal for bedding and for pot culture as well. They are available by colour rather than named variety, including light pink, rose, yellow, white, salmon and orange. Mixtures are also obtainable.

B. pendula are the graceful begonias of pendulous, drooping or trailing habit and these splendid plants with delicate foliage bear a profusion of semi-double flowers on long limp floral stems. Give them homes in hanging baskets, tubs or windowboxes and enjoy mass display all through the summer months. They are available with crimson, scarlet, rose, salmon, orange, yellow or white flowers.

CANNA

Cannas, members of the canna family, and known as canna lilies, are very well known in the United States and are now becoming more popular for bedding in Britain. These truly handsome plants with broad green or purplish leaves and flowers of bright red, carmine pink, salmon pink and bright orange on stems 2–3ft in height, are frequently seen in public parks, planted in borders or in tubs. They are probably one of our oldest decorative plants and were certainly grown in Italy as early as the middle of the sixteenth century. The name comes from the Greek 'kanna', meaning 'a reed' and the 50-odd species of the genus are related to the banana. They are native to tropical regions.

Cannas are not true bulbs for they have thick, fleshy rhizomes rather similar to those of the iris. Because of the multiple hybridisation of cannas over the years modern varieties are all botanically grouped together under the name Canna hybrids.

Canna lilies flower from summer into autumn and are quite easy to grow, although like begonias, they require an early start. The rhizomes should be planted in March in rich soil, preferably equal parts of loam, well-rotted manure, leaf-mould and sand, either in pots 4–5in in diameter or in flats. These should be placed in a sunny greenhouse or indoors at a temperature of about 65° F (20° C). The plants should be watered sparingly at first, increasing amounts as the foliage develops. In late April they can be hardened off in a cold frame or in sheltered positions outdoors if the weather is mild, and planted in beds in June, about 18–24in apart. The soil should be well dug over and enriched with decayed manure beforehand. Sunny positions and liberal watering are essential if really gorgeous flowers are to appear on the $2\frac{1}{2}$–3ft stems.

Cannas must be lifted before the first frost of autumn, dried off and placed in a well ventilated frost-free place. In February or March the rhizomes should be cleaned and divided before replanting. Garden centres and other retailers sell cannas by colour or named variety.

FREESIA

The latest introduction to the range of summer-flowering bulbs for the garden are freesias, which until recently have been grown only in greenhouses. By a very special method of treatment and storage the Dutch have been able to retard development of the corms so that they can now be planted outdoors from mid-April onward to flower from late July to October. Freesias are, of course, tailor-made for the warm climates of the United States and the corms do not require pre-cooling before being planted in sunny positions.

This is good news for every gardener for the delicate pastel flowers are every bit as colourful and sweetly scented as those tender winter-flowering freesias commercially forced under glass for the florists. The new outdoor freesias have the same narrow leaves and attractive tubular flowers of the greenhouse freesias but the stems are somewhat shorter, ranging between 10–15in, and there are not quite as many flowers per stem. They are delightful in sunny moist corners of the garden and should be planted 2in deep and some 2–3in apart in well worked over and fairly rich soil. They like sheltered positions and must be watered regularly in dry weather, particularly during the early growing stages. The corms should be discarded after flowering and a fresh supply purchased each spring.

There is a whole range of lovely colours—white, pink, yellow, orange, red, mauve, purple and blue. Each stem bears about half a dozen erect tubular flowers. Named after the German physician, Friedrich Heinrich Thoedor Freese, these members of the iris family are native to South Africa but no single pure species is cultivated these days. The Dutch have undertaken the selection and systematic hybridisation of freesias and the hybrids now available are superb flowers. You can buy outdoor freesias in gay rainbow mixtures (see page 173). Naturally, they make dainty and fragrant cut flowers.

GALTONIA

Galtonia (syn. Hyacinthus) **candicans** is the botanical name of the 'summer hyacinth' or 'spire lily', that tall, conspicuous, sweetly-scented pure white flower that rather resembles the more familiar hyacinth of spring. It is in fact closely related to hyacinths orientalis of the Middle East although this particular member of the lily family is native to South Africa. It was introduced to Europe much later than the hyacinth, about 1870, and was named after the British anthropologist, Sir Francis Galton.

The large bulbs, quite inexpensive, produce a tuft of large strap-shaped leaves and strong erect flower spikes on which in July–August appear loose racemes of 15–20 delicately scented and large drooping pure milky white bells. The stems, in contrast to the spring flowering hyacinth, soar 2½–4ft in height. Its stature coupled with the pointed shape of the floral raceme has earned it the nickname of 'spire lily'. It is a hardy bulb which need not be lifted except in the coldest areas but it does appreciate a winter mulch.

Galtonia candicans likes sunny, well drained positions and is a good subject for the back of borders, for planting among shrubs or for siting in clusters. Just half a dozen bulbs in a group will produce a bold and showy picture and, if left undisturbed, will provide a grand display for years. The bulbs can even be naturalised in grass if you take the trouble to lift the turf and thoroughly cultivate and enrich the soil beneath it.

The bulbs can be planted from March–April some 5–6in deep and about

Page 277 Galtonia candicans

6–8in apart. If you do not plan to lift them after the foliage dies down do double the space between bulbs to allow for the spread of clumps. I like planting them with acidanthera and find them particularly showy when interplanted with scarlet gladioli.

Galtonias make excellent cut flowers and many gardeners grow them in the cutting garden. Others grow them in pots in the greenhouse. If potted in early spring they will flower in summer but they can also be potted in early winter for unusual spring flower. Bulbs should be placed individually in 5–6in pots in fairly rich compost. After planting and watering place the pots in cold frames and cover with sand until growth begins, after which they can be brought into a warm greenhouse. They need water and liquid manure until they flower. Bulbs grown in pots cannot be used for potting again but can be planted in rich garden soil for outdoor cutting.

ISMENE

Anyone who has not heard of a summer daffodil should remedy the situation by becoming acquainted with a certain native of the Peruvian Andes. Bulb catalogues list these flowers with glorious umbels of 2–5 large pure white trumpet-shaped blooms of great fragrance as **ismene calathina** which is a synonym for the proper botanical name of hymenocallis narcissiflora. Botanists gave this large genus of the amaryllis family this particular name from the cup-shaped membrane which joins together the base of the stamens superficially like the corona of a narcissus.

The species **I. calathina** is almost hardy and an improved hybrid named **Advance** is now available to gardeners. In full bloom the flowers look like fantastic king-size daffodils for each white and fragrant bloom is a trumpet with long narrow reflexed segments. They flower in July–August on stems 18in or more tall, with decorative long leaves.

Another hybrid available is **Festalis** (see page 174), also with pure white elegantly curved flowers, sweet-scented and with gold-tipped anthers. It is very free-flowering on stems $1\frac{1}{2}$–2ft tall.

The fat bulbs of both must be kept dry and warm in winter and not planted in the garden until late May at the earliest. Choose sunny, sheltered positions and plant the bulbs 5–6in deep and 8–12in apart in well-drained soil rich in humus, consisting of a mixture of peat, leaf-mould and sand.

Page 279 Ismene festalis

These Peruvian daffodils, sometimes called 'spider lilies', grow very quickly, the first flowers appearing as early as a month after planting. They should be watered freely in dry weather. The plants must be lifted before the first frosts and bulbs stored in boxes filled with dry peat or sand and kept in a dry, warm store until planting time comes round again.

Spectacular in the summer garden both hybrids make long-lasting cut flowers. They will also thrive in pots in a cool greenhouse. Pot in spring or summer, when new growth is about to begin, with tips of bulbs just buried. Water freely during active growth and shade the plants from strong summer sun. Applications of dilute liquid manure during the growing period produce superior flowers. They need repotting only every few years but pots should be given a top dressing every spring. Night temperatures in the greenhouse should not be allowed to fall below 50° F (10° C).

MONTBRETIA

Montbretia (syn. Tritonia) (see page 174) are half-hardy relatives of gladioli but smaller, more graceful and more informal in growth. The leaves are sword-shaped and deeply grooved and each corm produces from July–September from 1–3 spikes between 1–2ft tall bearing a host of lovely tubular flowers in yellow, orange, copper, red or in combinations of these colours.

Like gladioli they are members of the iris family and although generally listed as montbretia in bulb catalogues are botanically classified as tritonia. Like most gladioli they are natives of South Africa. Like gladioli again they need plenty of water when growing and flowering. But unlike gladioli once established they multiply rapidly and do not require lifting in the autumn. As the corms spread rapidly, however, they do need lifting every 3–4 years for the clumps to be divided and immediately replanted.

Montbretia, named for Antoine de Montbret, one of the botanists accompanying Napoleon's forces to Egypt, are most useful summer flowering subjects for quite apart from enlivening any mixed border they flourish along the base of light hedges and between shrubs. And they make dainty and long-lasting cut flowers too.

Plant the inexpensive corms in deep, well drained soil with plenty of leaf-mould or well-decayed manure in sites which ensure they get sun for at least part of the day. Depth of planting is 3–4in, spacing is 4–5in, and planting time is from April through May. It is important, however, to plant the corms when you get them from your supplier and not leave them lying about. Splendid mixtures are available providing the widest colour range.

ORNITHOGALUM

This genus is covered fully in Chapter 9 but a reminder that **O. thyrsoides** or the chincherinchee which blooms from July–September should be planted from March–May is considered pertinent here.

OXALIS

There is one species in this vast genus of over 800 which should be planted in spring for summer flower. It is **O. deppei,** a native of Mexico, which is known as the 'good luck' plant or 'four-leaved clover' because its broad leaves have four red-spotted leaflets each, like those of red clover. It grows from 6–12in tall with dainty clusters of copper-red flowers blooming from July–September. **O. deppei alba** is the pure white form.

These are lovely little plants for sunny borders, semi-shady positions in rockeries or for growing in pots indoors. Plant them outdoors in March–April in any well-drained soil about 4–6in deep and about the same distance apart. The tubers should be lifted and divided about October and stored over the winter in a well-ventilated frost-free place. For indoor culture pot the tubers in spring before growth starts about 1–2in deep in 5in pots using a light but nourishing compost. Water sparingly at first but freely when in active growth. Keep dry when the foliage naturally dies down after flowering and dry when bulbs are dormant. The bulbs should be repotted in fresh soil every year.

RANUNCULUS

No plants produce a brighter or more gorgeous effect between late May and August than multi-coloured ranunculus (see page 174) with their large double or semi-double flowers in lovely shades of yellow, orange, scarlet, crimson, pink, purple and white and deeply scalloped leaves on 9–16in stems. This very large genus of fibrous and tuberous-rooted plants, among which is the common buttercup, derives its name from the Latin 'rana' or 'frog', apparently because so many species grow in damp places

Page 282 Ornithogalum thyrsoides

such as are inhabited by frogs. All cultivated or garden ranunculi stem from a single species, R. asiaticus, originating in Asia Minor, where it has been cultivated even prior to biblical days. They do not have true bulbs but fleshy tuberous rhizomes with clearly discernible divisions known as 'claws'.

Cultivation of ranunculi is similar to that of anemones. They are eminently adaptable to the warm climates of the United States and will produce a fine show of colour if the special instructions for the cultivation and care of anemones in warm climates (page 197) are followed.,

You can plant them from the end of February in any well-drained humus-filled soil, claws down, and cover them with sand and then soil so that the crown of the tuber is about 1½in below the surface. Space the tubers about 6–8in apart. Sites can be sunny or semi-shady but the soil should be moist when planting. Do not water too much after planting but watering should be liberal when the plants are in active growth. In warmer areas ranunculi can be planted in the autumn in the garden or cold frames and mulched 4in deep with dead leaves after the first hard frost. Ranunculi do not like clay soils and with garden soil of this nature it is advisable to plant the tubers in beds raised 5in above the normal soil level. Whether planted in groups on their own or combined with anemones, ranunculi provide glorious splashes of colour and are useful as cut flowers too.

Many interesting types and varieties of ranunculi have been developed from R. asiaticus as a result of much selecting and hybridising. The blooms range from 1–4in diameter according to type and variety. Four distinctly different types are available to gardeners today.

French ranunculus were evolved in France late in the nineteenth century and the semi-double flowers were later improved by the Dutch. This is a very vigorous type with large blooms and in many delightful colours, all having a central black blotch. They flower in May–June on 9–12in stems and like sunny sheltered positions. Best planted everywhere in February–March they can be purchased in choice mixtures or in named varieties.

Paeony-flowered ranunculus were developed during the first quarter of the twentieth century in Italy and possibly simultaneously in Holland. They have large double or semi-double flowers blooming from May to July on 10–14in stems and are notably free-flowering. They do best in sunny positions. Depending upon climatic conditions they can be planted from December through April. They too are available in rainbow mixtures or in named varieties.

Persian ranunculus have long been grown in Turkish gardens and were introduced into Europe about 1700. The flowers can be single or double on 10–16in stems but they are medium or small in size. Obtainable in mixtures or in named varieties they should not be planted until February–March.

Turban ranunculus are the hardiest of the lot and can be planted from autumn into spring. They have large globular or almost rose-shaped double or semi-double flowers on 9–12in stems and bloom as early as June. Their showy and brilliant colours look best in full sun. They too have long been cultivated in Turkish gardens and were brought to the attention of Europeans as early as 1580 by Carolus Clusius. This type can be purchased in mixtures or in named varieties too.

All ranunculi will welcome a mulch of peat in April or May. The tubers can be lifted when the foliage dies down and stored in a cool but frost-free, well ventilated space until planting time comes round again, or can be left in the ground for season after season of bloom if you give them a dressing of fertiliser each autumn and protect them carefully from frosts. Ranunculi can also be grown in a cool greenhouse, if planted in pots and plunged outdoors until well rooted.

TIGRIDIA

Perhaps the most exotic and spectacular of all summer flowering bulbs is the tigridia (syn. ferraria) which is popularly called the 'peacock tiger flower' or 'Mexican shell-flower'. The quaint shape, colours and habit of the flowers attract immediate attention. The blooms are open and shaped rather like a wide shallow bowl with three broad petals which seem to droop slightly and three much smaller inner petals which are flattened against the bottom of the bowl. The stamens and pistil are held erect in a long tube at the centre.

Tigridia, which are members of the iris family and are related to gladioli —apparent from the shape of the leaves—come from the mountains of Mexico and South America. But only one species, **T. pavonia** (see page 191), produces large 6in diameter blooms with unique combinations of rich colours. In July and August each 10–16in stem produces a sequence of up to 6 flowers. Each bloom reveals its beauty for a single day and fades away but the others follow on and succession is further maintained by planting the small, ovoid, elongated corms in clumps of about 2 dozen. Basically the flowers are orange scarlet, spotted with deep crimson at the base of segments, but in the mixtures available from garden centres and other suppliers there are colours ranging from white to violet.

Tigridia are easy to cultivate, as easy as gladioli. Plant the corms 3–4in deep and about 6in apart in well-drained humus-filled soil in late March or April, later in colder areas. They need warm and sunny border positions to give of their best, plenty of water just like gladioli, and applications of peat to keep them moist throughout the growing season. To induce richer colourings and continuous flowering add liquid manure to the water from the time the first bud appears. When they have finished flowering about the end of August allow the leaves to wither and then lift and store them for the winter in the same way as gladioli corms. In warmer areas they can be left in the ground if heavily mulched against winter frosts.

ZEPHYRANTHES

This is a most attractive genus of bulbous plants belonging to the amaryllis family and related both to the hippeastrum and habranthus. It is little known in Britain and Europe but can certainly be grown in the garden in warm and sunny positions if protected in winter. There is a certain amount of confusion about these plants, even in bulb catalogues, and they are known as 'flowers of the west wind', 'zephyr lilies', 'rain lilies' and 'fairy lilies'. They are native to both North and South America.

The flowers are always single on short stiff stems. The perianth is tubular or funnel-shaped widening into a trumpet with six equal and overlapping segments, joined at the base only.

Z. candida is the hardiest species, producing pure white flowers about 1½–2in long and rather crocus-like in September–October on stems up to 8in tall. The leaves of this species from Argentina are narrow and linear and longer than the floral stem. The ovoid bulbs multiply rapidly from offsets and consequently form large clumps, but require winter protection. The flowers enjoy warm sunny border positions and can be planted *en masse* or used as permanent edging. The bulbs can be planted in October or in April, about 4in deep and the same distance apart in porous soil containing plenty of leaf-mould and some sand. They are also excellent cool greenhouse subjects and can be potted in autumn or spring. About 5–6 bulbs should be planted in 6in pots in a mixture of loam, peat and sand in equal parts. They flower more prolifically if allowed to become pot-bound. The bulbs need 10–12 weeks of rest after flowering is over and the leaves have withered, during which period they should be

Page 286 Zephyranthes robusta

kept dry. If this method is followed it is possible to have Z. candida flowering under glass twice a year.

Z. robusta, also from the Argentine, is in fact botanically **Habranthus robustus** and can be catalogued either way. Its flowers are larger than those of Z. candida, measuring some 3in across by 3in long. They are single and funnel-shaped and open very wide. Flowering time is as early as June but can continue into September, and the flowers are a beautiful pale pink with deeper veining and with a greenish white throat. The base of the segments are green on the outside, while the pistil carries pink stigmata and the stamens are bright yellow. Stems are stout and range from 6–10in in height. The linear leaves, slightly glaucous, appear in spring. Plant the oval, long-necked bulbs with dark brown tunics in March–April, about 2–3in deep and the same distance apart in humus-rich soil in the rock garden or border and be sure to choose sunny positions. In autumn the bulbs must be lifted and stored over winter in a dry frost-free place. The bulbs which are propagated by bulb division like narcissi, can also be potted and grown in the cool greenhouse like Z. candida. Bulbs should be spaced about 2–3in apart. Water sparingly at first, moderately when in active growth, and withhold entirely when foliage dies naturally after flowering time. Repotting is necessary only every 3–4 years but pots should be top-dressed every year.

Chapter Fourteen

SOME TENDER BULBS FOR INDOOR BLOOM

THIS CHAPTER is devoted to just a few rather special tender bulbs suited solely or primarily for indoor cultivation.

HIPPEASTRUM

If I had to choose one bulb as the most striking and satisfying of all bulbous plants there is no doubt in my mind that it would be the hippeastrum or Royal Dutch Amaryllis. Although a member of the amaryllis family and almost universally called amaryllis it does not belong to the amaryllis genus but a quite separate one botanically described as hippeastrum. Call them what you like but these magnificent and spectacular plants are certainly the emperors of indoor bloom.

The bulbs, like the flowers, are enormous and often 4–6in in diameter. They are brown, tunicated, with flattened leaf scars at the top and semi-dry roots at the bottom, and, more often than not, you can see the green tips of the leaves or even of the flattened flower buds just emerging. The bulbs are not cheap but your investment produces massive dividends. The smallest bulbs, but still quite sizeable, are frequently obtainable in pre-packed containers but the largest bulbs are sold loose.

The recent extensive hybridisation programme in Holland has rapidly increased the number of giant modern hybrids on the market (see page 192). These hybrids, derived from H. vittatum from the Peruvian Andes, show refinement in texture and substance of the petals, richness and subtlety of colour, and the coarseness of the earlier hybrids has disappeared. The massive lily-like trumpet-shaped flowers—often larger than a man's outstretched hand—are superb and long lasting. Each fat light green stem, up to 3ft or more in height, bears from 4–6 of these giant flowers and the exhibition-size bulbs can have two or more stems and up to a dozen flowers. They come in a range of gorgeous colours.

The flower stalks usually appear before the bright green strap-shaped leaves but the latter develop quickly as the flowers open. Occasionally leaves will appear simultaneously with the flowering stems or even precede them from the neck of the bulb. The blooms, if kept cool, will last 3–4 weeks or more, particularly if the pollen is removed as they reach full flower. They make long-lasting cut flowers and cut hippeastrum are beginning to appear in leading florists.

Pre-packed smaller bulbs of hippeastrum hybrids can be purchased by colour and colours available include white, red, vermilion, scarlet orange red, bright red with a pure white star in the centre, rose, salmon, orange, pink, salmon pink, violet pink, cherry and white striped pink.

Specialist suppliers will have a wider choice and offer exhibition-size bulbs in colours or in named varieties. Among the latter, but not necessarily available from the same specialist supplier, are:

Appleblossom	pale pink with lighter throat
Beautiful Lady	mandarin red with pink throat
Belinda	dark velvet red
Bouquet	begonia pink blending to rose
Daintiness	porcelain rose with greenish veined throat
Easterflower	azalea pink edged white
Excelsior	clear orange
Fairyland	solid rose
Glorious Victory	salmon orange with darker throat
Hecuba	salmon
Joan of Arc	pure white with green throat
Minerva	white edged brick red
Mont Blanc	pure white with greenish tinged throat
Parsifal	orange scarlet
Peppermint	pure white with cardinal red streaks
Picotee	pure white speckled with red dots and edged red
Rembrandt	clear dark red
Striped Beauty	salmon pink edged white with carmine red lines
Wyndham Hayward	dark oriental red shading to blood red

There are a number of these hybrids which are specially prepared for Christmas flowering from October plantings but amateurs who have not grown hippeastrum before are advised to start with ordinary bulbs and plant from February, when the days are lengthening and there is some heat from the sun. The ordinary bulbs are available from early December but those potted early tend to have longer stems and smaller flowers.

It is well worth taking a little care in cultivating these bulbs and this can be done in the home, in a greenhouse or in a heated frame. Most amateurs manage successfully under normal centrally-heated conditions in the home.

The roots and lower parts of the bulbs obtained from your supplier should be soaked in tepid water for about five days before planting. Use ordinary clay pots with drainage holes but ensure that the pots are clean and at least 3in more in diameter than the bulbs. Mix a compost of three parts good loam and one part leaf-mould or peat, adding sufficient coarse silver sand to keep the whole porous. I also mix in a heaped table-spoon of bonemeal but this is not absolutely necessary. A rich potting compost like John Innes No 3 is a suitable alternative.

Place the big bulb on a cone of compost with the roots spread well out and fill up with compost leaving half to a third of the bulb exposed. Firm well without tightly packing the compost. To encourage vigorous growth bottom heat is most helpful. This is easy in a greenhouse but more difficult in a modern home. Potted bulbs should be placed on a shallow dish and sited on a radiator or mantelpiece to start them—if this is not feasible start them in a sunny window—but plants should be removed from bottom heat to a window when the buds have formed.

Watering correctly is important for success. Newly potted bulbs should not be watered until root growth is active, usually a matter of a couple of weeks. Then water sparingly, increasing the amount as the flowering stalk lengthens. Use tepid water on the compost only. The newly potted bulbs like a temperature of 65–70° F (18–21° C) and it must not be allowed to fall below 60° F (16° C). No period of darkness is needed, as is the case with hyacinths, tulips and narcissus, for the root formation period. Heat can be increased as the flower stalk lengthens.

Once the flowers open, however, the plant can be moved to a cooler position to make the blooms last longer. When a stalk has finished flowering cut it out with a sharp knife an inch or so from the bulb but keep the plant growing, allowing foliage to develop. After flowering the bulbs may have decreased in size and there are certain basic rules to build up the bulbs for flowering the following year. Give the plants plenty of sun and water freely. Add liquid fertiliser to the water at fortnightly intervals throughout the summer and then gradually withhold all water and fertiliser and dry them off in September. To dry off the bulbs simply lay the pots on their side, ensuring that they are protected from frost. When planting time comes again all you have to do is top-dress the pots with compost and start the bulbs again. Bulbs need to be completely repotted only every third or fourth year.

By planting hippeastrum bulbs from February at 2–3 week intervals through April you can have these giant and gorgeous flowers in bloom in your home from late March through June. From the time of planting to flowering time is between 7–10 weeks, depending upon the temperature of your home.

NERINE

The nerine is a most decorative genus of South African bulbs and like the hippeastrum, a member of the amaryllis family. Because the flowers are long lasting and have such attractive iridescent petals nerines are grown commercially on quite a large scale as cut flowers.

The flowers, which appear outdoors in September–October, are borne in umbels and usually appear before the strap-like leaves have grown to any extent. For the most part nerines, named after that engaging nymph in Greek mythology, are for indoor culture, although what I regard as the most beautiful species of the genus, **N. bowdenii** and its hybrids, can be grown outdoors in warmer climates. But even in the southern and western counties of England the bulbs have to be sited in sheltered positions, by preference at the base of a south wall.

For outdoor cultivation the bulb, which is shaped rather like a Chianti wine bottle, globose at the base but with a long, thin neck, should be planted in autumn or early winter very shallowly in a mixture of good garden soil, peat and sand. The neck of the bulb should just be covered and bulbs should be spaced 3–4in apart. A mulch of dried leaves or peat will be necessary for winter protection. The leaves emerge in spring and wither in summer and the flowers bloom outdoors in September or October. Once established nerine bulbs should not be moved and only divided when the clumps become very thick and begin to flower poorly. Top-dressings of rich compost and bonemeal should be applied every August before the flower spikes appear.

For indoor cultivation the bulbs should be planted in large pots in the autumn or early winter with the upper half of the neck of the bulb showing. One bulb can be housed in a 4in pot or three in a 6in pot and a fairly rich compost should be used. From April onwards, when growth appears, the pots are best plunged outdoors until August. When the flower spikes appear (about September) the pots should be moved to a cool greenhouse or cold frame and then be given an occasional application of well diluted liquid manure. The flowers will bloom from September to November. During the winter months, after flowering and when the bulbs are resting, they should be watered very sparingly indeed. Nerines in pots will need repotting every fourth or fifth year as the bulbs increase freely by division. Some crowding is beneficial for they bloom better when pot-bound. Any repotting should be carried out in August or early September before new flower spikes appear, and bonemeal should be added to the fresh compost when repotting.

N. bowdenii, named after Athelstan Bowden, who sent the bulbs from South Africa to England in the late 1880s, has large umbels of 8–12 pink flowers, 3–4in across with slightly waved and gracefully recurved petals, on 18–24in stems. This species flowers outdoors in September–October.

N. bowdenii Pink Triumph is a handsome hybrid, producing a lovely umbel of big deep pink flowers which are nicely crinkled. Stems are 18–24in tall too, but this hybrid flowers a little later than the species.

N. crispa (syn. **undulata**) is a small species with stems rarely more than 14in tall. The flowers which bloom in October, are rose-pink and grouped in a sizeable round umbel. The petals are oddly crisped and curled at the edges and the narrow leaves of this species are virtually evergreen. It is not hardy, however, and should always be grown in a cool greenhouse.

SPREKELIA

This genus consists of one species only, **S. formosissima** (see page 174), a member of the amaryllis family and related to the hippeastrum but differing in that it always has a solitary flower. Known as the 'Jacobean lily', the 'Aztec lily' or the 'St. James' lily', it is native to Mexico and Guatemala. It is usually grown as a pot plant but can be cultivated outdoors in all but the coldest districts if planting is delayed until the end of April.

Sprekelia boast a handsome red, orchid-like, six petalled flower on 1½–2ft stems with deep green strap-like leaves. Each large, oval shaped and long necked bulb with a black tunic sends up one or two pinkish floral stems. Although the flowers are single each one has a bunch of golden stamens in the throat. The foliage may appear before the floral stems or after them.

Plant the bulbs outdoors at the end of April or early May in well drained, humus-filled soil in sunny positions. Shallow planting is essential and the bulbs should be spaced 12–18in apart. Flowering time is June–July.

When growing sprekelia in the greenhouse or house, plant and handle them just like hippeastrum. Planting time in pots, with the top half to third of the bulb remaining exposed, is February. Watering freely should not begin until growth is evident. You can continue to give water liberally until September when the potted bulbs should be allowed to dry off and rest. Top-dressing is necessary annually but repotting should not be undertaken for three years after the initial planting.

Sprekelia bulbs are not hardy and should you plant some in your garden be sure they are lifted in the autumn, before the first frosts, and kept in a warm and dry storage place through the winter and early spring. The bulbs increase by division, but offshoots will take several years to produce flowers even with applications of liquid manure.

VALLOTA

The vallota genus also consists of one species only, **V. speciosa,** and is suitable for indoor cultivation only, but it is one of the most beautiful members of the amaryllis family from South Africa. Called the 'Scarborough lily' ostensibly because some of the bulbs were washed ashore from a shipwreck off Scarborough, it produces on stout stems up to 2ft tall umbels of 5–10 large brilliant scarlet flowers, funnel-shaped and up to 3in across. The anthers are golden yellow. It has broad leaves, rather like those of the hippeastrum, which appear at the same time as the flowers and are about 15–16in long. Flowering time is August–September.

Plant 2–3 of the large oval bulbs with brown tunics in a large pot in a compost of good fibrous loam, leaf-mould and sand. Planting time is June–July and the necks of the bulbs should protrude from the compost. Water thoroughly after planting and place the pots in a light sunny greenhouse or on the windowsill of a sunny room. Give the pots plenty of water and sun during the growing period. After flowering the leaves of the plant will continue growing and gradually die off in the winter. Watering should be reduced and completely stopped between February and May. Like all members of the amaryllis family vallota dislikes transplanting and should only be repotted every 3–4 years.

ZANTEDESCHIA

This genus of South African bulbous plants named after the Italian botanist, Giovanni Zantedeschi, has name trouble for it is also known erroneously as 'calla' and 'richardia' and more familiarly as the 'arum lily', the 'trumpet lily', the 'lily of the Nile' or the 'calla lily'.

The species and hybrids available are all perennial, with thick, fleshy roots and large, sometimes spotted, leaves. The flower consists of an erect, rather clublike spadix, more or less enclosed by a large funnel-shaped spathe. Zantedeschia, which are members of the Araceae or aroid family, are not difficult to grow and any amateur can bring these superb, if tender, plants to flower in the home or cool greenhouse. Commercial growers cultivate the better known white species, **Z. aethiopica,** which is widely used in church decoration, under glass in successive batches for year-round flower. This tropical African species can be kept growing almost continuously but the others, from South Africa, require a long rest period of complete dryness after flowering.

Plant the white arum or calla lily in 5–8in pots depending upon the size of the roots, using a good fibrous loam mixed with sand and bone meal, in August or September for spring bloom. The tops of the thick rhizomatous roots should barely be covered with compost but space should be left for 2in of additional compost to be added later. Water moderately after potting and stand pots outdoors or in a cold frame for about a month before bringing them into the home or cool greenhouse. Top dress with rich compost when the roots show plentifully at the surface. When the roots come through the top dressing apply dilute liquid fertiliser 2–3 times a week. These plants need plenty of water once the leaves appear. After flowering decrease supplies of water and once the danger of frost is passed, about early June, the pots can be moved to the garden until it is time to start them into growth again. Alternatively the plants can be removed from their pots and planted out into rich garden soil until September. They must be lifted and carefully potted again by mid-September. Propagation is by offsets or 'sucker rhizomes' which form on the side of the old roots. These should be detached when repotting. Once repotted place the pots in a cold frame until new growth indicates that it is time once again to bring them into the home or cool greenhouse.

Page 295 Zantesdeschia Elliottiana

The other species and hybrids are cultivated in the same way but will not require pots over 5in in diameter. After they have flowered, however, give them less water and finally withhold completely. The pots can be placed on their sides in a shaded cool place in the garden and kept dry until planting time comes round again. The roots should be repotted in fresh compost every year.

Z. aethiopica, from the marshlands of tropical Africa, was first grown in Europe in 1687 at the Amsterdam Botanic Gardens. The flowers have a large snow white spathe up to 10in long and recurved in the upper part surrounding the white spadix, which extends above the spathe and is yellowy orange at the tip, like a funnel. The stem is 2–3ft tall and the leaves are rich green without any mottling.

Z. albomaculata, introduced from South Africa in 1859, is a dwarf species with stems little more than 18in tall. The flowers are creamy white with a purple blotch or mark at the base of the narrower spathe. Because the dark green leaves have white spots this species is often called the 'spotted calla lily'.

Z. Elliottiana, Elliott's calla or the 'golden calla lily', is a natural hybrid introduced to Europe in 1886 and only recently becoming popular. It has a 5in long pure yellow spathe without a blotch or mark and dark green silvery leaves. The yellow spadix is about 3in long and the stems range from 20–24in in height.

Z. rehmanii is a dwarf species with stems 10–14in tall which was discovered in the mountainous regions of Natal about 1888. Its 4in spathe is dull white tinged pale to deep pink or even mauve and is sometimes referred to as the 'pink calla lily'. The slender green leaves are unmottled or only slightly mottled.

Z. Solfatare, not introduced until 1902, is a hybrid of Z. Elliottiana and the species adlami, which has a creamy white spathe with a large black basal blotch. The spathe of this hybrid is sulphur yellow with a black blotch and the flowers are large on 18–24in stems. The leaves are bright green and usually unmottled.

Amateurs will find Z. aethiopica and Z. Elliottiana the easiest to grow successfully in their homes.

LIST OF HORTICULTURAL SOCIETIES

Information about activities and applications for membership may be obtained from the secretaries of the specialist horticultural societies listed below. Every care has been taken to ensure accuracy but entries are subject to change at short notice.

BRITAIN

British Gladiolus Society
P. Holloway
9 The Drive
Shoreham-by-Sea, Sussex

British Iris Society
Mrs. T. A. Blanco White
72 South Hill Park
London, N.W. 3

Daffodil Society
D. J. Pearce
College of the Ascension
Selly Oak
Birmingham 29

National Begonia Society
F. J. Martin
50 Woodlands Farm Road
Erdington
Birmingham 24

National Dahlia Society
Philip Damp
26 Burns Road
Lillington
Leamington Spa
Warwickshire

The Nerine Society
C. A. Norris
9 Brookend House
Welland, Malvern
Worcestershire

Northern Horticultural Society
Harlow Car Gardens
Harrogate
Yorkshire

North Wales Horticultural Society
Mrs. G. Linhard
'Rhydycyrt'
Mochdre
Newtown
Montgomeryshire

Royal Caledonian Horticultural
  Society
John Turnbull
44 Melville Street
Edinburgh 3

The Royal Horticultural Society
Vincent Square
London, SW1P 2PE

Royal Horticultural Society of Ireland
16 St. Stephen's Green
Dublin 2

Wakefield and North of England
  Tulip Society

H. V. Calvert
7 School Crescent
Lupset
Wakefield
Yorkshire

CANADA

Canadian Gladiolus Society
Samuel Colhoun
646 Henderson Highway
East Kildenan
Winnipeg 5
Manitoba

Canadian Horticultural Council
219 Queen Street
Ottawa
Ontario

Canadian Iris Society
Lloyd Zurbrigg
33 College Street
Kingston
Ontario

National Tulip Society (of the United
  States)
Regional Office
P. Cade Browne
Sarnia
Ontario

Ottawa & District Gladiolus Society
A. R. Buckley
653 Highland Avenue
Ottawa 3
Ontario

Province of Quebec Gladiolus Society
Fred J. Coleman
426 Egan Avenue
Verdun 19, P.Q.

Thunder Bay Gladiolus Society
Eva Mekkonen
126 Pine Street
Port Arthur
Ontario

Toronto District Gladiolus Society
Mrs. Aubrey C. Dunn
405 Mill Street
Richmond Hill
Ontario

Vancouver Dahlia Society
D. L. Lock
4612 W. Ninth Avenue
Vancouver 8
British Columbia

Vancouver Gladiolus Society
Mrs. D. Lott
4517 Knight Street
Vancouver 12
British Columbia

Victoria Gladiolus Society
Mrs. B. A. Setchell
727 Newbury Street
Victoria
British Columbia

Winnipeg Gladiolus Society
Mrs. Marian Colhoun
646 Henderson Highway
East Kildenan
Winnipeg 5
Manitoba

UNITED STATES

American Begonia Society
Irma Jane Brown
3628 Revere Avenue
Los Angeles 39
California

American Daffodil Society
Mrs. Ernest J. Adams
1121 Twelfth Avenue
Huntington
West Virginia

American Dahlia Society, Inc.
Edward B. Lloyd
10 Crestmont Road
Montolair
New Jersey

American Horticultural Society
1600 Bladensburg Road N.E.
Washington 2, D.C.

American Iris Society
Clifford W. Benson
Missouri Botanical Garden
2237 Tower Grove Boulevard
St. Louis 10
Missouri

Bulb Society
5139 Hormosa Avenue
Los Angeles 41
California

Dwarf Iris Society
Mrs. Walter Welch
Middlebury
Indiana

National Tulip Society
Felix R. Tyroler
55 West 42nd Street
New York 36
New York

North American Gladiolus Council
J. Elton Carter
2514 East Twenty-fifth Street
Des Moines 17
Iowa

North American Lily Society
Mrs. W. T. Moars
R. R. 3, Box 99
Anderson
Indiana

*Enquiries on any aspect of Dutch bulbs
will be welcomed by:*

The Bulb Information Desk
Kimbolton House
117 Fulham Road
London, S.W. 3

INDEX